Drums and Shadows

Drums and Shadows

SURVIVAL STUDIES AMONG THE
GEORGIA COASTAL NEGROES

Savannah Unit

Georgia Writers' Project

Work Projects Administration

Introduction by

CHARLES JOYNER

Photographs by

MURIEL AND MALCOLM BELL, JR.

Brown Thrasher Books

The University of Georgia Press   Athens and London

© 1940 by the University of Georgia
Introduction to the Brown Thrasher Edition © 1986
by the University of Georgia Press
Athens, Georgia 30602
All rights reserved

The paper in this book meets the guidelines for
permanence and durability of the Committee on
Production Guidelines for Book Longevity of the
Council on Library Resources.

Printed in the United States of America

90 89 88 87 86   5 4 3 2 1

Library of Congress Cataloging in Publication Data

Drums and shadows.

"Brown thrasher books."
Bibliography: p.
Includes index.
1. Afro-Americans—Georgia. 2. Afro-Americans—
Georgia—Folklore. 3. Folklore—Georgia.
4. Superstition—Georgia. 5. Georgia—Social life
and customs. 6. Georgia—History. I. Georgia
Writers' Project. Savannah Unit.
E185.93.G4D78 1986   975.8'700496073   86-3370
ISBN 0-8203-0850-1 (alk. paper)
ISBN 0-8203-0851-X (pbk.: alk. paper)

Contents

◇◇◇◇◇◇◇◇◇◇◇◇

v

CONTENTS

vi

Illustrations

❖❖❖❖❖❖❖❖❖❖❖❖❖

ILLUSTRATIONS

Introduction to the Brown Thrasher Edition

◇◇◇

CHARLES JOYNER

LOOK AT THE PICTURES. HERE ARE CABINS AND PRAISE-
houses, oxcarts, banjos, and coiled baskets. Here are carved
chains and masks, wooden figures and walking sticks. Here
are the haunting faces of black coastal Georgians.

Here is Katie Brown, sitting on the sunny steps of her unpainted cabin, her head swathed in a white kerchief, her
body encased in a well-worn sweater. Her visitors have come
down the coast more than fifty miles from Savannah, crossing
over to Sapelo, one of the long chain of sea islands that
stretch along the South Carolina and Georgia coast. Passing
the sawmill village in the center of the island, they have
bounced through woods and underbrush over winding, tree-
shaded oxcart paths to the tiny settlement on the lower end of
the island. Here live the descendants of Sapelo's plantation
slaves. Katie Brown is a gracious hostess to the visitors who
ply her with pipe tobacco and questions about old-time customs and beliefs. They ask her about "sitting-up" with the
dead, about conjures and spirits, about the use of drums in
church services, and about animal trickster tales. "Yeah, we
hab set-ups wid duh dead," she acknowledges, but maintains,
"I ain know bout conjuh." As for drums in church, she recalls
that they "use to hab um long time ago, but not now on duh
ilun,—leas I ain heah um." Regarding Buh Rabbit stories,
she says, "I heah um, but I fuhgits." But she has not forgotten Belali Mohomet, her great-grandfather who came from

ix

Africa and became the driver on Thomas Spalding's Sapelo plantation. Belali Mohomet and his wife, Phoebe, prayed "wen duh sun come up, wen it straight obuh head an wen it set," she recalls. "Dey bow tuh duh sun and hab lill mat tuh kneel on." She also tells the visitors the story of her grandmother. "Belali he from Africa but muh gran she come by Bahamas. She speak funny wuds we didn know." On the same day, every year, her grandmother had made a strange, flat cake.

She wash rice, an po off all duh watuh. She let wet rice sit all night, an in mawnin rice is all swell. She tek dat rice an put it in wooden mawtuh, an beat it tuh paste wid wooden pestle. She add honey, sometime shuguh, an make it in flat cake wid uh hans. "Saraka" she call um.

Katie Brown has endured. She is one of the oldest dwellers on Sapelo. Her words gradually reveal to the visitors a portrait of Sapelo's black community, a culture in which the past still persists into the present, a culture shaped as much by remembered traditions from Africa as by encountered traditions from elsewhere.

Look at the pictures. Here is Tony William Delegal, the blind Ogeechee Town centenarian who toiled as a slave on Major John Thomas's Harris Neck plantation and who can still sing an African song for the Savannah visitors. Here is Henry Williams of St. Marys, born a slave of "William Cole wut live at Oakland Plantation." Williams recalls Daddy Patty, an Ibo who "use tuh talk tuh the mens in the tannin yahd bout weah he came from. He ain talk tuh me but I heah im." Patty had told the men of life in Africa. "Patty he wuz the chief son an he have three straight mahks slantin down on he right cheek an that wuz a bran tuh show who he wuz." And here is Jim Myers of Mush Bluff Island, sitting on the oak logs that serve as front steps for his cabin in a hard-packed clearing amid a grove of trees. Myers is slightly stooped from rheumatism and wears two brass wires around his ankles to help relieve the pain in his legs. His African-born grandmother, Bina, "tell me how she get heah on a big boat an she lan down theah on Cumberland Ilun on a big dock." He tells the visitors how the slaveholders "broke" newly enslaved Africans by confining them in a log house, chaining them to iron rings in the floor:

> They chained them wile Africans theah till they wuz tame. They'd take em out one by one and they'd give em a stick an put em in the fiel with people wut knowd how tuh wuk an that way they lun how too. They sked to give em a hoe. It's shahp and they might frail roun with it.

Look at his picture. A big, barefoot, very black man with a fringe of white beard, Jim Myers is a living link between Georgia and Africa.

FROM THEIR ENCOUNTERS with Katie Brown, Tony William Delegal, Henry Williams, and Jim Myers—and with 134 other people like them in twenty locations over a three-year period—the fieldworkers of the Savannah Unit of the Federal Writers Project fashioned a series of haunting portraits in words and pictures of coastal black Georgians. Their book, *Drums and Shadows*, is aimed at a general audience. It is organized by community and is presented in a straight-forward narrative spiced with long quotations in a readable literary adaptation of the black Georgians' speech. It is filled with rich examples of Afro-American folklore.

Drums and Shadows presents much information on folk speech and naming patterns, including the use of day names and the folk etymology of Gullah. Here are examples of numerous African words used in coastal Georgia. Here is *deloe* (water), *juba haltuh* (water bucket), *sisure* (chicken), *gombay* (cow), *nyana* (fish), *flim* (pancakes), *mosojo* (pot), *diffy* (fire), *nyam* (eat), *mulafo* (whiskey), and *musongo* (tobacco). Here are *ma-foo-bey* (an expression of surprise) and the expletive *skinskon*. Here are folk narratives of Buh Rabbit, mysterious spiders, magic hoes, landing Ibos, flying Africans, and various supernatural spirits. Here are African songs—*a-shou-tu-goula*, the lullaby *nikki-yimi, nikki-yimi*, and the refrain *yeribum, yeribum, yeribum, by*. Here is the ballad of Bo-cat, the wife murderer. Here is instrumental music on banjos, bones, drums, and gourds. And here are such dances as the Buzzard Lope, the Camel Walk, Come Down to the Mire, the Fish Bone, the Fish Tail, and the Snake Hip. Here are examples of folk religion in descriptions of Moslem ancestors and African prayer rituals. Here are the chanted *Belambi, Hackabera, Ameela, Mahamadu*, and *Ameen, Ameen, Ameen* during prayers, followed by *Meena, mino, mo* at the end of prayers, and *Kum buba yali kum buba tambe, kum kunka yali, kum kunka tembe*, said before flying back to Africa. Here are river baptisms, and sermons, and guest appearances by Father Divine and Daddy Grace. Other folk beliefs are exemplified in conjure bags and conjure doctors, graveyard dirt, mojoes, such charms as Adam and Eve Root, Black Cat Bone, Lucky Heart, and High John the Conqueror. Here are examples of customary folklore in birth customs and death customs as well as festival celebrations. And here are descriptions of material culture, including folk architecture and such foodways as the use of benne seeds, palm cabbage and palm wine, palmetto cabbage and palmetto wine, peanuts, ashcakes, and African rice cakes. Among the folk crafts produced by black coastal Georgians are baskets, beads, bowls and utensils, musical instruments, walking sticks, and carved wooden spoons.

In its concentration on local folklore *Drums and Shadows* was pursuing a policy encouraged by the national office of the Federal Writers' Project. An agency of the New Deal's Work

Projects Administration, the Federal Writers' Project employed over six thousand jobless persons, some of whom were experienced in putting words on paper—novelists, poets, Ph.D.'s, journalists, and free-lance writers. They interviewed sharecroppers and living exslaves; they transcribed court records and inventoried cemeteries; they collected oral history and folklore. Through their state guides and other publications they contributed materially to a better understanding of America. Jerrold Hirsch writes that the national director, Henry G. Alsberg, and the folklore editor, Benjamin A. Botkin, shared a vision that attempted to reconcile cosmopolitan and provincialism. They respected the provincial sense of place and understood that every place possesses its own unique qualities and heritage, but they did not believe a sense of place was incompatible with a more cosmopolitan perspective informed by knowledge of other traditions. They saw American culture as pluralistic, a mosaic of different traditions, each contributing to the whole. But they found it difficult to communicate such a vision to state and local units. There are advantages to both provincial and cosmopolitan perspectives—that of the insider and that of the outsider—but rarely did any one person possess both. According to Hirsch, southern fieldworkers were closer to their folk roots and were more sensitive to local folklore than those outside the region and largely avoided the condescending tone that distanced the collector from the folk. When white southern fieldworkers reported black folklore and folkways, however, they could be as patronizing as their counterparts in other states. The national office worried that their encouragement of local folklore might contribute to a divisive regionalism. Botkin, hoping to emphasize the process of cultural interchange, wished a line "to be clearly drawn between the acculturative and contra-acculturative phases of regionalism." The Savannah Unit's concentration on African survivals rather than on black acculturation in Georgia found itself in conflict with the vision of the national office, which felt that *Drums and Shadows* promoted a racist theory of cultural evolution in which cultural traits might "survive" from earlier, more "primitive" stages of culture but would eventually disappear under contact with more "advanced" cultures.[1]

Drums and Shadows was also in conflict with popular stereotypes. Published in 1940, it was offered to an American public whose image of black Georgians was formed by *Gone with the Wind*. Margaret Mitchell's novel had won the Pulitzer Prize in 1936, and David O. Selznick's film version had enjoyed enormous popular and critical success in 1939, setting box-office records and sweeping the Academy Awards. Black Georgians, as portrayed in *Gone with the Wind*, were either loyal, unsupervised field hands like Big Sam—so grateful to be allowed to be "de one dat sez when it's quittin' time at Tara" that he is later proud to dig trenches to help the Confederates win the war—or loyal, unhurried house servants like Prissy (who "don't know nothin' 'bout birthin' babies"), or the butler Uncle Peter (whose incongruous dignity is presented as faintly comical), or the bossy, influential Mammy (the Emily Post of Tara, arbiter of what is appropriate and what "ain't fittin'"). Unlike David Wark Griffith's *The Birth of a Nation*, the images are sentimental rather than paranoid, patronizing rather than vicious; but they are nonetheless inaccurate and demeaning.[2]

Seduced by such affectionate and appealing stereotypes, Americans were ill prepared for the real black Georgians presented in *Drums and Shadows*. It presented a world far removed from the traditional South of sentimental romances in which Colonel Massa sips mint juleps on the magnolia-shaded piazza of the white-columned Big House, while happy, carefree slaves prance about, rolling their eyes and strumming their banjos. The real world of rural black Southerners in the 1930s was one in which families lived on less than two hundred dollars a year in leaky, tin-roofed houses lacking either glass or screens in the windows. It was a world in which children walked miles to rickety schools and the elderly walked miles to rickety churches. It was a world in which farmers borrowed small sums at indefinite rates of interest and lost their lands at indefinite rates of foreclosure. The major impact of the Great Depression on this world of perpetual depression was to bring in fieldworkers from the Federal Writers' Project.[3]

Drums and Shadows was sparsely reviewed at the time and did not enjoy large sales. The *New York Times Book Review* buried its notice on page 17, and the critic damned the book with faint praise. In a joint review of *Drums and Shadows* and Mason Crum's *Gullah*, C. McD. Puckette said that both books performed "a real service to folklore." He lamented that the "generation of Negroes raised under the tutelage of former slaves is thinning and sophistication is coming even to the last point of the outermost barrier island." And he praised the interviewers who "convince one that a faithful task has been done and Georgia can justly be gratified at this addition to the annals of the State." By comparison with Crum's book, he said that *Drums and Shadows* "covers the fresher ground only because fewer chronicles have recorded the stories of Sapelo, St. Simon's and St. Mary's."[4]

THE IMPORTANCE OF *Drums and Shadows* is much clearer in retrospect. It was the pioneering book in demonstrating the continuing, living influence of African folklore among Afro-Americans, not through bits and pieces of shadowy survivals gathered in small numbers over scattered wide areas, but through concrete examples gathered in massive quantities within a small area of the United States. In his foreword the sociologist Guy B. Johnson termed it "probably the most thorough search for African heritages among Negroes in a small area that has ever been attempted in this country up to the present time."[5] The Savannah Unit was aware that the local folklore collected on the Georgia coast had implications extending far beyond the state of Georgia. The writers presented their material in the explicit hope that it might be "useful as an outline for further investigations in this and related fields."[6]

In choosing to focus on African survivals, *Drums and Shadows* was consciously departing from a generation of scholarly consensus in the fields of history, folklore, sociology, and anthropology. The leading university historian of the Afro-American experience in slavery was Yale's Georgia-born scholar Ulrich Bonnell Phillips. His *American Negro Slavery*, published in 1918, remained the standard work on the subject until the 1950s.[7] Studies of Georgia slavery by Ralph Betts Flanders and Albert H. Stoddard were written in the Phillips tradition.[8] In *American Negro Slavery*, Phillips revealed a certain ambivalence regarding the amount of African inheritance by Afro-Americans. Occasionally he seemed to believe in African cultural continuity among the slaves. "While produced only in America," he wrote, "the plantation slave was a product of old world forces. His nature was an African's profoundly modified but hardly transformed by the requirements of European civilization. The wrench from Africa and the subjection to the new discipline while uprooting his ancient language and customs had little more effect upon his temperament than upon his complexion." Yet only a few sentences later Phillips quoted with approval a saying of the slaveholders that "a negro was what a white man made him." On the slave plantation, the slave left Africa behind. "Ceasing to be Foulah, Coramantee, Ebo or Angola, he became instead the American negro."[9] In any event, Phillips's view of Africa was terribly negative. "No people is without its philosophy and religion," he admitted, but "of all regions of extensive habitation equatorial Africa is the worst." As for the Africans, "the climate in fact not only discourages but prohibits mental effort of severe or sustained character, and the negroes have submitted to that prohibition as to many others, through countless generations, with excellent grace." Such

xvi

African continuities as he acknowledged, he deplored. Slavery he regarded as a school—mostly successful—for civilizing savages.[10]

American sociologists expressed a more clear-cut catastrophist interpretation of the black cultural experience, following the position enunciated by the Chicago sociologist Robert E. Park in 1919. According to Park, "the Negro, when he landed in the United States, left behind him almost everything but his dark complexion and his tropical temperament. It is very difficult to find in the South today anything that can be traced directly back to Africa."[11] The foremost black sociologist of the first half of the twentieth century, E. Franklin Frazier, became a leading spokesman for the catastrophist position. "Probably never before in history," he wrote in his 1939 book *The Negro Family in the United States*, "has a people been so completely stripped of its social heritage as the Negroes who were brought to America." The positive result of losing their African heritage, however, was that they had "gradually taken over the more sophisticated American culture."[12] These sophisticated restatements of part of Phillips's position reveal a certain embarrassment over the African past and the shameful experience of slavery.

Sociological studies of the South Carolina sea islands followed the catastrophist interpretation of Park and Frazier. In his 1930 book *Folk Culture on St. Helena Island*, Guy B. Johnson traced the genealogy of black speech, songs, and folk beliefs mainly to white sources. "The Negro's almost complete loss of African language heritages is startling at first glance," he wrote, "but slavery as practised in the United States made any other outcome impossible." On the sea islands, "the Negro took over the English of the whites with whom he was associated, and he did it remarkably well." Gullah grammar, he said, "is merely simplified English grammar." As for songs, "the general pattern and many of the particulars of the music developed in slavery were borrowed from white folk music." Even "superstitions," so often regarded as evidence of the primitive African origins of black southerners, were attributed by Johnson to white sources. "A surprisingly large proportion of the Negro folk beliefs found in the South is of European descent." Other studies in the St. Helena project by Guion Griffis Johnson and T. J. Woofter, Jr. were in the same tradition.[13]

While black scholars such as John Wesley Work, James Weldon Johnson, and N. G. J. Ballanta had claimed African origins for the Afro-American spirituals, the only white scholar who had shared that view was the music critic Edward Krehbiel in 1914. In the 1920s and 1930s a number of white scholars, including Edward M. von Hornbostel, Newman Ivey White, Robert Winslow Gordon, Guy B. Johnson, and George Pullen Jackson, had contended that the Afro-American spirituals represented selective borrowings from white folk hymnody.[14] For the most part folklorists of the period tended to publish large collections of lore without drawing many conclusions about them. Elsie Clews Parsons collected black folklore in the sea islands off South Carolina and in the Caribbean. She refrained from inferences, but her careful annotations showed the similarity of her material to folklore collected in Africa. On the other hand, Newbell Niles Puckett, in his *Folk Beliefs of the Southern Negro* (1926), said that, while most whites believed black "superstitions" to be relics of African heathenism, "in four cases out of five it is a European dogma from which only centuries of patient education could wean even his own ancestors." The black folklorist Zora Neale Hurston suggested a more complex relationship between African and European elements underlying Afro-American folklore but was somewhat vague about their proportions.[15]

Both Elsie Clews Parsons and Zora Neale Hurston were trained anthropologists who had studied with Franz Boas at Columbia University. Boas—eager to combat the evolutionary tradition in anthropology that considered blacks to be at an earlier, less advanced level of civilization than whites— denied any enduring influence of African culture. According to Boas,

> The traits of the American Negroes are adequately explained on the basis of his [sic] history and social status. The tearing away from the African soil and the consequent complete loss of the old standards of life, which were replaced by the dependency of slavery and by all that it entailed, followed by a period of disorganization and by a severe economic struggle against heavy odds, are sufficient to explain the inferiority of the status of the race, without falling back upon the theory of hereditary inferiority.

Another Boas student, Ruth Benedict, wrote of black Americans in her book *Race:* "Their patterns of political, economic, and artistic behavior were forgotten—even the languages they had spoken in Africa." She accounted for this loss in the same way that E. Franklin Frazier and Guy B. Johnson had: "Conditions of slavery in America were so drastic that this loss is not to be wondered at." [16]

By the 1930s one anthropologist was beginning to ask if scholars might not, upon close examination of Afro-American culture, find "that there are some subtle elements left of what was ancestrally possessed." Himself a student of Boas, Melville J. Herskovits had early in his career scorned the idea that there were even lingering traces of Africa among black Americans and had doubted that there was any separate Afro-American culture. "That they have absorbed the culture of America," he wrote in 1925, "is too obvious, almost, to be mentioned." As he began to conduct comparative research in New World Afro-American cultures, he began to question his earlier position. As late as 1937, however, when he published his *Life in a Haitian Valley,* he declared that "going native" (being a participant-observer) was "neither possible nor of benefit among West African Negroes and their New World descendants." His stated reason was that the failure of the fieldworker to observe the racial etiquette of segregation would embarrass informants and subject the fieldworker to community ridicule.[17]

Herskovits published his most significant work, *The Myth of the Negro Past,* in 1941, following several years of fieldwork in the Caribbean, in Brazil, and in West Africa. In it Herskovits proposed a general theory of culture change that posited the persistence of such African survivals in Afro-American cultures as *Drums and Shadows* had already demonstrated. *The Myth of the Negro Past* was immediately controversial. Nearly all American intellectuals, black and white, denounced his thesis as misguided and exaggerated. Racial integrationists such as E. Franklin Frazier and Guy B. Johnson were concerned that segregationists might use Herskovits's arguments to build a case that black Americans were unassimilable. Herskovits, a long-time foe of white supremacy, was no supporter of segregation (even though much of his *Myth of the Negro Past* was built upon the scholarship of Ulrich B. Phillips, whom he quoted approvingly a dozen times). But few Americans other than ardent white supremacists were prepared to accept his thesis of African survivals in the New World.[18]

DRUMS AND SHADOWS preceded *The Myth of the Negro Past* by a year. In some ways, as in its fascination with primitivism and its sometimes patronizing tone, *Drums and Shadows* reflects the time and place of its inception. What is remarkable about *Drums and Shadows,* however, is not the occasional minor lapse but the determined and generally successful effort the whole project made to overcome such attitudes.

How did *Drums and Shadows* come to focus on African survivals among coastal black Georgians, then, since most scholars of black America emphasized the loss of African culture? Melville J. Herskovits was an advisor to the project. One might suspect that he imposed the theme on the Savannah Unit of the Federal Writers' Project. On the other hand, Guy B. Johnson was another major advisor. Was Johnson, identified with the white-to-black school of acculturation, outmaneuvered for influence by Herskovits? Was that why he was rewarded with the consolation of writing the foreword?

In fact, Mary Granger, district supervisor of the Savannah Unit, seems to have originated the survivals emphasis and to have chosen the project's advisors because of that emphasis. Granger—a woman of formidable intellect—was a cosmopolitan and well-traveled novelist. Her choice of Herskovits as advisor was an obvious one. Less obvious was her choice of Johnson. Johnson, however, maintains that he was never as hostile to the notion of African survivals as he has been depicted. He never denied the existence of African survivals nor opposed their study, although he believed that they played a less significant role in Afro-American culture than European elements did. He describes his position, then and now, as a middle position between the Africanist and Europeanist extremes. He believed, and still believes, that the balance lies somewhat closer to the Europeanist position. Johnson encouraged the Savannah project's search for survivals, and it was he who suggested the inclusion of an appendix documenting African parallels for the Georgia material. Furthermore, Johnson and Herskovits were social friends and visited Georgia together.[19]

Drums and Shadows certainly reflects the influence of Herskovits's earlier work in Dutch Guiana, Haiti, and West Africa rather more than it does Johnson's earlier sea island investigation. Not only are *Rebel Destiny, Suriname Folk-Lore, Life in a Haitian Valley,* and *Dahomey* listed in the bibliography—along with Johnson's *Folk Culture on St. Helena Island*—but they are cited time and again in the annotations of black folklore from coastal Georgia.

Herskovits and Johnson were not the only advisors chosen by the *Drums and Shadows* team. Among other outside consultants were the anthropologist William R. Bascom, the sociologist Charles S. Johnson, the folklorist Newbell Niles Puckett, the linguist Lorenzo Dow Turner, and the poet Sterling Brown. Three of the consultants—Johnson, Turner, and Brown—were black. Brown was perhaps the most influential upon the Savannah Unit. In his poetry he had already moved away from the pseudo-folk persona of the minstrel-show tradition to an authentic black folk voice. Perhaps the more literary orientation of the Savannah Unit gave Brown greater influence upon them than the social scientists could exert. The Georgia fieldworkers would have been familiar with a tradition in Afro-American literature that extolled—however equivocally—the African inheritance. Alain Locke had spoken ambivalently in 1925 of black Americans as "the advance guard of the African peoples in their contact with Twentieth Century civilization." In the same year Countee Cullen's poem "Heritage" proposed that a black God would better understand the Afro-American's roots in Africa and anomalous position in America. Even earlier, in 1921, Langston Hughes had published a Whitmanesque identification with his African ancestors:

I bathed in the Euphrates when dawns were young.
I built my hut near the Congo and it lulled me to sleep.
I looked upon the Nile and raised the pyramids above it.
. . . .
My soul has grown deep like the rivers.

Muriel and Malcolm Bell, photographers for *Drums and Shadows*, were inspired by their literary reference point to see Robert Lucas, whom they photographed at St. Marys, in the context of Richard Wright's Bigger Thomas. And they saw Katie Brown in the context of William Faulkner's Dilsey.[20]

xxii

Sterling Brown insisted that "half truth is not enough, however picturesque." He urged fieldworkers to avoid taking
white southern opinion as the arbiter of authenticity in black
southern folklore. If, on the other hand, the accounts were
genuine, if they went beyond a simplistic and misleading
treatment of serious sociological issues, then as a result both
blacks and whites could lay down the burden that stereotypes
had put upon them. That, he believed, could ultimately bring
about a revitalization of American culture.[21]

Perhaps neither the consultants nor the national officials
were completely happy with *Drums and Shadows*. Like many
pioneering efforts, it picked its way cautiously through underbrush and thickets that obscured what lay ahead. The
Savannah fieldworkers could see where they had come from
more clearly than where they were going. Unlike Herskovits's
Myth of the Negro Past, which propounded theories of reten-
tion, reinterpretation, and syncretism, *Drums and Shadows*
eschews analysis. Seventy African parallels are cited and
documented in the appendix, but the book ignores European
parallels and the influence of culture contact. "Though European parallels could be cited for many of the cultural patterns," Mary Granger acknowledges, "the citations in the
appendix have been limited to African material both because
the European material is better known and because the African parallels suggest interesting lines of investigation." In
his foreword Guy B. Johnson emphasizes that *Drums and
Shadows* "wisely refrained from attempting to include an
investigation of subjects like folk music and dialect, which
require special training and technical analysis." Perhaps because of having eschewed such analysis, *Drums and Shadows*
seems fresher nearly half a century later than the theoretical
works of the period. Scholars now recognize that coastal
blacks of Georgia and South Carolina developed a creole language that played a crucial role in shaping a creole culture. If
the Savannah fieldworkers mistakenly considered their infor-

xxiii

mants to be speaking in "dialect," in contrast to speaking "correctly," they nevertheless render that speech so accurately that scholars can reconstruct the grammatical rules of the creole language as spoken in coastal Georgia. Furthermore, the Savannah fieldworkers make a determined effort to note generational and educational differences in speech and to demonstrate such sociolinguistic features as code-switching ("excitement or emotion often throws the speaker back into a type of speech which ordinarily he no longer uses"). In the pages of *Drums and Shadows* modern readers can find the evidence to support a far more sophisticated understanding of the creolization of Afro-American culture than those put forward by Phillips, or Park, or even Herskovits.[22]

LOOK AT THE PICTURES. Among the notable features of *Drums and Shadows* is a series of sensitive and evocative photographs by Muriel and Malcolm Bell, Jr. These pictures transcend mere illustration; they are, in fact, a scholarly photographic essay. In the original publication the photographs followed the text almost as an afterthought. For this Brown Thrasher edition new prints have been made from the original negatives. Some additional photographs made for the original project but not published in the first edition are now included. The photographs have been printed and their sequence organized under the supervision of Muriel and Malcolm Bell for this edition, and the photographic essay is now printed where it should be—at the beginning. It is an essay that amplifies and comments on the life of these people visually, an essay that says things about their culture that cannot be said in words.

Look at the faces of these people of coastal Georgia. Look at the way they sit or stand. Look at their houses and their surroundings. Listen to their voices. In these pictures and in these words a portrait emerges: a portrait of a certain time and place, a portrait of an important part of southern culture.

INTRODUCTION

Notes

1. Jerrold Hirsch, "Portrait of America: The Federal Writers'
Project in a Cultural and Intellectual Context" (Ph.D. diss., Uni-
versity of North Carolina, 1984), pp. 30–66, 351–81, 389–90.
Botkin's quote is on p. 40.

2. Margaret Mitchell, *Gone with the Wind* (New York, 1936); Jack
Temple Kirby, *Media-made Dixie: The South in the American Imagi-
nation* (Baton Rouge, La., 1978), pp. 73–74, 169; Edward D. C.
Campbell, Jr., *The Celluloid South: Hollywood and the Southern
Myth* (Knoxville, Tenn., 1981), pp. 3–4, 17–19, 128–29, 133–34;
Rudy Behlmer, ed., *Memo from David O. Selznick* (New York,
1972), p. 151; Gavin Lambert, *GWTW: The Making of Gone with the
Wind* (Boston, 1973), p. 70.

3. Cf. Clarence Cason, *90° in the Shade* (Chapel Hill, N.C.,
1935); Allison Davis, Burleigh B. Gardner, and Mary R. Gardner,
Deep South (Chicago, 1941); John Dollard, *Caste and Class in a
Southern Town* (New York, 1937); Charles S. Johnson, *Shadow of the
Plantation* (Chicago, 1934); Hortense Powdermaker, *After Freedom*
(New York, 1939); and Arthur F. Raper, *Preface to Peasantry: A Tale
of Two Black Belt Counties* (Chapel Hill, N.C., 1936).

4. C. McD. Puckette, "Sea Island Negroes," *New York Times
Book Review*, April 6, 1941, p. 17. See also Mason Crum, *Gullah:
Negro Life in the Carolina Sea Islands* (Durham, N.C., 1940).

5. Guy B. Johnson, Foreword to 1940 edition of *Drums and Shadows*, p. vi.

6. *Drums and Shadows*, original dust jacket.

7. Ulrich B. Phillips, *American Negro Slavery* (New York, 1918).
For explications of Phillips's life and works see Eugene D. Genovese, "Ulrich Bonnell Phillips and His Critics," Foreword to
American Negro Slavery by Phillips (Baton Rouge, La., 1966); Eugene D. Genovese, "Race and Class in Southern History: An Ap-
praisal of the Work of Ulrich Bonnell Phillips," *Agricultural History*
41 (1967): 345–58; John Herbert Roper, *U. B. Phillips: A Southern
Mind* (Macon, Ga., 1984); Merton L. Dillon, *Ulrich Bonnell Phillips, Historian of the Old South* (Baton Rouge, La., 1985); and John
David Smith, *An Old Creed for the New South: Proslavery Ideology
and Historiography, 1865–1918* (Westport, Conn., 1985).

8. Ralph Betts Flanders, *Plantation Slavery in Georgia* (Chapel Hill, N.C., 1933); Albert H. Stoddard, "Origin, Dialect, Beliefs, and Characteristics of the Negroes of the South Carolina and Georgia Coasts," *Georgia Historical Quarterly* 28 (1944): 186–95. For more recent perspectives, see Betty Wood, *Slavery in Colonial Georgia, 1730–1775* (Athens, Ga., 1984); Julia Floyd Smith, *Slavery and Rice Culture in Low Country Georgia, 1750–1860* (Knoxville, Tenn., 1985); and Clarence L. Mohr, *On the Threshold of Freedom: Masters and Slaves in Civil War Georgia* (Athens, Ga., 1986).

9. Phillips, *American Negro Slavery*, p. 291.

10. *Ibid.*, pp. 3–5, 42–44, 342.

11. Robert E. Park, "The Conflict and Fusion of Cultures with Special Reference to the Negro," *Journal of Negro History* 4 (1919): 116. For an interesting perspective on conservative and radical manifestations of the catastrophist school see Orlando Patterson, "Rethinking Black History," *Harvard Educational Review* 41 (1971): 299–304.

12. E. Franklin Frazier, *The Negro Family in America* (Chicago, 1939), pp. 21–22, 479. See also his "Traditions and Patterns of Negro Family Life in the United States," in *Race and Culture Contacts*, ed. E. B. Reuter (New York, 1934), p. 194; and his *The Negro Church in America* (New York, 1963).

13. Guy B. Johnson, *Folk Culture on St. Helena Island, South Carolina* (Chapel Hill, N.C., 1930), pp. 10–11, 128, 171; Guion Griffis Johnson, *A Social History of the Sea Islands* (Chapel Hill, N.C., 1930); T. J. Woofter, Jr., *Black Yeomanry: Life on St. Helena Island* (Chapel Hill, N.C., 1930). For a discussion of Guy B. Johnson and his role in the St. Helena project, see Daniel Joseph Singal, *The War Within: From Victorian to Modernist Thought in the South, 1919–1945* (Chapel Hill, N.C., 1982), pp. 315–27.

14. John Wesley Work, Introduction to *Folk Song of the American Negro*, ed. Frederick J. Work (Nashville, Tenn., 1907); James Weldon Johnson and J. Rosamund Johnson, *The Book of American Negro Spirituals* (New York, 1925); Nicholas George Julius Ballanta, *Saint Helena Island Spirituals* (New York, 1925); Edward Krehbiel, *Afro-American Folksongs: A Study in Racial and National Music* (New York, 1914); Edward M. von Hornbostel, "American Negro

Music," *International Review of Missions* 15 (1926): 748–51; Newman Ivey White, *American Negro Folk Songs* (Cambridge, Mass., 1928); George Pullen Jackson, *White and Negro Spirituals* (New York, 1943). For studies of the controversy over the spirituals, see Charles Joyner, "Music: Origins of Spirituals," in *Encyclopedia of Black America*, ed. W. Augustus Low and Virgil A. Clift (New York, 1981), pp. 591–96; John David Smith, "The Unveiling of Slave Folk Culture, 1865–1920," *Journal of Folklore Research* 21 (1984): 47–62; D. K. Wilgus, *Anglo-American Folksong Scholarship Since 1898* (New Brunswick, N.J., 1959), pp. 345–64.

15. See the following by Elsie Clews Parsons: *Folk Tales from the Sea Islands, South Carolina* (Cambridge, Mass., 1923); *Folk Tales of the Andros Islands* (Cambridge, Mass., 1918); *Folklore from the Cape Verde Islands* (Cambridge, Mass., 1923); *Folk Lore of the Antilles, French and English*, vols. 1–3 (Cambridge, Mass., 1933–35, 1943). See also Newbell Niles Puckett, *Folk Beliefs of the Southern Negro* (Chapel Hill, N.C., 1926), pp. i–ii; Zora Neale Hurston, *Mules and Men* (Philadelphia, 1935).

16. Franz Boas, *The Mind of Primitive Man* (New York, 1938, 1963), p. 240; Ruth Benedict, *Race: Science and Politics* (New York, 1940, 1959), pp. 86–87.

17. Melville J. Herskovits, "The Negro in the New World: The Statement of a Problem," *American Anthropologist* 32 (1930): 141–55; Melville J. Herskovits, "The Negro's Americanism," in *The New Negro*, ed. Alain Locke (New York, 1925), pp. 359–60; Melville J. Herskovits, *Life in a Haitian Valley* (New York, 1937), pp. 326–27.

18. Melville J. Herskovits, *The Myth of the Negro Past* (New York, 1941; Boston, 1958), pp. 8, 25, 37, 40, 41, 45, 88, 118, 120n, 126, 127, 304. See Guy B. Johnson's review in *American Sociological Review* 7 (1942): 289. Cf. John F. Szwed, "An American Anthropological Dilemma: The Politics of Afro-American Culture," in *Reinventing Anthropology*, ed. Dell Hymes (New York, 1972), pp. 153–81.

19. Muriel and Malcolm Bell, Jr., interview with author, Savannah, Ga., September 22–23, 1985; Guy B. Johnson, Chapel Hill, N.C., telephone conversation with author, September 14, 1985.

20. *Drums and Shadows*, p. ix; Locke, *The New Negro*, pp. 14–15; Countee Cullen, "Heritage," in *On These I Stand* (New York, 1947);

Langston Hughes, "The Negro Speaks of Rivers," *The Crisis*, June 1921; Bell interview.

21. Hirsch, "Portrait of America," pp. 49, 301, 388.

22. For an analysis of the structure of the creole language, Gullah, and a history of how it came into being, see Charles Joyner, *Down by the Riverside: A South Carolina Slave Community* (Urbana, Ill., 1984), pp. 196–224.

Photographers' Note

❖❖❖❖❖❖❖❖❖❖❖❖❖❖❖❖❖❖❖❖

LANDSCAPES AND NATURAL HISTORY PROVIDED SUBJECT matter for our start into what we thought for a time would lead to careers in professional photography. The first serious project was a series of pictures of Savannah houses and buildings for a history of the city's architecture, a venture that was inadvertently put aside. We had our own darkroom, in which we did our developing and printing. We used a German-made Eastman Kodak, a 2¼ × 3¼–inch ground glass camera called a Recomar. A sturdy tripod and a large black cloth enabled us to stop the lens down to its limit of f/32 and to bring forth a sharp image on the inverted glass screen. The stationary subject permitted ample time to compose our picture; first one of us, then the other made the necessary adjustments from under the black cloth. It was always an interesting maneuver and one that stood us in good stead when we came to the *Drums and Shadows* project.

Mary Granger, our older and interesting family friend, was the unquestioned leader of the Savannah section of the "writers" who were trying to break the depression's grip through the Work Projects Administration of the federal government. It was as district supervisor of the Savannah unit of the Georgia Writers' Project that she told us of her proposed study of African cultural survivals she believed to be extant along the Georgia coast. We were interested and from the outset believed we could photograph coastal blacks using the same technique we had found successful on Savannah architecture. We had seen the Julia Peterkin–Doris Ulmann

xxix

collaboration, *Roll, Jordan, Roll,* and resolved that our photographs of the Negroes would be as sharply focused as had been our Savannah houses. The soft focus of the Ulmann portraits was not to our liking, nor was the poor quality of their reproduction. Ulmann's remarkable ability to capture an attitude and to reflect her subject's character we hoped to emulate. We soon learned that to photograph a person, particularly a child, was far removed from making a portrait of an eighteenth- or nineteenth-century building.

Our picture-taking expeditions were always led by Mary Granger. If our subjects were to be close by Savannah she would have made arrangements with friends or with members of her staff who conducted earlier interviews. The usual procedure was for our leader to engage the subjects in conversation at a spot we had chosen with an eye to light and background. The camera on the tripod and the black cloth that we were forever ducking under to focus and compose invariably provoked their interest and usually put them at ease. Mary Granger's confident and cheerful demeanor and her good sense of humor accounted for the bright, responsive expressions that show on the faces of many of the older people. She questioned as she talked, made notes on interesting responses, and often would chant the African song "Kum Baba Yano," which she had learned from old Tony Delegal. This never failed to bring a look of incredulity to the faces of our subjects.

On the island trips and those to distant and remote areas our arrival was unannounced. Mary Granger was always ready to reward cooperative subjects or to persuade reluctant ones to be photographed with an offer of sweet rolls, tobacco, or old but serviceable clothes, all of which Miss Granger seemed to have in endless supply.

The *Drums and Shadows* photographs have appeared in any number of publications, the artifacts and the Bowen grave markers more frequently than the portraits. The latter,

xxx

particularly those of Katie Brown, Shad Hall, the young girl at Pin Point, and old Jim Myers, have been used in numerous photographic exhibits in Savannah and elsewhere. When Katie Brown's likeness was on display in a Savannah bank, one of the employees recognized her as a much-loved grandmother. The incident prompted a gathering of members of the Brown descendants—schoolteachers, principals, postal workers, young and old, sons, daughters, grand- and great-grandchildren.

Our contract with the federal government permitted the use of twenty-five of our photographs. We retained the ownership of the negatives and of the rights to reproduce. We were paid two dollars for each print. Most of the reproductions used in this new edition of *Drums and Shadows* were made from the old negatives by Savannahian Jack Leigh, a sensitive and understanding technician and a very able photographer.

The *Drums and Shadows* project became a meaningful episode in our lives. The simple dignity, the presence and pride of the people we photographed won from us lasting respect.

MURIEL BARROW BELL
MALCOLM BELL, JR.

Savannah, 1986

xxxi

Ia. Carved masks and wooden chains

Ib. Carved wooden figures

 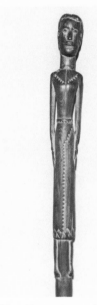

IIa. Carved wooden spoon   IIb. Carved wooden stick
with figure

IIc. Coil basket and carved wooden objects

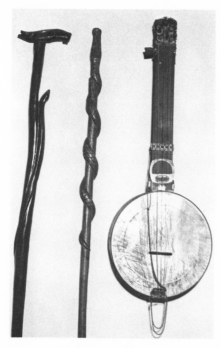

IIIa. Carved sticks and
handmade banjo

IIIb. Carved sticks

IIIc. Carved stone fig

IVa. Carved head of man on stick

IVb. Painted wooden figure

IVc. Carved wooden frog

IVd. Goatskin-covered log drum
made by James Collier

V. Julian Linder at Brownville

VI. James Collier at Brownville

VII. Tony Delegal at Ogeechee Town

VIII. Woman and baby at Pin Point

IX. Girl at Pin Point

X. Boy at Pin Point

XI. Lewis McIver, fisherman at Pin Point

XII. Wooden grave markers at Sunbury

XIII. Alec Anderson at Possum Point

XIVa. Rachel Anderson at Possum Point

XIVb. The Andersons' granddaughter at Possum Point

XIVc. Woods worker at Possum Point

XVa. Katie Brown with Flint

XVb. Katie Brown with pestle and mortar

XVc. Cuffy Wilson and granddaughter at Sapelo

XVd. Nero Jones at Sapelo

XVI. Julius Bailey and ox cart at Sapelo

XVIIa. Shad Hall at Hog Hammock, Sapelo

XVIIb. John Bryan at Raccoon Bluff, Sapelo

XVIIIa. Praise House at Sapelo

XVIIIb. Ryna Johnson, her daughter and son-in-law
at Harrington, St. Simons Island

XVIIIc. Ben Sullivan at St. Simons Island

XIX. Henry Williams at St. Marys

XX. House of Henry Williams at St. Marys

XXI. Artie and Enoch Jones at St. Marys

XXII. Robert Lucas at St. Marys

XXIII. Jim Myers at Mush Bluff Island

XXIV. Jim Myers at Mush Bluff Island

Foreword

◇◇◇◇◇◇◇◇◇◇◇◇

THE COASTAL REGION OF GEORGIA AND SOUTH CAR-
olina is a fertile field for the study of old cultural heritages.
Artists, poets, and novelists are not the only ones who have
felt the allure of this region with its old plantations, its
sleepy towns, its cypress swamps, its moss-hung trees, its ox
carts, and its Negro peasantry. The works of C. C. Jones,
Jr., John Bennett, Marcellus Whaley, Ambrose Gonzales,
Reed Smith, Elsie C. Parsons, Ballanta-Taylor, T. J. Woofter, Jr., Guion G. Johnson, Guy B. Johnson, Robert Gordon, Lorenzo Turner, and others testify to the continuing
interest of scholars in the history, folklore, folk music, and
dialect of the Negro people of this region. These Negroes,
more perhaps than any others in the United States, have
lived in a physical and cultural isolation which is conducive
to the survival of many old customs and thoughtways, both
African and European. The present work represents an
effort to go a bit deeper than any other work has done into
certain aspects of the folk culture of these people in the
coastal area. It is particularly welcome at this time, for it
not only covers an area which has not received as much attention as have other areas, notably those around Charles-
ton and Beaufort, but it is oriented toward the problem of
African heritages in this country, a problem which is coming
to be more and more important to the cultural anthropologist.

Readers of *Drums and Shadows* will encounter much that
is familiar, for many of the customs and beliefs found

among the Georgia Coastal Negroes are not peculiar to them. Indeed, many of these traits, such as the belief in ghosts, witches, and conjure, are either known or practiced by thousands of white and Negro people in other parts of the United States; while the dogmas and methods of Father Divine and Bishop Grace seem to flourish best among the proletariat of Harlem, Chicago, Detroit, Washington, Richmond, and other urban centers. Nevertheless, one finds much in these pages which is new, and one senses the great virility of old heritages in the daily lives of the coastal Negroes.

Drums and Shadows makes no pretense of offering a complete picture of the life and culture of these people, but limits its scope of inquiry to certain definite types. In undertaking the work, Miss Granger, the supervisor, also wisely refrained from attempting to include an investigation of subjects like folk music and dialect, which require special training and technical analysis. The visits, interviews, and observations were made by the workers on the Georgia Writers' Project. The investigators were enthusiastic and persistent, and, in spite of the fact that they had had no formal training in ethnological methods, they have made a real contribution to knowledge. They have recorded what is probably the most thorough search for African heritages among Negroes in a small area that has ever been attempted in this country up to the present time.

This question of the nature and importance of African heritage in America bids fair to develop into something of a controversy. At one extreme are scholars like Robert E. Park and E. B. Reuter who would not even consider the matter debatable since they virtually deny the existence of *any* significant Africanisms in the United States. Toward the other extreme is Melville J. Herskovits, who believes that African heritages are very significant, that they have contributed much to the culture of white America, and that the

study of these heritages may point the way to racial understanding and the alleviation of friction between the races in
the United States. My own position lies somewhere between
these two, since I believe that there are a few important
African survivals in the United States, but that the degree
of significance of these African heritages is questionable in
view of the overwhelming tendency of the culture of the
white man to displace the Negro's African culture, and that
their influence on the everyday problem of race relations is
relatively inconsequential.

However, regardless of differences of opinion as to the
nature and importance of African heritages in our civilization, almost everyone would agree that the question is interesting and worthy of study. Such study may not only satisfy a wholesome curiosity but may throw light on the
scientific problem of the processes which go on when two
different cultures come into contact. In dealing with the
material collected for this book, Miss Granger makes no de-
cision as to the African sources of particular traits. She
has, however, included a valuable appendix on West African
culture patterns and has cited therein numerous possible
parallels between these patterns and the culture of Georgia
coastal Negroes.

Drums and Shadows will interest the scholar as well as the
general reader, for it has combed over a strategic area, has
discovered clues, has raised problems, and thus made easier
the way of any cultural anthropologist who might want to
follow and attempt a definitive scientific study of the question of African heritages and influences in American civilization.

GUY B. JOHNSON
University of North Carolina
1940

Acknowledgements

✧✧✧✧✧✧✧✧✧✧✧✧✧✧✧✧✧✧✧✧

GRATEFUL THANKS ARE DUE TO MELVILLE J. HER-skovits and Guy B. Johnson whose unfailing interest has been an inspiration and whose critical advice and untiring encouragement have been a valuable aid to the project. The project also wishes to thank William Bascom, Sterling Brown, Benjamin L. Hubert, Charles S. Johnson, William F. Ogburn, Newbell Niles Puckett, and Lorenzo Turner for helpful criticism and to acknowledge the outstanding work of Virginia Thorpe, project editor, and Albert Dunbar, project research field worker, in connection with the manuscript.

Notes to the Reader

◇◇◇◇◇◇◇◇◇◇◇◇◇◇◇◇◇◇◇◇◇◇◇◇

PRONUNCIATION OF INDIVIDUAL WORDS, ELISION, and emphasis play almost equal roles in the Negro speech of this section. Except for the spelling of surnames, dialect in the interviews has been faithfully transcribed. Great care has been taken to try to represent the pronunciation, but to have represented literally the elision and emphasis would have made the text unintelligible to the average non-scientific reader. Therefore the elision has been moderated and the emphasis left to the reader. Diacritical marks have not been used because it was thought it would give the text too foreign an appearance, and apostrophes commonly used in dialect have been discarded for simplification. Many variations in pronunciation occur even in a small area; younger members of a community speak differently from older, the better educated differently from the less well educated. Excitement or emotion often throws the speaker back into a type of speech which ordinarily he no longer uses. Almost universally *uh* is substituted for *er* and *d* for *th*, though there are more exceptions to the latter than to the former. An *h* is nearly always substituted for an *r* following a vowel and *ah* is substituted for the terminal *re;* thus *here* becomes *heah.* This latter spelling is as near as can be achieved, and though the diphthong is present the *e* is very short. In certain cases persons have learned to pronounce certain words correctly while other words of the same type will still be spoken in dialect. *Mother* is a common example of this. The *th* in this word has often been deliberately learned though the final *er* will still be pronounced *uh*. Initial syllables are often pronounced differently from the same syllable occurring in the middle of a sentence. The pronoun *I* at the beginning of a sentence is almost always pronounced correctly, whereas *I* in the middle of the sentence is usually pronounced *uh*. Thus the same word often varies according to its importance and the need of the speaker for emphasis, and so on, *ad infinitum*. Some of the above mentioned points may not seem worthy of mention to the student familiar with white speech of the same section. But because the white speech has many similarities of pronunciation, it does not make the recorded speech of these studies any less of a dialect nor any less of a variation from standard speech.

African parallels will be found in the appendix. These have been grouped according to subjects and the subjects arranged alphabetically and numbered consecutively. Text reference numbers (Arabic) refer to the appendix numbers where pertinent parallels may be found. Where an appendix number is followed by a letter, the parallel under this heading is especially noteworthy. Though European parallels could be cited for many of the cultural patterns, the citations in the appendix have been limited to African material both because the European material is better known and because the African parallels suggest interesting lines of investigation.

Introduction

◇◇◇◇◇◇◇◇◇◇◇◇◇◇◇◇◇

THE AFRICAN NEGRO, INTRODUCED AS A SLAVE INTO
Virginia in 1619, had been a part of the plantation life of
the older colonies of America for more than a century before
the Colony of Georgia was founded in 1733. Almost two
decades passed before the Trustees of Georgia legalized
Negro slavery. Thus it was the middle of the eighteenth
century before Georgia became an open market for slaves.

By this time certain land restrictions had been removed
and the consequent development of large plantations, for
which the Negro was an economic necessity, greatly stimu-
lated the slave market. During these early years the plantations that developed in the tidewater regions of coastal
Georgia planted principally rice, a wet culture necessitating
a high percentage of Negro laborers. Later, as additional
acres of adjoining higher ground were planted in sugar cane
and cotton, the demand for slaves persisted.

For more than a hundred years (1750–1858) this demand
steadily increased, and it was the common habit to dump
from 300 to 400 "prime Africans" on the Savannah market. Under these conditions Georgia, and more particularly the coastal region, was being supplied with Africans
when much of older America was already sufficiently supplied or oversupplied with native born slaves bred for the
domestic trade. Thus in many regions the long period of
white contact was beginning to obscure tribal customs when
Africans were being brought in great numbers to Georgia
soil.

Although in 1798 the Georgia Constitution prohibited slave importation directly from Africa and in 1808 the Federal Constitution made the African slave trade unlawful, the favorable topography of the Georgia coast encouraged smuggling. The tidewater coastline and large navigable rivers penetrating for miles into the interior facilitated the landing of cargo. Consequently illegal slave traffic flourished in this region until 1858, when the slave ship *Wanderer* landed its cargo on Georgia soil.

Newspaper advertisements indicate that a large proportion of these early cargoes came from the Gambia River and Niger River sections; later the coast from the Congo River to the southern end of Portuguese West Africa was the base of operation. Accounts of various explorers' travels through Africa at that time, however, indicate that native traders frequently collected their slave cargoes from interior sections and shipped them from the west coast of Africa. Although to the white man, Negroes of an average cargo might have seemed similar in type, it is possible that in many instances they were brought from widely separated regions.

The coastal Negroes of Georgia are sometimes called Gullahs, although in general parlance the term is applied only to the Negroes of coastal South Carolina. Because of the similarity in type and speech, however, it is sometimes loosely extended to include the Georgia coastal Negroes as well. The place name, Geechee, derived from Ogeechee River, near Savannah, is also used locally to designate the Negroes of this district.

The coastal plantations that absorbed the slave traffic were remote from one another. The jungle swamps of the low country and the wide expanses of water separating the coastal islands made communication difficult among the plantation laborers of this section. With the continued arrival of Africans to these isolated plantation communities, native ceremonies and customs were renewed or exchanged.

This continuous exchange and renewal of folk customs intensified the folk urge fostered by isolation. This naturally delayed the intrusion of white culture and the Negro kept intact much of his racial heritage. For these reasons the student of Negro folklore turns to coastal Georgia for source material. Here he may still find living Negroes who remember parents or grandparents born in Africa.

Much research has been done and many books written on the folk customs and beliefs of the Negro. In this section, however, where the Negro has been kept more or less racially distinct the field is so rich that intensified study in special areas still reveals valuable information.

In an effort to present an accurate pictorial account of this type of Georgia coastal Negro these field reports have been compiled. They endeavor to present the customs and beliefs of what is left of a generation closely linked to its native African origin. Some of this generation of Negroes were slaves; many of them are the children of former slaves and the grandchildren of native Africans. Their customs and tales are their own special heritage. Knowledge of them must be recorded now while this generation lives or they will lose much of their accuracy and value.

No attempt has been made to give a cross section of the Negro scene as a whole, but only that part of it which would seem to indicate the survival elements. This limitation of the field necessarily concentrates this study on the more primitive aspects of a comparatively small group of persons and ignores a large section of the Negro population whose interest and point of view are vastly different. Effort has been made to base the studies on source material provided by the Negro himself. Footnotes which give African parallels have been used. Though an African parallel does not confine the custom or belief to Africa alone, it provides interesting comparative material for the reader.

Visiting the communities was an interesting experience.

xliii

Repeated visits were necessary to complete the studies. For the sake of simplicity and clarity, however, each report is presented as the result of one visit of continuous interviews. Though this necessitated telescoping the time element, it in no way affects the material contributed by the persons interviewed.

Today sorcery is still practiced. Modern root doctors, visited frequently by their superstitious clients, perform mystic rites and promise to work miracles and cures. Many coastal Negroes view adversity not as the workings of fate but as the revenge of a personal enemy brought about by the mystic working of the conjure doctor. To this type of Negro there is little talk of "bad luck." To him it is "bad mouth" set against him by an enemy.

It is understandable that the older coastal Negro's use of ceremony and even the ordinary routine of his daily life are influenced profoundly by his beliefs. His imagination continues to crowd his world with spirits, both good and evil. Spirits of the departed are still believed to make frequent visitations to the earth and are as real to this type of Negro as his next door neighbor. Into his Christian ceremonies these superstitions and customs have been injected, lending a distinctiveness not found in many of the white man's ceremonies.

As the field of opportunity widens for the Negro and as his culture begins to approximate that of his white neighbor, it is among this fast vanishing type that the remnants of folk memories still live, without which this collection of source material could not have been compiled.

MARY GRANGER, *District Supervisor*
Georgia Writers' Project

Savannah, Georgia
November 4, 1940.

Drums and Shadows

Old Fort

◇◇◇◇◇◇◇◇◇◇◇◇

DUSTY, WINDY LANES BORDERED WITH ROWS OF squat wooden houses, wide paved streets lined on each side with paintless one-story frame structures, the smells of river, fishboats, fertilizer plants and escaping gases, and overshadowing all, the gigantic gas reservoirs. That is the impression given by the Negro section of the Old Fort, located in the extreme northeastern section of Savannah. Here life goes on serenely for days, months. Then suddenly, as it happened only a short time ago on a calm Sunday morning, a woman is stabbed in the back and left writhing on the pavement to die before a swiftly gathering crowd. It was whispered among the frightened spectators that the death was caused by conjure, for despite all efforts to remove the knife it remained firmly embedded in the victim's back.

The streets present a monotonous aspect because of the absence of grass and trees. Yet the pedestrian is frequently surprised to come upon a dead-end alley blocked by an old brick tenement house with lovely arched windows or to find gay flowers in boxes and tin cans on some of the low stoops. On several corners the houses abruptly give way to small grocery stores or beer parlors.

There are two Baptist churches and one Sanctified church in the Negro part of the Old Fort. Although the people are devout believers in all the tenets of the Christian faith, many of them, particularly the old ones, are bound by older beliefs and superstitions. There exists among them a deep-

1

rooted fear of the unknown. Spirits, ghosts, and "cunjuh" all powerfully influence their daily existence.

Young and middle-aged persons, reticent before strangers, appear dubious and suspicious. They profess great knowledge of conjure and superstitions, but they hasten to say that they "sho ain't gonuh tell nobody" what they know about these things. The old inhabitants, more loquacious, enjoy relating their beliefs and customs to a willing listener.

Among the older inhabitants is Aunt Mary,* the daughter of a slave, who remembers the days when rice fields lay east of the town and it was no unusual sight to find a big " 'gatuh" caught in the rice canal. Early morning finds Aunt Mary hobbling to her work of scrubbing the entrances to stores. In going to and from work she always drags a broom behind her. When we asked the reason for this, she answered, " 'Cuz uh dohn wants none uh deze fixuhs tuh git muh foot track, cuz den dey kin hanl yuh jis lak dey wants tuh." [7]

"Do you really believe that, Aunt Mary? Do you believe in dreams and ghosts too?"

"I sho does belieb in dreams an ghoses. Ef uh hab suttn dreams, dey sho comes true. Tuh dream uh fresh poke some uh yuh kin folks gwine die; fresh beef mean duh det uh some wite pusson yuh knows well. Tuh dream uh a dead pusson is a sho sign uh rain, an anudduh sign uh rain is wen a suttn place on muh head itches."

The old woman switched her broom around under the other arm and continued, "As fuh ghoses, ain't uh got tuh belieb in um? [59] Wy, I kin see um muhsef. Yuh see, I wuz bawn wid a double caul obuh muh face an anybody knows dat a pusson bawn wid a caul obuh dey face kin sho see ghoses.[4] Deah's mo dan one kine uh ghos. Some come befo yuh natchul an pleasant; den some kin sho make yuh sked. I kin tell long fo anyting happen wen it gwine happen.

* *Mary Hunter, 548 East St. Julian Street.*

2

Nuttn ebuh happen tuh me widout me knowin it long fo it come." [22a, e]

Another old woman * can recall when her slave mother used to carry her on her back to the spring on their plantation. This woman wears large earrings of gold which she has worn since her mother pierced her ears in childhood. Each wrist is encircled by a band of copper wire. She smiled and inadvertently touched the wire as she explained its presence.

"Ef yuh wuks hahd aw does much washin, it heps duh nerbes." [8, 12]

At the mention of "cunjuh" the old woman lit her pipe, smiled pathetically, and shook her head. As the blue smoke curled upward, she told of having been conjured and of how it had changed her whole life in a few short weeks.

"Yeahs ago," she sighed, "I hab a huzbun wut treat me well an uh wuz libin good. Dis wuz jis fo muh twins wuz bawn. Ise a twin too, an it sho is bad luck.[67] Deah wuz somebody wut want muh huzbun tuh leab me an go off wid um, so dey hab me fix.[15] Wen uh come home one day, I step in a hole by duh doe an deah wuz a bottle fix wid some tings in it. Right den an deah I took sech a misery in muh lef side an den uh swell up all obuh; muh hands wuz twice deah size.[8, 12, 15] I stay dataway till I fine out wut tuh do. Den I sprinkle black peppuh an potash in duh hole weah duh bottle wuz an it bile up. Den some friens wash me off in wiskey ebry day an soon uh wuz all right.[6] But wen duh twins wuz bawn duh boy twin hab a lill hole right in is lef side weah I hab duh misery frum duh fixin. He lib nine days fo he die."

"But the person did not succeed in getting your husband after all, did she?" we asked.

"Yes'm but she sho did. Whoebuh fix me fix muh huzbun too, cuz he go off an leab me an I know he ain nebuh done dat lessn he bin fix. Muh son die wen he wuz twenty-tree an

* *Dye Williams, Old Fort.*

wuz a fine lookin boy. Deah wuz so many women attuh him, lots uh people tink one uh dem fix im,[15] but duh doctuh say he die frum pneumonia.

"I knowd he wuz gwine die cuz I heahd a owl jis a hootin duh day befo.[44] Deah's udduh signs uh det too, sech as ef yuh sees a buzzud sailin roun duh elements, das a sho sign. Ef a rat eat yuh dress, yuh musn patch it yuhsef lessn yuh bun duh place fo yuh sew on it, cuz das a sign uh det. Dat happen right heah in dis house fo muh faduh die."

She folded her hands in her lap and slowly rocked her chair as she continued. "Wen a pusson die in duh house, ef yuh take em out fo duh ministuh say a few wuds, den deah spirit will hant duh house,[36c] cuz dey jis caahn be happy till dey hab ebryting done propuh an right.[36] I hab heahd spirits roun dis house. Sometime dey call yuh. Wen dey call yuh, dey done come tuh hant yuh an git yuh tuh go weah dey is. Wen dey call, yuh mus say, 'I ain ready tuh go yit.' "

The old woman stopped rocking, sat upright, and removed the pipe from between her stained teeth. "An spirits ain all. Deah's witches. Wy, deah's a ole uhmun neah yuh wut people say is a witch wut rides folks.[69] We all leab uh lone. We shuts duh doe ef we sees uh comin. She come lak a nightmeah tuh duh folks wile dey sleepin. But ef yuh puts duh bruhm cross duh doe, yuh kin keep any witch out duh ruhm at night. Witches jis caahn cross obuh a bruhmstick."

Another woman * was scornful about conjure. She tossed her head indignantly as she made known that most of her neighbors for blocks around, her friends, the members of her church, believed in the infallibility of the root worker.

"Wy," she said, "they all believe that everything that happen tuh anybody is cause by some root wukuh.[48] They don't leave anything fuh God tuh do. Ef anybody takes sick, yuh'll fine somebody theah sayin sumpm is wrong with yuh sickness, that somebody 'put down' sumpm fuh yuh. Ef

* *Katie McCarts, 744 Hull Street.*

4

anybody dies roun heah, some root wukuh is responsible fuh the death.[15, 69b] Now, me, I don't believe people kin put sumpm unduh steps aw unduh yuh house that will hahm yuh. Some time ago my son, my only chile, wuz drownded. Well every time I tun roun some of my neighbuhs wuz tellin me my son's death wuzn't fair. They say 'somebody hoodood yuh chile an cause him tuh git drownded.' "

She hastened to add, however, that she did believe "fuh sho" in some signs and omens, concerning which she has been "plenty sperienced."

"Take fuh instance," she explained, "ef I staht out an have tuh tun back, I know it's bad luck less I makes a cross mahk an spits in it. I try tuh keep a woman frum bein the fust pusson tuh come tuh my house on Monday mawnin even ef I have tuh call in a man passin by. Fuh a woman tuh be yuh fust visituh on Monday mawnin means bad luck the balance of that week. I won't borruh aw len salt, fuh my mothuh alluz said it wuz bad luck. I believe in all the ole signs I ebuh heahd my parents talk bout. I wouldn't sweep trash out of the house aftuh dahk fuh anything cuz it'll sweep yuh luck away. Nevuh shake a tablecloth out duh doe aftuh dahk cause it means the death of yuh kin. Nevuh sew aw make a piece fuh a sick pusson aw that pusson will die.[49] An dreams, I sho do believe in em. Jis fo my son wuz drownded I suttnly have a dream that mean a death in the fambly."

The next person * we interviewed several blocks away expressed an absolute faith in the return of the dead in various shapes. This was a man, who spoke with great earnestness of two experiences he had undergone, one with spirits, the other with a witch. He, too, had been born with a caul.[4]

"Muh fus time tuh see a ghos wuz in a rainstawm. Me an muh brudduh wuz caught, so we run tuh a ole vacant house an soons we git inside, duh doe slam shut. We tought it wuz

* *S. B. Holmes, 716 East Perry Street.*

5

duh win, but wen uh look roun deah wuz standin in duh cawnuh two men wid no head. I tought muh brudduh see em too. Wen duh rain stop, we lef. Muh brudduh didn say nuttn, so I say, 'Did you see dem mens in dat house?' He say, 'No, wut mens?' Wen I tole im, he tought I bin crazy. But lots uh time attuh dat I seen ghos." He folded his lips and nodded sagely.

"Now bout witches. Yuh know ghos an witches is diffunt. Witches is libin people an ghos is spirits uh duh dead. I know a ole uhmun ebrybody say wuz a witch. Well, bery soon she wuz ridin me.[69] I could eben see uh come. Duh winduh—it would go up, an den uh would begin tuh choke an smudduh till somebody wake me up. I git reel tin an po. Den cross duh street wuz a man wich wuz complainin bout his wife bein rid by a witch. It seem lak duh witch would ride me, den go obuh tuh his house. So he say he would trap uh. He stay up. When he heah his wife strugglin, he git a axe hanl an begin frailin roun in duh dahk till he hit sumpm. It let out a screech an a cat run out duh winduh an down duh paat. So duh nex mawnin duh man git his dog an put im on duh cat's trail.[68] Well, suh, bout half a mile down duh road in duh fence cawnuh wuz ole Malinda Edmonde wid tree rib broke. She beg im not tuh kill uh, but dat broke up duh witch ridin."

Further verification of the belief in the existence of spirits and witches was given us by Jack Wilson * who operates a small junk shop in the vicinity. We visited the elderly Negro in his residence and place of business, a small, queerly shaped shack that entirely blocks the narrow lane on which it stands. The lodging is hardly more than a shelter made by driving several long poles into the ground, suspending on these a frame-work of rope and wire, and piling on this foundation pieces of tin, iron, cardboard, and other junk. A small opening left at each end reveals on the inside no furni-

* Jack Wilson, 272 McAlister Street.

ture, only some old pipes and pieces of scrap iron, heaps of burlap sacks, and ragged clothes. Outside is a small vegetable garden, and clustered around the house in confusion are the odd automobile parts, lengths of pipe, parts of stoves, rags, and other miscellaneous items that make up the old man's stock in trade.

Wilson acknowledged a firm belief in the supernatural. He told us, "I wuz bawn wid spiritual knowledge which gib me duh powuh tuh read duh mines uh people.[22a, e] I kin see people wut bin dead many yeahs. Duh dead know wut duh libin is doin an come roun deah close kin an friens wen dey is in trouble.[56] I kin speak tuh duh dead folk in song an dey kin unduhstan me.

"I kin see ghos mos any time. Dey seem lak natchul people. Duh way I know it's a ghos is cuz I kin nebuh ketch up wid um. Dey keep jis a suttn distance ahead uh me.

"Witches an cunjuh is jis groun wuk. Ef yuh keep way frum um dey sho caahn hut yuh. Some hab magic powuh wut come tuh um frum way back in Africa. Muh mothuh use tuh tell me bout slabes jis brung obuh frum Africa wut hab duh supreme magic powuh. Deah wuz a magic pass wud dat dey would pass tuh udduhs. Ef dey belieb in dis magic, dey could scape an fly back tuh Africa.[69c] I hab a uncle wut could wuk dis magic. He could disappeah lak duh win, jis walk off duh plantation an stay way fuh weeks at a time. One time he git cawnuhed by duh putrolmun an he jis walk up to a tree an he say, 'I tink I go intuh dis tree.' Den he disappeah right in duh tree."

These interviews, chosen at random from among the Old Fort Negroes, afford some small glimpse behind the scenes of this section's placid daily routine. They give significance to the penny often seen nailed to the bone-white doorstep and help the outsider to understand the mojo ring or luck piece worn by almost every man, the silver dime tied around many a woman's ankle.[8, 12a, e, d]

Near this section lives a Negro basketmaker * who claims that he is carrying on the tradition of his ancestors. He stated that for generations the men of his family had engaged in wood carving, basket making, and various phases of weaving, and that the craft had been passed on from father to son.[70] He himself only makes baskets. White oak and bulrushes are selected as the material from which to make the baskets and they are stitched with scrub palmetto. Those made of bulrushes are of the coil type (Plate IIc). A kind of thin rope is made from this grass which is then twisted around and around and sewn tightly together. The baskets made from white oak are plaited.[70] The types of baskets include hampers, flat clothes baskets, farm and shopping baskets, and the popular "fanner" which the Negro venders balance gracefully on their heads as they walk about the city, displaying a colorful array of merchandise.

Some years ago an unusual discovery was made near this district when a boy noticed a carved spoon ** lying on top of a rubbish heap. This spoon (Plate IIa), which has been carefully preserved, is made of teak, and, judging from the dark polished surface of the wood and its general appearance, it might well be more than a century old. The bowl is shallow and about two by three inches and the whole length about seven inches. The most unusual feature of the spoon is the carved figure of the disproportionate little man forming the handle. Of particular interest are the flat cranium, the exaggerated ears, the gash-like mouth, the queerly shaped nose, the long dangling arms, and the short tapering legs which appear to be far too small for the rest of the body.[41b]

Near the Old Fort is the Peace Mission of Father Divine.†
This comparatively new religious sect has an estimated mem-

* *John Haynes, 933 Wheaton Street.*
** *Property of Edward A. Sieg, 128 West Jones Street.*
† *Though the meetings of Father Divine are common to many parts of the United States, especially in the North, where white worshippers form a sizable proportion of the followers of Father Divine, this description ac-*

bership of two million and a local membership of about fifty. There is nothing prepossessing about the small white building. The wooden floor is sprinkled with sawdust and except for the piano the only furniture is several roughly built wooden benches. The walls of the mission are hung with placards bearing inscriptions, of which the following are a few: "Peace—the Kingdom of Heaven is not meat and drink, but joy, peace and good will," "Peace and Good Will to the World," "Peace, Father Divine is God, Salutation is Peace."

At about eight o'clock in the evening members begin straggling in, two or three at a time. They are dressed soberly, with a noticeable lack of bright colors and ornamentation of any description, as one of the precepts of the cult is the sacrifice of all worldly possessions. Upon joining the church they must surrender everything of material value to Father Divine. The old life is a thing of the past. The convert must accept new habits, new names, and an entirely new scheme of existence.

The ardor of followers is not dampened by the fact that their leader has never been known to visit the Savannah branch. They claim that he is always present spiritually and can in this manner accomplish his miracles. At the meeting a major part of the service is given over to a number of testimonials, presented by many of those present. One by one the converts intone their devotion to Father Divine * and vividly recount what he has done for them.

A stout Negro woman bearing the name of Sister Patience

curately portrays the House as it was found in this community. For this reason it was thought well to include it.
* Father Divine is said to have been born George Baker on a Hutchinson Island rice plantation near Savannah about sixty years ago. Sometime in the late 1890's it appears that he opened a meeting house in the Negro section of the Old Fort, calling himself "The Son of Righteousness." His activities in the community abruptly ceased when, after some trouble with the authorities, he fled from Savannah to escape a gang of whites who aimed to make him prove himself the reincarnation of Christ by walking on the Savannah River.
Arriving in Baltimore, Maryland, he joined a religious sect headed by

Peace * gives the following testimonial: "Once it wuz muh highes ambition tuh know duh tings uh duh worl. I loved cahds an drink an udduh vices. No day passed wen I wuz not so drunk dat I would gib out an hab tuh go tuh bed. Now it is not so. I hab nebuh seen duh Fathuh in duh body, but I know dat he is God, fuh I hab made spiritual contac wid him. Because uh rightous libin I am now weighin two hundud pouns. Praise Fathuh."

A thin, wiry little Negro man, ** whose eyes gleam with a fanatical light, speaks next. He gives his name as Noah's Ark and states that Father Divine has given him the power to raise his wife from the dead and has caused him to enter upon a new and sanctified life. Faithful Patience, the wife, is also present and in turn testifies as to the truth of his statement and as to her own faith in Father Divine.

Triumphant Virgin, † happy in the knowledge that she is now leading a blameless existence, steps forward and gives the following statement: "I know Fathuh Divine tuh be God cuz he lifted me out uh duh guttuh and changed me frum a drunkud an all udduh low tings dat I use tuh be.

Father Jehovia. Later, in New York City the new disciple decided to open his own cult. It was then that he adopted his present name and that his converts created the maxim "Father Divine is God."

Converts both white and Negro were eager to join the new order. Today Father Divine computes his followers as being between 21,000,000 and 30,000,000, although outsiders give a more conservative estimate. The leader travels extensively and "heavens" have been established in various parts of the country. His weekly income is reputed to be $20,000 and is derived from the many business establishments operated under his supervision.

He has a fondness for flashy clothing, wears a five dollar gold piece for a stickpin, and rides about in a pale blue Rolls Royce and a scarlet monoplane.

The self-styled Messiah has now extended his activities to the field of politics, both national and international. There is a variance of public sentiment concerning him. To followers he appears to be "reincarnated God," while enemies insist he is a fraud, a hypnotist, and a remarkably clever actor who is at present growing a little tired of the role he has chosen to enact.

Robert Allerton Parker, "The Incredible Messiah" (Boston, 1937), pp. 80, 93, 94, 106, 183, 188, 209–36.
* Sister Patience Peace, Old Fort.
** Noah's Ark, Old Fort.
† Triumphant Virgin, Old Fort.

Muh ole name is dead an now tings reign tru Fathuh Divine. Peace Thanks, Fathuh."

As the evening wears on, more of the devotees join in the chanting and in the spirited singing of the hymns. Demonstrations become more and more violent. Several of the congregation, caught in the throes of a powerful religious intoxication, begin to dance and sway with abandonment.[19] Others in the group encourage the dancers with a rhythmic clapping of hands and stamping of feet.

On and on the dancers whirl while the piano pounds out its accompaniment; above the din rises the wailed repetitious version of an improvised hymn. The participants in the dance seem oblivious to everything except the series of contortions in which they are indulging. Eyes half closed, fixed smiles on their faces, every muscle in their bodies aquiver, they stumble blindly on. Some bump into the wooden benches, others fall exhausted to the floor. Still the dance goes on.[46]

Over and over can be heard the hoarse chanting of the worshipers as they continue to give praise to Father Divine, the man who, according to their own account, was not born in the ordinary manner but was "combusted" one day in New York City and who was sent to earth to save his followers from destruction.

Tin City

◇◇◇◇◇◇◇◇◇◇◇◇

EASTWARD FROM SAVANNAH IN WEED-GROWN FIELDS
lies Tin City, born of the depression and nurtured by the
lean years that have followed. The little settlement, with
its uncertain lanes winding through a maze of grass and
tall shrubbery, stretches out over two hundred acres of land
where long ago slaves labored in the black muck of rice fields.

To the west and south this land is touched by the ragged
fringe of Savannah; to the north it sweeps away to the
murky waters of the Savannah River. In 1819 the city of
Savannah condemned the wet-culture rice lands and attempted to build up the unhealthy, low-lying acres with
leaves and trash. With the passing years the place has been
marked with peculiar ridges and mounds, the result of this
building-up process. A wild growth of tall greenery covers
the land.

About 1929 Louis Ellis, an old Negro who had been
evicted from his home for non-payment of rent, secured per-
mission from Savannah to settle on the land. His shack of
discarded tin and his patch of a garden soon attracted other
poverty stricken Negroes, and around him grew up a small
community, self sufficient in its rent-free houses and its produce of garden and river. Although some of the settlers
have abandoned the community and only about twenty remain, Tin City still leads its own independent existence.
Within its precincts the fresh atmosphere of a country
district prevails, for here and there a clump of chinaberry
trees or an oak tree spreads shade, rows of sugar cane and

green corn grow tall, and sweet potato and pumpkin vines wander at random. The rusty little huts are built of scrap tin, bits of cast-off shed roof, salvagings from automobile junk yards, even discarded signs advertising soft drinks or headache tablets. Each house is surrounded by a garden, fenced either with uneven poles driven into the earth or with ingenious odds and ends of junk. Now and then through the coils of an old bed spring that serves as a fence a wild morning glory vine climbs riotously, or beside a wall hangs a yellow gourd effectively decorative above a row of "greens."

Two men claim the mayoralty of the settlement. One, through natural ability, has held the office almost from the founding of the town. The other, settling later, simply announced that he was mayor. Both officials have a following of political supporters.

Nathaniel John Lewis,* the first mayor, has a neat little one-room dwelling behind a board fence. As he politely apologized for not being at his best, a certain amount of schooling was evident in his speech, which was extremely soft, slow, and careful. He smiled with grim amusement when we asked if he knew anything about conjure or spells.

"Cunjuh?" he repeated. "That's what is wrong with this ahm of mine. As I sit heah, I know that my enemy brought about this affliction.[15] One night two, three yeahs ago, I put out my hand to open my gate. Pain went into my palm jus like stabbin with a shahp needle. This ahm has been no use since then."

"Perhaps it is rheumatism?" we suggested.

"No, sir. It isn't. I know. An cunjuh must be fought with cunjuh.[6] If I know my enemy's name I could get somethin frum a cunjuh doctuh to help me seek revenge. But I am helpless."

"What would the doctor do about it?" we asked.

* *Nathaniel John Lewis, Tin City.*

"The toe nails, the finguh nails, even the scrapins frum the bottom of the foot are all very powuhful.[10] If the doctuh could get any of these frum my enemy, he would mix them in whiskey an make my enemy drink. That is all."

"Would the enemy die or just get sick?"

But the old man was brooding with a faraway look in his eyes and would not answer our question.

"Cunjuh," he said again. "You ask me if I know about these dahk things. I know too well. My wife Hattie had a spell put on uh fuh three long yeahs with a nest of rattlesnakes inside uh. She jus lay theah an swelled an suffuhed. How she suffuhed! Jus like the foam that comes on a snake's mouth when he is hungry, she would foam. But she couldn't eat."

"Did she die of snakes?" we wanted to know.

"No. It was predicted that she would have a spell put on uh to die by fyuh and sho enough one night she was burned to death with the snakes still inside uh." [15]

"But how were the snakes given to her?"

"That I can't tell. She maybe drank them in a little whiskey. But I can't tell."

Nathaniel Lewis' somber gaze had all this time been directed through the open door to his garden. It was a pretty little green inclosure with rustic benches set hospitably about. We commented on the vines and ferns, which showed careful cultivation.

"You like my gahden?" Lewis said mournfully. "That's all I can think of, my gahden. Theah's a bush out theah that's goin to protect me frum any othuh enemies.[34] Nobody can cunjuh me now because of that bush. If only I'd had a little piece of that plant befo, Hattie would be alive an me well an strong. But I kept puttin off goin to get a piece. You have to go to the woods in the dahk of night an find it faw yuhself. If you get caught at sunrise in those woods, you can't get out till night again. You plant a piece of the bush in somebody's yahd. They can't go out till you let them. You plant it in yuh own yahd. Nobody can get in to do you hahm. That's why I'm safe now. But," he concluded, with a melancholy look around his meagerly furnished domain, "I should've had it befo. My enemy has even prevented me from gettin on relief."

Lewis showed us his single treasured book, which he said contained magic art.*

"This book has helped me some," he said, "but I didn't really need it. I was birthed with my wisdom because I was the seventh child an bawn with a caul." [4]

We asked if he could see and talk with spirits.

"I see them," he said simply. [54, 55, 59] "Theah is a little ghos that stays right roun this house. The firs night I moved in heah he walked right in an jumped on me. I managed to throw him off. Now he comes every night. Sometimes he stands at the gate with his feet so high off the groun," measuring about a foot, "an his face is turned backwards,[57] but he can always see you. I don't talk to him any aw try to come close, because he would hahm me aw cause me to hahm myself. I jus pass him by as if he wasn't theah. But I see him.

"I know theah must be buried treasure wheah this house is built, fuh wheahevuh theah is money aw othuh treasure a ghos is put theah to gahd it.[61] One time I went out to Deptford with two othuh men to dig up a pot of money that I knew was buried theah. I saw three spirits, one man an two women. We dug and dug an finally we could see the pot of money. Jus then one of the women laughed, 'Ha! Ha! Ha!' The pot sunk down deepuh in the groun. We all ran.

"The laugh that spirit gave went right through me. I nevuh tried to dig up the money again. Right now I know

* L. W. de Laurence, "The Book of Magical Art, Hindu Magic and East Indian Occultism." Chicago: The de Laurence Company, Twelfth Edition, Revised, 1914.

theah is treasure buried heah unduh me, but I wouldn't try
to get it. It is bad luck. That spirit warned me.

"I see witches, too," he continued. "Not everybody can
tell a witch, but I can. Theah's an old woman on Gwinnett
Street with some cows. Othuh people don't know it, but
she's the worse kind of witch. Not very long ago she came
and rode a woman heah in Tin City and sucked uh blood.[69c]
You ought to see that woman. She's so thin and weak she
can't stand up."

"But isn't there some way to keep witches out?" we asked.

"Yes, you can lay a bruhmstick cross the doe befo night
an they can't come in. A little salt is good. They don't
take to salt." [69a]

Then he insisted on returning to the subject of his magic
book. We evinced the proper interest and he showed us a
strange recipe jotted down in almost illegible writing on the
flyleaf of this book.

Eggs—2
carisin—1 pint
turpentine—1 pint
vinegar
cy pepper
table salt—1 box

"That's a cunjuh mixin," the old man explained. "I
don't know what it's faw. It was in the book when Joe
Fraser, a root doctuh,[48] gave it to me."

"Where is Joe Fraser?"

"He is dead these long yeahs. All the real old root doctuhs are passin on to the beyon." And Nathaniel Lewis
sadly stroked his lame arm.

We left him standing in his garden and went on down the
winding path. On each side, closed away behind their fences,
stood the little houses of the town. One was made entirely of
old signs; another was merely a battered automobile body

16

with a rickety chimney sending up smoke from the roof.

From the doorway of one of the little tin houses, two heads peered out curiously at us. We stopped and talked for a few minutes with Paul Singleton * and his wife.

The old man told us that he had been born during slavery times on a plantation near Darien. His master had owned about thirty-five plantations in the vicinity. He added that he had been brought to Savannah in 1869.

"Muh daddy use tuh tell me all duh time bout folks wut could fly back tuh Africa. Dey could take wing an jis fly off," he confided. "Lots uh time he tell me annudduh story bout a slabe ship bout tuh be caught by revenoo boat. Duh slabe ship slip tru back ribbuh intuh creek. Deah wuz bout fifty slabes on bode. Duh slabe runnuhs tie rocks roun duh slabes' necks and tro um ovuhbode tuh drown. Dey say yuh kin heah um moanin an groanin in duh creek ef yuh goes neah deah tuh-day.

"I bin seein ghos all muh life.[59] One time a ghos try tuh skeah me an uh git mad and den he leab me. Muh fus wife is dead, an muh second wife heah kin see uh come roun mos any time. She kin see any uh duh kin folks wut dead.

"Ef I goes tuh duh cimiterry at twelve o'clock at night I kin see any one uh duh dead folks standin at duh head bode uh deah grabe. Den dey settle down an disappeah."

Mose Brown ** who lived near by told us, "I bin rid by witches [69] an seed a thousandn mo ghos.[59] I see um mos any time. Dey jis float long bout two feet frum duh groun. Sometime dey come in a wirlwin.

"One day at duh rosin yahd deah come up a wirlwin. I see a big wite man in it. I show im tuh duh udduh men but dey dohn see im. I kin see im cuz uh wuz bawn wid a double caul [4] an foot foemos. Dat gib yuh duh powuh tuh see um. A ghos come heah ebry night an peep in duh soouh obuh deah. He look in duh soouh, walk tuh duh cawnuh, an den disappeah. Any night I'm on dis stoop I kin see im.

"My gran use tuh tell me bout folks flyin back tuh Africa. A man an his wife wuz brung frum Africa. Wen dey fine out dey wuz slabes an got treat so hahd, dey jis fret an fret. One day dey wuz standin wid some udduh slabes an all ub a sudden dey say, 'We gwine back tuh Africa. So goodie bye, goodie bye.' Den dey flied right out uh sight."

"No, I nebuh see no ghos, but uh kin feel em," [59] said another resident of the community. This was Emma Monroe,* an elderly woman who had formerly been a slave on a plantation known as Wilton Bluff Plantation. "Wen a ghos is roun muh haiah rise up on muh head an sumpm tech me an uh feel strange all tru. It's duh same wen witches is roun. Deah's plenty folks roun yuh duh witches ride.[69] Dey kin git in yuh house nebuh mine how yuh shut up.

"Duh ole folks use tuh tell us chillun duh story bout people dat flied off tuh Africa.[69c] I blieb um bout flyin. Some folks kin wuk roots too. Dey hab duh powuh tuh lay down sumpm tuh hahm yuh,[15] an udduhs hab duh powuh tuh moob wut dey done put down fuh yuh.[6] I ain nebuh bin rooted yit, cuz I stay way frum sech people.

"One ting I do blieb in is signs. Ef yuh watch signs, dey alluz mean good aw bad luck tuh yuh. Ef muh lef eye jump, I kin look fuh bad nooz, and ef muh right eye jump, I kin look fuh good nooz. Same ting wen yuh han itch. Yuh lef han mean yuh gwine tuh git a piece uh money; yuh right han say yuh gwine shake hans wid a strainjuh. Wen yuh foot itch, yuh gwine tuh walk on strange lan aw go tuh duh grabeyahd. Dogs an chickens an buds all make signs dat mean sumpm. Ef somebody is comin, a roostuh come right up tuh duh doe an crow. Ef a dog sets up a howlin, somebody in duh neighbuhhood gwine die. A screech owl screechin roun tells yuh somebody neah by gwine die." [44]

* *Emma Monroe, Tin City.*

Christine Nelson,* a middle-aged Negro woman, admitted that she, too, believed in witches and ghosts and that she knew there was a good deal of conjuring going on in the neighborhood.[15]

"Cunjuh is magic some folks is bawn wid," she explained. "It gibs um powuh obuh tings udduh folks dohn unnuhstan.[22a, e] Dey kin wuk dat powuh fuh good aw bad. Dey kin put spells on yuh an lif duh spell some udduh root wukuh hab put on yuh.[6] Ef a root wukuh break yuh spirit, he kin hanl yuh lak he want tuh. A witch is a cunjuh man dat somebody paid tuh tawment yuh. I know uh folks dat wuz rid so much by witches dat dey jis pine way an die." [69b]

The case of a man who had been conjured was described to us by James Moore.** "He jis mope roun—couldn git spirit nuff tuh wuk. Den all ub a sudden he swell up an duh doctuhs couldn tell wut ail im. We tink he gonuh die.[15] Den long come a man we call Professuh.[48] He say ef we kin git any money he kin lif duh spell.[6] We git some money tuhgedduh and he go out in duh stable an wen he come back he hab a lill black sack. He say dis hab duh cunjuh in it.[8a, h] Den he bile up some mullen leaves and bathe muh frien in um. He tell us tuh keep on doin dis. In two weeks duh swellin go down an he all right. Deah's root men wukin gense yuh all duh time. Dey kin lay tings down fuh yuh an ef yuh walk obuh dis, yuh fall unduh duh spell. Less yuh kin fine somebody else wut kin wuk roots an kin lif duh spell,[6] yuh is doomed.

"I kin see duh spirits uh people fo dey die.[59a] Duh spirit is most lak duh natchul pusson but wen I see it I know dat duh pusson will soon die. Attuh a pusson die, I see duh ghos [56] an sometime dey is lak animals,[54] and den agen lak people, jis floatin long lak a piece uh papuh in duh win. Sometime dey hab no head aw feet an dey's alluz dressed in wite.

* *Christine Nelson, Tin City.*
** *James Moore, Tin City.*

"Witches done ride me plenty times.[69] I spicioned who dey wuz but nebuh could ketch one. Dey alluz tun out tuh be somebody right in yuh neighbuhhood. Yuh kin keep em away by puttin sulphuh roun yuh house aw by placin a knife aw a Bible unduh yuh pilluh.

"Deah's lots uh strange tings dat happen. I seen folks disappeah right fo muh eyes. Jis go right out uh sight. Dey do say dat people brought frum Africa in slabery times could disappeah an fly right back tuh Africa. Frum duh tings I see mysef I blieb dat dey could do dis."

Ozie Cohen * said that he too saw the spirits of people just before they were about to die.[59a] He told us, "Not long ago a frien uh mine wuz sick. Duh night befo he die I see his spirit floatin long befo me in duh street. Duh nex day he pass away. Eben aftuh some uh muh friens die, I see deah spirits nuff tuh know em.[56]

"Hags worry me too. I see um slide in frum noweah. I try tuh call out, den all at once I'm hepless an strugglin.[69] Ef I membuh tuh put a Bible unduh muh pilluh, dey dohn bodduh me.

"I hab heahd duh story bout folks flyin back tuh Africa. I tink it mus be true wen I tink bout how witches kin come tru a keyhole tuhday.[69c]

"Yuh heah lots bout roots an fixin.[15] Folks is alluz sayin somebody bin rooted mos anytime somebody git sick fuh a long spell. Den yuh heah dem sayin, duh sickness ain feah. Dey bin rooted."

Down one long lane and up another we came upon the two or three-room dwelling of the second mayor, George Boddison,** built on the banks of the old rice canal. Boddison came out of his home to meet us. His wrists and arms were encircled by copper wire strung with good luck charms; [8] his fingers were covered with several large plain rings. A copper wire was bound around his head and attached to this wire were two broken bits of mirror which, lying flat against his temples with the reflecting side out, flashed and glittered when he moved his head.

"Yes, Ise duh mayuh," he admitted. He was reluctant to talk of what he termed "mysterious tings uh duh elements." But after a few minutes' conversation, he told us that he believed there was "sumpm" to certain beliefs and superstitions.

"I hab a deep suspicious mine dat way muhsef. I know deah is luck an unluck an some people kin wuk it. It's a science in mos ebryting dey does. Dey kin swap yuh frum good luck place tuh bad luck place." [15]

"Has anyone tried to harm you?"

"Yes, dat dey hab." He smiled at this, and we saw that a brass ring had been inserted in his mouth in the place of a lower jaw tooth. "Some days I feel lak uh jis caahn make it. It seem lak sumpm hab a holt on me an uh caahn wuk. Den I know strong currents is directed tuh do me ebil. If dey res on me, uh would be sick, maybe die. But deze dat I weahs," indicating the copper wire, the mirrors, and the other charms, "keeps all deze tings frum huttn me. Duh ebil caahn dwell on me. It hab tuh pass on.[12a, c, d]

"Many tings kin be done tuh cause people hahm aw make em disability," he went on. "Dis is wut I hab confidence in. A pusson kin take sech as a cat aw dog aw a lizud, sech creatures as libin. Dey kin kill dis animal an dey hab some way tuh cause its spirit tuh be ebil. Dis spirit moobs on currents tuh somebody duh pusson do not lak an is so powuhful dat it cause eben duh flesh tuh rot.[5]

"So I weahs deze," he ended. "Long as I weahs em deah is nuttn kin do me reel hahm." [8]

When we thanked him, he did not smile but only bowed his head. To the end of the interview he kept his dignified and serious demeanor.

As we drove away, he stood there before his little house with the tall butterbean vine covered fence encircling it and the wild greenness of uncultivated fields growing all around. The last glimpse we had was of the fragments of mirror bound to his head glittering in the sun.

Yamacraw*

◇◇◇◇◇◇◇◇◇◇◇◇◇◇

YAMACRAW TAKES ITS NAME FROM THE LITTLE IN-dian town that Tomochichi, chief and friend of General Oglethorpe, established on the Savannah River bluff west of the township of Savannah over two hundred years ago. To-day waterfront industries have pushed the Negro district southward from the bluff, but it is still so close to the river that some of the small shanties rattle when winds roar across the water.

In this community the residents are drawn largely from coastal counties of Georgia and South Carolina. At one time an unruly element gained Yamacraw the reputation of being the toughest section of Savannah, but the presence of an un-usual number of churches of various denominations seems to have improved law and order in recent years. Intense re-ligious interest is aided by pride felt in the fact that the first Negro Baptist church in America was established here and also that Methodism gained an earlier start among Yama-craw Negroes than in any other part of the county.

In spite of the difference in religious doctrines there seem to be certain common beliefs handed down in families. We found an implicit and readily asserted faith in the power "tuh do unnatchul ting." Ghosts are everyday experiences. Root doctors are in constant demand.

---

* Old Yamacraw has gone. Since late in 1939 there has been a radical physi-cal change under the program of the Federal Housing Administration. Two thirds of the tumble-down brick houses and wooden shanties in the once crowded area have been replaced by modern concrete buildings with low rentals for Negro tenants.

Eighty-year old Martha Page,* a small and frail woman, remembers her African grandfather and the strange "talk he use tuh make wid two udduh slabes on duh plantation."

"Wen dey git tuh gabbin, yuh couldn unnuhstan a wud dey say," Martha informed us. "Muh gran sho hab funny name fuh call ting, too. He lub tuh hunt an fish an he use tuh hab a lill piece uh wood wid a string on each en tuh kill squhrel an hawk wid. He call it he 'wah-hoo bahk.' Sometime he use tuh sing a song das staht off like dis, 'Dody boda do dandy.' He say it mean, 'We come fuh make waw tuhday.' "

"Did your gran tell you about magic and conjure?" we asked.

"Dat he did. I sho wuz sked ub im wen he use tuh talk bout dem ting he people in Africa could do.[15, 22a, e, 48] Some ub em could make yuh disappeah, he say, an some could fly all roun duh elements an make yuh do anyting dey wants yuh tuh do. Wen I growd up, I discobuh dat plenty uh duh tings gran tell me is sho nuff true."

"You've had personal experiences?" we queried hopefully.

"Me an muh sistuh bote. Witches use tuh ride uh regluh till it seem she gwine swivel away an die.[69] One day a man tell uh tuh tro salt on duh bed an no witch would bodduh uh. So dat ebenin muh sistuh sprinkle a heap uh salt on uh cubbuh.[69a] Soon attuh we git tuh bed, I seen a cat come [68] right in duh doe an look me in duh eye. I try tuh holluh but uh couldn make a soun. Nex ting I know sistuh wuz poin watuh in muh face.

"I dohn take tuh witches," said Martha Page. "I dohn mine ghos, cuz I caahn see em as I wuzn bawn wid a caul.[4] But I dohn want no mo sperience wid witches. Das wy uh sprinkle salt down ebry night uh muh life."

The broom precaution against witches is also believed in

* *Martha Page, 606 Zubly Street.*

among Yamacraw residents. Martha Major,* aged sixty, related to us the time a witch had "worried" her.[69] She was alone in a basement in an empty house, as the landlady was out of the city. No sooner had she gone to bed than she heard "sumpm comin down duh steps."

"It jump on me," she declared, "an it choke me neah tuh det. But I knowd who it wuz. She come tuh see me duh bery nex day but she ain nebuh been back sence, cuz I put a bruhm by duh bed."

We noticed that as Martha Major had risen from her chair in excitement over her story, she had exhibited a slight limp.

"Have you hurt your foot?" we asked.

"Oh, it mos well. Mos all duh wuhrums done crawl out now." [5, 5c]

"Worms?"

At our astonishment she was instantly on guard.

"Muh foot all right," she said crossly, but her brown face was a mask of brooding. Finally she volunteered the information that she had been conjured the previous October, almost six months past.[15]

"I dohn know who done it, but all ub a sudden muh leg begin tuh swell an swell. I call a regluh doctuh, but he didn seem tuh do no good; so tree weeks ago I went tuh a root man.[48] He gimme sumpm tuh take an sumpm tuh put in muh bed.[6] In a few days knots come out all obuh muh leg an wuhrums staht tuh crawl out. Only one knot lef. I guess I soon be well."

Out beyond Yamacraw, where the old brick and dirt streets of the community give way to the broad, paved Augusta road, an old Negro named James Cooper has for years conducted a miscellaneous business in a ramshackle push cart.** James sells lunches to the workers at the Savannah Sugar

---

* *Martha Major, 542 West York Street.*
** *James Cooper, Port Wentworth.*

Refinery; he also cobbles shoes and repairs anything from broken pots to roller skates. Because of his skill as a wood carver, particularly of walking sticks, he has become known in the vicinity as "Stick Daddy." A decidedly original technique is evident in his carving, but he smiled when this was mentioned.

"I nevuh bin taught," he said. "I took up cahvin as paht time jis fuh the fun of it. Muh granfathuh, Pharo Cooper, he used tuh make things frum wood an straw, sech as baskets an cheahs an tables an othuh things fuh the home. I guess I sawt of inherited it frum him."

One of "Stick Daddy's" canes is a slender, snake-encircled rod with a handle made from a large black and white die. Another, slightly thicker, is carved with a single crocodile. The third, a heavy stick topped with a flashlight handle in which the snapshot of a young Negro girl has been inserted, is artfully decorated with a turtle, a large crocodile, and a small, sinuous snake (Plate IIIb). The chief characteristic of "Stick Daddy's" work is the boldness with which the carved figures, dark-stained and highly polished, stand out against their unfinished natural wood background. Very different is another stick that was found abandoned in an office building in the city. This has a man's head for a handle but the stick proper is so covered with minute, unpatterned crisscrosses that the little figure of a man upside down, a horned head also upside down, and an undetermined object which may be either man or animal, are noticed only when the cane is carefully studied.

"Stick Daddy," besides being a general repair man and carver, knows a few "sho cuos" for illnesses.

"I kin make a sho cuo fuh chills an fevuh. Yuh take some cawn fodduh an boil it an make a tea. Yuh drink some an bathe in some an yuh'll git well soon. Fuh a cold yuh git some life-evuh-lastin and make a tea tuh drink, aw git some Jack-O."

We asked about roots.

"I dohn believe in them things," asserted "Stick Daddy." "I dohn believe in nuthin like that. It's too dangerous. But I do believe in some signs. Yuh watch em and yuh'll see that they dohn nevuh fail. If somebody borruh salt frum yuh, 'tis not wise tuh accept it back; 'twill cause trouble. If yuh throw out stove an chimney cleanin aftuh sundown, 'tis sho death."

Fred Jones,* a tall Negro of nearly eighty, with brown complexion and piercing eyes, sternly forbade us to discuss conjure.

"Dohn yuh know," fearfully, "dat yuh might bring trouble on yuhsef? Das ting ain nobody ought tuh mess wid."

"How do you know that?"

"Ain no mattuh how come I knows. I seen it. I seen pusson wid duh powuh tuh tun hesef intuh any shape he got a mine tuh.[68] Dey kin cause yuh plenty trouble an duh only ting kin sabe yuh is tuh git tuh a root man on time." [6, 48]

Our surprise and interest drew him in spite of his fears to speak in a low voice of several instances where he had seen conjure working.

"Deah wuz a man wid duh powuh.[48] He draw a ring roun anudduh man an dat man couldn git out dat ring till duh root man come an wave tuh um. Den deah wuz a uhmun done up so bad by somebody dat ants wuz crawlin out tru uh skin.[5c] Wenebuh a pusson go crazy, wut is dat but cunjuh? [15]

"I dohn lak tuh talk bout muhsef, but I caahn nebuh fuhgit duh time I hab a dose put on me by a uhmun uh didn lak. I wuz a good frien ub uh huzbun an she didn lak fuh us tuh go out tuhgedduh; so she tole me not tuh come tuh uh house no mo. I ain pay no tention. Well, suh, duh nex night soon as uh laid down, uh feel muhsef swoon. Ebry night it happen. Dis ting keep up till uh git sick. I couldn eat an jis

* Fred Jones, 607 West Congress Street.

27

git tuh pinin way.[15] Duh doctuh he caahn hep me none.
Finally I went tuh a root man.[48] He say right off somebody
done gib me a dose. He say 'I'll be roun tuhnight. Git
some money tuhgedduh cuz I caahn do yuh no good less yuh
staht off wid some silbuh.'

"Wen he come dat night an git duh silbuh, he look all roun
duh house an den dig a hole unduh duh doe step. Deah he
fine a bottle. He tro it in duh fyuh an holluh, 'Git gone,
yuh debil.' Attuh dat I git bettuh, but I ain nebuh bin tuh
dat uhmun's house since. An I dohn lak tuh talk about it."

Another octogenarian, Thomas Smith,* told us that the
same magic power that Moses had used when he turned his
rod to a snake before Pharoah still exists today among
Negroes.

"Dat happen in Africa duh Bible say. Ain dat show dat
Africa wuz a lan uh magic powuh since duh beginnin uh
histry? Well den, duh descendants ub Africans hab duh
same gif tuh do unnatchul ting. Ise heahd duh story uh duh
flyin Africans [69c] an I sho belieb it happen. I know doze wut
could make a pot bile widout fyuh. Jis sit it anyweah on
duh flo aw in duh yahd an bile deah meals. Dey could make
a buzzud row a boat an hab a crow fuh pilot.

"Long yeahs ago deah wuz a cunjuh man wut could git
yuh out uh jail by magic. A frien uh mine at Hilton Head
git rested fuh stealin. He sen fuh duh cunjuh man [48] an
duh man say, 'Dohn worry. Duh jedge gwine tun yuh
loose.' Wen duh hour uh duh trial come, duh cunjuh man
tell me, 'See dat bud on duh cote house? I sen im up deah.
Deah wohn be no trial.' Sho nuff, wen duh case wuz call fuh,
duh jedge git tuh suchin roun tuhnin up ebryting tuh fine
duh chahge gense muh frien. Attuh wile he git disgusted an
tell duh cote, 'Case dismissed. I caahn fine duh papuhs.'
Wen we git outside duh bud done fly away."

Thomas Smith's reference to flying Africans caused us to

* *Thomas Smith, 37 Ann Street.*

mention this story to Carrie Hamilton,* whom we next visited.

"I hab heah uh dem people," said this seventy year old woman, who has the tall, heavy frame of a plantation hoe hand. "Muh mudduh use tuh tell me bout em wen we set in duh city mahket sellin vegetubbles an fruit. She say dat deah wuz a man an he wife an dey git fooled abode a slabe ship. Fus ting dey know dey wuz sole tuh a plantuh on St. Helena. So one day wen all duh slabes wuz tuhgedduh, dis man an he wife say, 'We gwine back home, goodie bye, goodie bye,' an jis like a bud dey flew out uh sight.[69c]

"Muh mudduh use tuh tell me all kine uh ting cuz I wuz bawn wid a caul [4] an wuz diffrunt frum duh res. Ebry now an den I see ghos. Dey hab all kine uh shape, sometime no head, sometime no feet, jis floatin by.[59a] Dey is duh spirits uh duh dead, but ef yuh dohn meddle in deah business, dey ain gwine meddle in yoze."

Not only among these older Yamacraw Negroes but among younger residents we found a solid background of ancestral beliefs and practices, for here little of modern progress has touched the dirt streets, pebbly walks, and tumble down houses of another day.

Ellen Dorsey,** forty years old, born in Savannah, gave us a detailed description of the conjure her husband put on her.

"Me an him couldn git long so I lef im. He went tuh a root doctuh [48] fuh him tuh make me come back home. Den duh root doctuh put me down sick so duh wite people I wuz wukin fuh would dischahge me. I had pains runnin up an down muh whole body, an I knowed I wuz cunjuhed but uh wouldn gib in.[15] I call me in a man who use tuh try tuh sell me a han tuh wawd off cunjuh.[12a, c, d] He rub muh legs down twice a day, an one mawnin a big black snake run outuh muh big toe.[50] 'Deah goes duh devil,' say duh root man, an frum den on I git bettuh. A cousin uh mine git a dose once an wen duh root doctuh rub uh all ovuh wid a cleah liquid, bugs begin crawlin out of uh skin.[5, 15] Duh doctuh say if she had wait one mo day it would uh bin too late."

"Did your husband ever try any more conjure on you?"

She laughed with great amusement. "He sho did. He went tuh duh same man dat cuo me an give him thutty dolluhs tuh make me go back tuh him. One Sunday attuh chuch wen I ain had thought of evuh livin wid muh huzbun agen, I walked out duh chuch straight tuh muh huzbun's house. An dis happen," concluded Ellen, "widout duh root man evuh seein me. I didn know nuthin bout it till long attuh we wuz reconcile."

Evans Brown * is only fifty years old. To see him going daily about his duties as janitor of the West Broad Street Negro School, no one would suspect unusual powers at work beneath his good-natured exterior. Yet he not only said that he believed absolutely in the supernatural but proudly asserted that he could work magic himself.

"It come natchul tuh me, duh powuh tuh do suttn ting. Since I wuz lill I could see ghos, sometime two feet off duh groun, sometime walkin. Wen muh haiah rise on en an hot eah pass muh face, I tun roun an deah's alluz a ghos. Lots uh time it's duh spirit ub a frien. Many wintuh mawnins wen I go tuh school early tuh make fyuhs, uh heah doze open an shut an den uh see duh ghos dat do it.[59]

"I didn know I hab powuh tuh do tings till muh mudduh wuz fixed. Yuh know, a man kin fix a dose fuh a suttn pusson an only dat pusson will git caught. Fo women wuz in duh house wid muh mudduh, but duh doe knob wuz dressed fuh huh. All dem women pass out befo she did, all tuhnin duh knob. But wen she come out, a pain strik uh in duh side. We hab doctuhs but nuttn done no good. Uh whole side tun black an she die.[15]

* *Evans Brown, West Broad Street School.*

"Dat cause me tuh make a special study," Evans Brown quietly added, "an soon uh realize uh wuz bawn wid duh [48] powuh. I ain nebuh use it much, cuz I dohn lak tuh bodduh wid dem ting. But I knowd a man name Doctuh Buzzud wut git yuh out ub any trouble yuh wuz in. He would chahge yuh so much an tell yuh tuh hide duh money in a suttn place. Duh money would disappeah an yuh trouble wid it.

"Duh poeleece rested a man right yuh in Yamacraw. Dey hab him by duh pants' wais takin him tuh duh box tuh ring up fuh duh wagon. Wen duh poeleece git tru ringin an tun roun tuh look, dey holdin a ole gray mule an duh man done disappeah." [68d]

Frogtown and Currytown

◇◇◇◇◇◇◇◇◇◇◇◇◇◇◇◇◇◇◇◇◇◇◇◇◇◇◇◇◇◇◇◇◇◇◇

WITHIN THE WESTERN LIMITS OF SAVANNAH ARE Frogtown and Currytown, through which flows Musgrove Creek, narrow and sluggish, on its way from "Big Ogeechee" to the red Savannah River. These are two poor communities, as can be seen from the paintless little houses on dirt streets that often lack sidewalks. With the canal cutting the center of the district, there is scant space for gardens; but in spite of this, there are small patches of earth green with collards and turnips, and almost every "stoop" is decorated with a row of plants in tins of assorted dimensions.

During week days, with many persons away at work in other sections of the city, it is mostly the old who are found at home. Grandmothers and grandfathers "mind" the small children while the mothers work out.

One old woman, Anna Miller,* had lived most of her youth on a Butler Island plantation, where some of the older workers had occupied the same cabins given to them before emancipation.

"Sebral uh dem hans wuz bery ole people," said Anna Miller. "Dey speak a funny language an none uh duh res ub us couldn hahdly unuhstan a wud dey say. Dey hab special name fuh all kine uh ting, but duh only ting I kin membuh is dat dey call a watuh bucket a 'juba haltuh'."

We found here, too, that in certain households certain foods are considered to bring bad luck.

"I dohn eat peanuts," Millie McKen ** told us, "an I dohn let a soul in muh fambly eat em."

* Anna Miller, 1018 Cuyler Street, Currytown.
** Millie McKen, 409 West Duffy Street, Currytown.

32

"Can you tell us why?" we queried, but she only shook her head.

"All I know is dat dey's bad luck. I foun dat out, an I wohn leh one come in muh house."

Handicraft objects in this section were more numerous than in many of the other communities. We found a most unusual brush * made from the palmetto.[45a] It was about four inches in length and two inches wide; both bristles and back had been made from a single piece of the rough fiber of the palmetto bark, spliced into splinters on one surface to form the bristles.

The work of two wood carvers was brought to our attention. One of the carvers ** made a specialty of small wooden figures (Plate Ia, Ib). He showed us several full length human figures, two or three busts mounted on square blocks of wood, and two oddly shaped objects, each with mask-like features carved on one surface.[41i] When we remarked on the originality of his work and its symmetry of design, he said simply, "I jis picked it up wen I wuzn wukin."

The other carver † had made several nondescript figures, but we were chiefly interested in two linked wooden chains (Plate Ia). One of these, which had an attached box with a ball enclosed, was similar to a chain previously shown us by another man in the community. Each man had cut his chain with all its details from a single block of wood.[70f, h]

In Frogtown and Currytown there is intense interest shown in witches, spirits, and conjure. Personal experiences were related to us by several old residents, who had come in contact with supernatural elements.

Old Henry Gamble ‡ told us that he has been accustomed to "seein tings" since childhood. Particularly on rainy nights ghosts appear to him. He said, "Sometimes dey float

* *Made by and property of Professor Redmond, Park Avenue and West Broad Street, Currytown.*
** *Jerome Carter, 445 Jefferson Street, Frogtown.*
† *Preston Coleman, 532 Charles Street, Frogtown.*
‡ *Henry Gamble, 519 West Broad Street, Currytown.*

right at muh side.[59]   Ise use tuh um now an it's jis lak
natchul people tuh me.   Yuh kin skeah witches an ghos ef
yuh make a cross mahk.   Dis will stop um frum followin
yuh."

Seventy-five year old Henry Bates * readily acknowledged
a belief in the supernatural.   "I done seen all kine uh strange
ting happen in muh lifetime.   Yuh wahn me tuh tell yuh
bout some uh dem ting, missus?

"One night I finished eatin dinnuh.   Den I walk tuh duh
kitchen doe.   I see a strange man comin down duh road; he
wuz twenty yahds away.   I tun muh head tuh look in duh
house an wen uh look back he done disappeahed.   I know he
mustuh been a ghos.[59]

"Anudduh time I heah a knock on duh doe.   I heah it tree
times. Bam! Bam! Bam! Wen muh dog heah dat knock,
he holluh lak he wuz sked tuh det.   I git up an go tuh duh
doe an muh haiah riz up on muh head.   Wen uh gits tuh duh
doe, uh see sumpm as big as a cow, only it look lak a dog.[54]
Den it vanish lak a shadduh.

"One night muh wife an me git ready tuh go tuh bed.
We fasten duh doe an winduh.   Attuh a time we heah a
noise.   Den we heah a click.   Duh winduh come open jis lak
somebody open it.   I strike a match an uh see a big yulluh
cat walkin long side duh bed.   It hab a face jis lak a pusson.
It go right out duh winduh.

"I fine out latuh dat duh cat wuz a witch.[68]   Witches is
jis livin people wut bin sole tuh duh debil.   Lots uh nights I
kin feel em ridin me.   Jis duh udduh day I wuz sittin in a
cheah an I dozed off tuh sleep.   All at once a hag jump on
me an staht ridin me.[69]

"Wen I wuz a boy I heah lots uh stories bout people flyin.
Some folks brung obuh frum Africa could fly off aw disappeah anytime dey wanted tuh.   I alluz belieb dat story.

* Henry Bates, 1118 West Waldbury Street, Currytown.

I know folks right now dat kin make duh spirits uh dead people come back.[56]

"Wen I wuz jis growin up I knowd a boy dat hab a strange powuh. Eben ef he wuzn wid duh udduh boys he could tell each one wut he bin doin.[22a, e] One day attuh we grown up he say dat he could bring back folks dat hab lef town an gone away.

"Now deah wuz a uhmun whose huzbun hab lef uh. Dis uhmun wuz jis frettin uhsef tuh det. Muh frien go tuh uh an say, 'I will cause yuh huzbun tuh come back tuh yuh. I will chahge yuh ten dolluhs. Yuh needn pay me till he come back, but ef yuh dohn pay me den, he wohn stay.'

"In a week's time duh uhmun's huzbun wuz back. He stay home till he die. Duh uhmun pay muh frien in piece payments till she pay im duh ten dolluhs."

Living in a dirt lane on the fringe of Currytown is Chloe West * who was born at White Bluff and cannot remember her exact age. She told us that she frequently sees ghosts [59] and that a spirit warns her when anything out of the ordinary is about to happen.[22a, e]

"One time I wuz bodduhed by duh folks nex doe wut wuz tryin tuh cunjuh me. Somebody tell me tuh git some hot watuh an tro it wen I heah duh noise. Jis as I git duh watuh hot, duh spirit ub a wite uhmun I use tuh wuk fuh peahed an tell me tuh pray an duh witches would go way. Attuh she spoke, duh witches went out an nebuh did bodduh me since. Duh witches wuz two men. One ub um went crazy an duh poeleece foun duh udduh one out in duh woods. He died in duh po house.

"One night I heah a noise at muh winduh. A voice say, 'Chloe, dohn go neah duh winduh.' I stop a minute, den uh go tuh duh winduh. Some kine uh powduh wuz trone in muh face dat bline me.[8b] Den duh voice tell me tuh wash muh

* Chloe West, 623 West Waldburg Lane.

face quick in karisene. I do dat an duh blineness leab me.

"Anudduh time duh uhmun wut lib nex doe want me tuh moob an she git a cunjuh bag an bury it unduh muh step.[15] Duh spirit wahn me agen an tell me a man would fine duh cunjuh fuh me. Duh nex day Doctuh Johnson, a root man,[48] come by. He say sumpm wuz laid down fuh me an he would take it up fuh fifty cent. I paid him duh money. He come back dat night, dig unduh muh steps, an take out a bunl. It hab some dut an some haiah[10] an sulphuh in it. Doctuh Johnson say it wuz grabe yahd dut.[9] Bin a long time since I bin bodduhed but uh sho belieb in all dem tings.

"Duh fus time I ebuh see ghos wuz long yeahs back. Once wen I wuz young an receivin compny, deah wuz two men comin tuh see me. I lak one man duh bes an duh udduh man wuz jealous. Well, duh jealous man die. Aftuh dat many a time uh see a shadduh lak him come right up tuh muh doe an disappeah. One night he come, stretch he ahm cross duh doe, an say jis as plain as anyting in a big loud voice, 'Is dat udduh man still comin roun yuh?' I wuz sked stiff."

D. C. Kelsey,* who has been blind for six years, told us that conjure had caused the loss of his sight.

"An I ain had duh money tuh git nobody tuh tun dis ting back on duh one dat put it on me," he complained.

He looked pleased when a piece of money was placed in his hand. When we asked why he blew on the coin, he smiled slowly. "Dat make mo luck. It'll hep me tuh git mo. Yuh know, a root man, he wohn take money out yuh han. He tell yuh tuh put it on duh table aw duh shef."

We encouraged him to continue on the subject of root men.

"Dey kin fix yuh wid mos anyting," Kelsey said. "Duh chinch bug is use a lot an Ise sked ub em. I wouldn put muh han on dem ting fuh ten dolluhs. I hab a sistuh name Ida Walker wut wuz fix wid candy. She ate duh candy an den

* D. C. Kelsey, 521 West Gaston Street, Frogtown.

uh ahm swell up an tun blue. Yuh could see lill animals runnin up an down uh ahm. She got a root doctuh name Sherman. Soons he look at it, he know wut it wuz. He come Toosday an he gie uh a rub tuh use, and he say tuh rub down an he would come back Friday. Wen he come, duh tings all done come intuh duh finguhs. He tuk a basin wid some wome watuh, an he put muh sistuh han in it. Den he ketch hol uh duh han an duh tings run out in duh watuh. Dey wuz puppy dogs.

"He ax uh did she want em tuh go back weah dey come frum, an she say yes. So he say he know duh man wut sen em, an he went tuh duh winduh an tro duh watuh wid duh puppy dogs in it in duh direction uh duh man house an say, 'Go.' One week latuh duh man wuz in he fiel ploughin an he drop duh plough an fall down. Wen duh people git tuh im, all he could say wuz, 'Dis is my wuk. Dis is my wuk.' He went plumb crazy an died, but muh sistuh got well an fine. She lib neah Millen now."

Springfield

◇◇◇◇◇◇◇◇◇◇◇◇◇◇

ROWS OF FADED GREY HOUSES, HUDDLED CLOSE TO-
gether and facing on narrow dirt lanes, house the population
of Springfield, a Negro community lying west of Savannah
near the city waterworks. In the neighborhood are several
wooden churches of various denominations, a well constructed
modern brick school building, and a number of stores that
supply the six hundred odd Negroes of the community.

Many of the houses are shuttered, dim and quiet. So
somber an atmosphere prevails that it is easy to imagine the
spectral figures that the Negroes claim they see wandering
at night along the twisting pathways. It is not surprising
to be told of the sinister powers which are constantly at work
and against which many inhabitants of this locality are always on guard.

A familiar figure in the neighborhood is James Washington,* famed locally as a fortune teller and root doctor. I
is said that Washington's patronage is growing steadily; [22a, e, 48] each day new clients visit his dilapidated house,
seeking advice or perhaps a cure for some puzzling ailment
that has descended upon them.

The consulting room is smoky, airless, and reeking with a
queer pungent odor. The shades are drawn down tightly,
and when a visitor is being given advice the door is shut securely against intrusion. The furniture is scant, consisting
of a lamp on a plain table, a couch for the visitor, and placed
directly across the room a wooden armchair in which sits the
dealer in magic. The most remarkable object in the room is

---

* *James Washington, Springfield.*

a "spirit picture," showing the head of one of the creatures of the "shadduh worl." The eyes are closed, the face bears a rapt, exalted expression, and the picture fades off into a dim mist of clouds.

Washington uses no cards or crystals. "I kin tell duh fewchuh jis by lookin at duh pusson," [22a, e] he told us, "cuz I wuz bawn wid a double cawl [4] wut wuz sabe fuh me till I wuz grown. Duh spirit show me ebryting. Ain many people hab duh powuh tuh see tings, but I got dis gif frum Gawd.

"I hab a deep knowledge uh magic. Deah's magic wut gahd yuh frum hahm an deah's ebil magic wut kin put yuh down sick aw eben kill yuh.[8] Wen yuh bin fix, yuh caahn git well wid regluh medicine.[15] Yuh got tuh git a han gense duh fixin.[6] Magic roots hep a lots.[48] Duh haiah is one uh duh mos powful tings yuh enemy kin git hole ub [10] cuz it grow neah duh brain an a han made outuh haiah kin sho affec duh brain."

The credulous neighbors constantly seek Washington's aid, for there is much talk of conjure among them. His recent acquittal on a charge of assault and robbery was interpreted as evidence that he possessed the ability to "fix duh cote so dey couldn nebuh sen im up."

We were told of a woman who had a spell cast upon her by her own sister.[15] Wishing to verify our information, we decided to pay the unfortunate victim a visit.

The house stood at the dead end of a narrow street. A high wall separated it from its neighbors and the barren ground encircling it was littered with refuse, tin cans, and large piles of rocks. A fierce looking dog prowled restlessly near the high arched gateway and bared his teeth at the intruders. At our request a neighbor obligingly called over the fence to the sick woman,* who a moment later came limping towards us.

* Ryna Bryant, Springfield.

Her age was uncertain; she was gaunt and sickly in appearance. Her outfit consisted of a dull gray waist with a turban to match and a faded blue skirt. Large brass earrings dangled from her ears, making her lean face appear still more woebegone. Certainly there was something wrong with the woman, for she dragged listlessly with the effort of walking the short distance from the house.

We inquired about her health but when we asked about the "cunjuh" which had been put upon her, she looked at us distrustfully, saying, "Muh huzbun tell yuh bout dat." With that she left us abruptly.

Soon the man * appeared, a bent figure in ragged blue overalls, with a battered felt hat on his grizzled head. Unlike his wife, Stephen Bryant was talkative and friendly, and he told us readily of his wife's strange predicament. "She wuz cunjuhed by uh own sistuh," he began. "Some days she all right an kin cook an clean up; den all at once tings git tuh runnin all obuh uh body.[5] Sometimes she fall down an hab tuh be put tuh bed."

We asked Stephen if he had consulted any root doctors [48] about his wife's condition and he said, "I hab monuh dozen root doctuhs tuh uh but dey dohn do uh no good. I keep on tryin an maybe some day I fine duh right un tuh reach duh cunjuh."

In this instance retribution seemed to have come swiftly, for Stephen told us that the sister who had caused the conjure was now "laid up uhsef wid cunjuh, fuh someone cas a spell on huh too."

When we asked Stephen if he believed in evil spirits, he nodded in affirmation. "I sees um all duh time," he said. "Dey is lill an wite an hab no head.[54, 55] Yuh nebuh see um till attuh duh sun gone down. Yuh dohn bodduh um none an dey leab yuh lone.

"Deah use tuh be a ole house right pas ours. Ebry night

* *Stephen Bryant, Springfield.*

40

we would be woke up by a loud bangin noise. Ef we look out duh winduh we could see dis spirit. He wuz alluz wanduhin roun. Ebry now an den he would tro a rock at a ole gasoline tank an it would make dat noise we heah.[55] We alluz use tuh tink deah wuz buried treasure neah an dis spirit wuz gahdin it.[61] I nebuh did look fuh duh treasure, I dohn wahn tuh fool wid no spirits. Attuh a time dey tuk down duh house an duh spirit nebuh did come back no mo."

Another victim of conjure,* a Negro man of about eighty-eight, told us that although he did not usually believe superstitious tales, his own strange experience had forced him to realize that "folks kin fix yuh." "One time I fall down sick frum a puhculeyuh disease. Nuttn didn do no good till uh hab a root uhmun come in. Right away she tell me a enemy done put down a dose fuh me.[15] She say I wuz fined in fish. Well, den, she tell me tuh drink a haffuh pint uh wiskey and tro way duh udduh res uh duh pint. Attuh uh done dis, uh git well agen.[6]

"I knows a case uh fixin right now. It's a young man wut dohn lib fah frum yuh. He alluz complainin bout crickets crawlin unduh his skin an some uh duh neighbuhs say dey see um. I blieb dis mus be so cuz deah's a uhmun roun yuh wut kin make a han tuh put any kine uh insec in yuh body.[5] She kill duh insec an grine it tuh powduh an rub it on duh skin uh duh pusson aw gib it tuh um tuh drink. Wen it entuh duh body, it tun back intuh insec, sometime a lizud aw a frawg aw a snake."

The old man continued, "Ise had plenty sperience bout root wuk,[48] but I alluz try tuh keep way frum dat kine uh folks. I membuh ole Doctuh Sheppard who use tuh op-purate yuh. He hab hunduds uh folks come tuh him day an night. He mustuh been bery good.

"Deah wuz a uhmun name Clara an she wuz good too. She use tuh ketch lots uh Doctuh Sheppard's customuhs. I

* *Charles Singleton, Springfield.*

41

went tuh uh house once. She show me a box full uh packages an she say dat ebry one wuz a han fuh diffrunt tings.[8b-e] I reach out tuh git hole ub em, but she stop me an say ef uh touch em, dey lose all duh powuh. Clara and Doctuh Sheppard bote dead now.

"Ise heahd lots uh stories bout folks wut could fly. Some time back I wuz libin in Woodville wen a man come tru deah. He wuz frum Liberty County. Dis man talk lot bout duh story uh duh Africans wut could fly. He say all dis wuz true. He say he wuz takin awduhs fuh wings an dey wuz all yuh need tuh fly. A peah uh wings coss twenty-five dolluhs. Duh man take yuh measure an a five dolluh deposit an say he collec duh balance wen he delibuh duh wings. Lots uh people gib deah awduh fuh wings, cuz all deah libes dey been heahin bout folks wut could fly. Duh man jis go roun takin awduhs an collectin five dolluhs. Das duh las any ub us ebuh heah uh duh man aw duh wings."

Clara Smith,* a resident of this community, told us that she too remembered the time when Dr. Sheppard and the woman called Clara, who it appeared was her aunt, had operated a thriving business. "I didn unduhstan much wut dey did," she said, "but dey wuz bote kep busy all uh dat time. Deah wuz alluz a long line uh folks waitin tuh see em.

"Dey say my Aunt Clara wuz bery good. She could wuk roots an gib good luck hans an tell fawchuns, and fix yuh enemies.

"One time a man come an git muh aunt. He say somebody cunjuh his wife.[15] She ack queah an run away an stay fuh days at a time. My aunt go tuh duh house an dig all roun. She fine a sack filled wid sulphuh, an haiah,[10] an matches, an grabeyahd dut.[9] Den she look in duh house an she fine mo sacks in duh mattress, in duh pilluh, an in duh dressuh draws. Deze cunjuh sacks wuz wut causin duh woman tuh be crazy. My aunt destroy duh sacks an gie duh woman a

* Clara Smith, 1139 East Duffy Street.

good luck han tuh weah [6, 12a, c, d] so no udduh root wukuh could hahm uh. Attuh dis duh ebil spell went away an duh woman wuz cuod."

One of the interesting characters of the section is Ellen Jones,* better known as "Pipe Ellen" because of a very evident liking for tobacco. The old woman, an ex-slave, claims to be almost one hundred and twenty-two years old and walks almost daily from Springfield to Savannah. Winter and summer, her frail figure is snugly buttoned into a heavy top coat, so long that the hem trails on the ground. On her white head she wears a dark wool skull cap.

"Pipe Ellen" told us that she firmly believed in conjure and in proof of this she related the following instance: "Right yuh in Savannah a uhmun wut claim tuh be muh frien root-mahk me.[15] I ain fraid tuh tell uh name, cuz she dead now. It wuz Flossie Hopkins.

"She fix me wid tuhbaccuh. Yuh see she knowed I lub tuhbaccuh. She wuk a root on me so strong dat she put a big snake in muh bed, an uh could feel tings moobin all tru muh body. I could feel duh snake runnin all tru me.[5, 50] Den I heah a noise an it keep on, so uh say tuh muhsef, 'A snake is in yuh.' I git up an set duh lamp in duh middle uh duh room. Duh snake show up. I close all duh cracks roun duh house, so nuttn couldn git out.

"Nex ting I know dat uhmun wuz knockin at muh doe. Wen I let uh in, she grab dat snake, tro it cross uh shoulduh an walk out.

"Ef uh hadduh kill dat snake, a man tole me, it sho would uh bin Flossie Hopkins. He tole me tuh git a box uh Debil Lye. Denne dug unduh muh doe step an took a bunle uh roots. Deah wuz red peppuh, an sulphuh, an salt, an some udduh kine uh powduh. He sprinkle dis all roun duh place an say I need nebuh be fraid cuz dis would kill any cunjuh put down fuh me." [6]

During the course of an interview, which was held later

* Ellen Jones, rear 1304 Stiles Avenue.

with another woman * in the community, we again discussed the subject of conjure. This woman told us, "Deah's plenty cunjuh in dis neighbuhhood. Deah wuz a man and his wife libed yuh. Duh man couldn git wuk an he went away. Attuh he lef, duh wife wuz took sick; dey say she wuz cunjuhed,[15] an dey sen fuh duh huzbun. Wen he git home he git a root doctuh tuh visit uh.[48] Duh root man go tuh duh back step an dig a hole, an deah he fine nails an sulphuh an haiah an some grabeyahd dut. In duh pilluhs an mattresses an in duh dressuh draws, dey fine duh same ting. Dem tings run uh crazy. She ack queah an run away an stay fuh days at a time. Duh root doctuh moob duh cunjuh an she wuz cuod. He gie uh duh powuh tuh disappeah an appeah any time she want tuh. I heah bout lots uh folks wut kin disappeah lak dat. Duh ole folks use tuh tell bout duh people wut could take wing an fly right back tuh Africa.[69c]

"I alluz know deah wuz witches an ghos. Attuh I gits married muh huzbun tell me dat he sees ghos.[59] He describe duh ghos tuh me. It wuzn long fo I wuz seein duh ghos too. Sometime he would say tuh me, 'Deah go a spirit. It jis floatin long, ain got no head.' Sho nuff, deah I would see a shadduh floatin by me.

"Sometime muh huzbun see duh spirit uh some frien ub ours. Dat wuz a sho sign sumpm gwine happen tuh dat pusson, eeduh sickness aw det. One day he see a ghos ub a close frien uh his. Duh nex day he git a tiligram wut say duh frien wuz dead.

"I knowd folks dat wuz witches; dey nebuh bodduhed me but jis picked on muh huzbun. Ain a night hahdly pass wen dey ain ride im.[69] Deah wuz a uhmun libed on duh same street we did. We use tuh call uh An Sally, duh cunjuh uhmun. She could tell fawchuns [22] an gib hans [8c, d] an fix yuh enemies fuh yuh. She ain seem tuh like muh huzbun. Ef she pass our house durin duh day, dat night she come an

* Dorothy Johnson, 1201 Murphy Avenue.

44

ride im.[69] Dis went on till he staht pinin away. He git disagreeable roun duh home an denne went away. He ain nebuh come back. I tink somebody git uh tuh fix im.[15] Dat sho convince me uh duh powuh uh cunjuh."

The spirits of the dead are believed to return and visit their former neighbors, sometimes as frequently as in life.[56] Their presence is not always regarded with dread but is often looked upon as a natural incident. One woman made the following statement: "I know deah's ghos, fuh I kin see um. Ef any uh muh friens die, I kin see um mos anytime. Dey peah jis as natchul as wen dey wuz libe."

On the fringe of the community was a small store at which we stopped for a few minutes. The proprietress, a robust, good-natured Negro woman of middle age, talked with us amiably and verified the numerous reports regarding superstitions that her neighbors had already confided in us. In parting we inquired if she thought the people's faith in the supernatural was weakening. The woman regarded us with a wide smile. Shaking her head she declared emphatically, "No, ma'am, dey sho ain losin no faith in magic an sech tings. All deah libes dey heah bout um frum duh ole folks. Seem lak tuh me dey beliebin in um mo an mo all duh time."

45

Brownville

◇◇◇◇◇◇◇◇◇◇◇◇◇◇◇

BROWNVILLE, MORE PROSPEROUS OF ASPECT THAN the Negro communities usually fringing business and industry, spreads westward along the edge of Savannah. Though on its Currytown boundary it, too, contains the inevitable shacks in lanes, several of its streets, paved and tree shaded, are lined with good frame and brick houses which are occupied by the more well-to-do Negroes, among them teachers, doctors, lawyers, and business men. A substantial school building and the Charity Hospital speak of advanced social consciousness.

On Bismark Street is found the House of Prayer, one of the many churches established throughout the country by Bishop Grace. Here several times each year the leader visits his congregation, and the day on which "Daddy Grace" *[16] returns to his flock is always a gala occasion. Regular members and visitors from outlying districts crowd the heavy lumber benches of the House of Prayer. The air is tense with excitement. Above the confusion can be heard the strident but rhythmic beat of drums.[23] Bright splashes of color are given by the crepe paper decorations and the vividly contrasting military costumes of members of the church organizations, among which are the Lilies of the Valley, the Queens, the Royal Guards, the Silver Leaf Band, the Transportation Committee, Male Ushers No. 1, Male Ushers No. 2, and the Sons and Daughters of the Prophet. Others in the

---

* *Though the meetings of Bishop Grace are common to many parts of the United States, it was thought well to include an accurate description of the House of Prayer as it was found in this community.*

congregation don their newest and most colorful garments.

Preparation has been made for all emergencies. In attendance are burly guards whose duty it is to see that nothing occurs to disturb the smooth performance of the ceremonies. The floor has been thickly sprinkled with sawdust and the stout posts at the front of the church are padded to prevent injury to overzealous worshipers.

At the sudden sharp sound of a whistle all activity ceases; there is silence in the church. The Armor Bearers leave the building to escort the Bishop to his seat of honor. Soon they return, followed by the Queen who is arrayed in a pale green satin evening dress over which is worn a black velvet cape lined with scarlet. A double line of uniformed guards follows, and marching proudly between the lines is the Bishop. According to his own statement, the Holy Prophet, as his followers call him, is of Portuguese birth. His long dark hair which falls to his shoulders, his piercing eyes, his pointed beard, and sideburns all combine to give him a distinguished and unusual appearance.*

The procession continues to the front of the church, where, with much ceremony, the Bishop seats himself upon a lofty throne set far back on the spacious platform. The

---

* *Details of the early life of "Daddy Grace" are clothed in obscurity and little can be learned of the real origin of the House of Prayer. Some claim that he is of West Indian birth, others that he was born Marcilino Manuel Garcia in Portugal, and still others interpret his references to " a land beyond the sea" as indication that he hails from Egypt. All members of the cult must be baptized and during a four-week session in 1936 1,789 candidates were ministered to at a charge of $1.00 each. The Bishop advocates that members give generously of their material goods to the church and he has been known on occasions to go about among his congregation seizing purses and demanding that worshipers sacrifice treasured jewelry. It is a well known fact that his profession of "spiritual leader" has proved a vastly profitable one, and in the course of the last several years he has amassed a huge fortune. Many of "Daddy's" enterprises are looked upon with disfavor and suspicion by the police department. His frequent clashes with the law over various matters of an extremely worldly nature serve only to increase the attendance and the collections at the church and also give the Bishop much desired publicity. Followers are unimpressed by his occasional arrests, secure in the knowledge that no earthly force can ever conquer "Daddy." See* Time *(New York), March 7, 1938, XXXI, No. 10, p. 30.*

Queen stands at the Bishop's right, facing the congregation. The music blares forth with renewed intensity and the entire multitude, led by the uniformed guard, passes in single file before the throne. As members approach the Bishop, they pledge themselves to him by removing their hats and bowing low. In the midst of all this commotion "Daddy" sits, a remote, detached figure, his downcast eyes seemingly indicating that he is scarcely aware of this carefully planned reception.

Between the musical numbers several of the congregation rise and loudly testify to the miracles that Bishop Grace [22] has performed in their behalf. A flourishing sale is conducted in consecrated handkerchiefs and copies of a newspaper published by the cult. These are believed to possess unusual healing powers.[8, 12] A ready market is also found for large pictures of the Bishop, for it is said that to chew up his likeness will cure many kinds of illness.

The grand march is spectacular. All those present assemble in the large center aisle. The band strikes up a lively measure and the procession starts. At the front of the church the line of march divides, half the people going down one side aisle, the other half going down the opposite one. At first the procession is orderly and fairly quiet, but as time passes, the music becomes increasingly loud. Above the brass instruments the steady throb of the drum can be heard. Voices are raised in accompaniment, feet stamp, shoulders sway, and hands clap.[19]

Around and around the procession winds. The singing and dancing become wilder and more abandoned. Many now close their eyes, dancing blindly and stumbling into those near them and into the benches and posts. By this time the music is almost deafening and the noise made by the worshipers is equally loud. The muscles of their bodies twitching convulsively, they continue in their dance.[46]

Occasionally one of the participants stops, and, regardless of the hindrance to the rest of the worshipers, jumps up and down wildly, crying out in a shrill, hysterical voice. At length, exhausted, he sinks to the floor and is dragged by friends from under the whirling feet of the others.

One woman, seized by such a paroxysm, falls to her knees, screaming incoherently. Exhausted by her violent emotion, she lies on the rough board floor, her jaws hanging open loosely, her eyes closed. Slowly, she raises her hands and beats them together muttering, "Praise Daddy. Praise Daddy Grace."

The pulsating rhythm of the instruments increases in tempo. A man leaps high into the air, gesticulating and babbling; faster and faster he whirls, until he too falls from utter exhaustion. Still the wild display continues. The terrific nervous strain is taking its toll, and now all but a few of the dancers stumble wearily. The steady, insistent sound of the drum urges them on; feet still shuffle, hands beat out the rhythm, and voices chant an incoherent incantation.

Abruptly the band ceases and members straggle back to their places. Those who have fallen out from exhaustion are dragged to the benches by their friends.

The service continues. During the evening many collections are taken up. Two of the deacons, acting on behalf of the Bishop, urge the people to contribute freely. Their methods of approach present a strong contrast. One, stout, dark-skinned, and clad in a pearl gray suit, has a gentle and persuasive manner. He says softly to the congregation, "Precious Haht, hep us tuh raise fawty bucks fuh Daddy Grace right quick. Wile duh Prophet sits on duh throne befo us, let us all contribute freely tuh him."

The other deacon, short and wiry, darts about among the congregation. His manner of speaking is quick, and he barks his orders to first one and then another of the church members. "Step right up now," he advises. "Dohn hole back on us. Anybody else now, come right up an contribute.

Ebrybody gib at leas one nickel now wile we still hab duh privilege uh gibin tuh Daddy. Step up, ebrybody."

Until this point Bishop Grace, apparently indifferent, has had no active part in the ceremony, but he now steps forward. There is a sudden hush.

"Daddy" becomes an intimate, vivid part of the group. Coming down among the congregation, he addresses his talk now to one individual, now to another, dropping frequently into the southern Negro dialect. The theme of his address is, "Whatsoever a man soweth, that also shall he reap." The main issue, however, is often sidetracked, and the speaker comments in turn upon world politics, the war, anecdotes of his own trips abroad, his persecution by enemies, all of whom "the Lord struck down dead," and the general condition of the local community. The entire discourse is interspersed with humorous sayings that find a delighted response. "Daddy" advises his followers strongly against trusting anyone. "If the angel from Heaven comes down an wants an extra pair of wings, don't trust him," he warns. "Tell him you ain't got no time to keep books today. He have to pay cash." Near the conclusion of his talk the Bishop says that he can accomplish anything he chooses, even to sinking ships, destroying fleets of planes, or conquering entire nations. He is not the actual power, he says, but he is so close to it that he has only to reach out his hand and pull the switch.

After every sentence or two that "Daddy" utters his listeners echo his statements with such remarks as "Ain't it so, Daddy," "Dat is duh trute," "Yes Daddy," "You tell em, Daddy," "Hallelujah," "Amen." These utterances do not always agree with what the speaker has just said but nevertheless are meant to express thorough approbation. At one time "Daddy" tosses to a woman in the congregation a rose he has used in illustrating a point in his sermon. This unexpected honor overcomes the recipient to such an extent that she is seized with violent convulsions.

Noticing that the hour is growing late, the Bishop abruptly ends his talk. There follows a prayer, led by one of the deacons and chanted rather than spoken. At the end of each line the man's voice catches on a high sob verging on hysteria, and those in the congregation murmur an almost inaudible echo of the speaker's plea. The other deacons join in the recital and in the wild sobbing. At the conclusion of the prayer a high pitch of excitement is reached.

It is now time for the Bishop to take leave of his flock. Slowly, reverently, his attendants bring him his top coat and high Stetson hat. From his pocket "Daddy" draws out a large white handkerchief which he waves slowly in accompaniment to the closing hymn, a corrupt version of *Nearer My God To Thee*. The worshipers, too, wave their handkerchiefs in solemn tribute to their departing leader.

Shortly after a visit from the Bishop we pursued our course of research in Brownville. We found a number of people who had been named for week days or the month in which they had been born. Thursday Jones,* when questioned about this particular custom, replied, "Dey name me dat way jis cuz uh happen tuh be bawn on Tursday, I guess. Sech tings seem tuh be in our fambly. I hab an uncle whose name is Monday Collins. It seem tuh come duh fus ting tuh folks' mine tuh name duh babies fuh duh day dey is bawn on." [20]

Another man ** told us, "We hab membuhs in our fambly name Monday, Friday, July an Augus. Dey jis didn tink ub any name tuh call em but duh day dey wuz bawn.[20] Deah wuz two brudduhs call July an Augus an deah two sons wuz name aftuh um. Some uh deze names go all duh way back tuh slabery time. Duh chillun jis name aftuh duh kin."

* *Thursday Jones, Brownville.*
** *John Blackshear, 625 Grapevine Avenue.*

"Ise quainted wid two ole men, one call Uncle Friday, duh othuh Uncle July," was the statement of a third Brownville resident.* "One wuz bawn on Good Friday an duh othuh on duh Foth uh July." [20]

We learned that certain foods are viewed with suspicion and are never eaten or allowed to be brought into the house.[65] The exact reason why these foods are forbidden was not explained to us. One woman said, "One ting I do lak is peanuts, but I dohn eat um. An I dohn let nobody else eat um in muh house. I dohn know jis wy, but it bring bad luck all duh week." **

The palmetto tree, Robert McNichols † told us, supplies an edible substance in the form of palmetto cabbage taken from the center of the tree, about a foot below the top. This is the terminal bud of the tree, white in color, tender, and resembling the ordinary northern cabbage. It may be eaten cooked or uncooked.[45a]

From the same tree a wine is made. We learned two different recipes for the preparation of this beverage. The wine is sometimes made from the cabbage, which when first cut contains a white sap. The chopped cabbage is put in a container where it is allowed to ferment, after which it is strained and sugar added.‡[45b] The wine may also be made from the dark blue palmetto berries. These are placed in a container until fermentation occurs after which the juice is extracted and sweetened. The wine is a clear dark brown and is said to have an excellent flavor. Incidentally, the palmetto tree serves a variety of other purposes. Palmetto fibre is used in making baskets, rugs, bottle holders, and numerous other objects.[45]

Many of the Brownville residents are skilled in palmetto weaving and also in woodcarving. Walking sticks (Plate

* *William Mikell, 616 West 32nd Street.*
** *Beatrice Ward, 832 West 35th Street.*
† *Robert McNichols, Brownville.*
‡ *Ibid.*

IIIa, IIIb) were brought to our attention. One had a lizard carved on its handle,* while the likeness of a snake twisted its body realistically about the length of the stick.[50, 70a-h] On a similar stick of dull, yellowish wood the tense, erect head of the large reptile which wrapped itself about the cane formed the handle.[50]   In the gaping mouth was held a ball. Even the smallest detail had been delicately and artistically executed. We could learn little of the history of the stick except that it had been carved many years ago by an old Negro who had given it to the present owner and soon afterward moved away from the section.** The snake decorating [50] a third cane had eyes of rhinestones [41c] which gleamed and flashed as the stick was moved about.†

Crude hand-carved wooden table utensils were in use in several households.[70a-h] We were shown a fork (Plate IIc) with only two prongs set wide apart on the far sides of the base. One of the spoons (Plate IIc) was about the size of an average tablespoon, but with a bowl of considerably greater depth.‡

One Negro showed much ingenuity in the carving of a linked chain § with a box-like object attached (Plate Ia). Inside the box was a small wooden ball. This entire contraption had been made from one solid piece of wood.[70f-h] Another man employed his spare time in the carving of small wooden dolls, jointed and so designed that they could stand alone.[41e-i] §§

An old Negro (Plate V) living in very poor circumstances owned a number of interesting objects.‖ These he said he had inherited from a grandfather who had come to this country from Santo Domingo, West Indies. Among the ob-

---

* *Made by and property of William Brown, Florence Street.*
** *Property of Henry Haynes, 41st and Harden Streets.*
† *Crawford Smith, 1704 Ogeechee Avenue.*
‡ *Made by and property of Alfred Wilcher, 610 West 31st Street.*
§ *Ibid.*
§§ *Made by and property of Marion Ralph, 2411 Harden Street.*
‖ *Julian Linder, 612 West 36th Street.*

jects were old coins, a pistol, and a pocketbook made of shells clamped together with metal bands. The most significant item, however, was a carved stone fig (Plate IIIc). The grainy texture and the slight splits in the skin had been executed with great skill. The fig had been carried as a charm by the old man's ancestor, but where this forebear had obtained it we were unable to learn.[8, 32, 34c]

On the Ogeechee Road not far from Brownville we came in contact with a Negro * whose favorite pastime was carving.[70a-e] He showed us the figure of a man (Plate IVb), about twenty-seven inches high, with heavy shoulders and torso overbalancing the lower part of the figure. The head was large and square, the eyes were painted on roughly, and the nose and mouth were attached pieces of wood. A wooden crane and other birds carved by the same man bore a crude, primitive stamp.[70c, d, g]

Near by on the Ogeechee Road we found Tony William Delegal,** an old man (Plate VII), well over one hundred years old, who was formerly a slave of Major John Thomas, Harris Neck, plantation owner. His dark eyes are filmed, his once powerful shoulders are bent, but Uncle Tony can still recall incidents which took place during his childhood on the plantation. Sitting on the front porch of his daughter's house, he sang an African song to us. Unfortunately he did not know the English translation. The old man sang the song over and over and we were finally able to take down the following:

> Wa kum kum munin
> Kum baba yano
> Lai lai tambe
> Ashi boong a nomo
> Shi wali go
> Ashi quank.

* Lee Ross, Ogeecheetown, near Brownville.
** Tony William Delegal, Ogeecheetown, near Brownville.

Kum baba yano
Lai lai tambe
Ashi lai lai lai
Shi wali go
Dhun.

In the heart of the thriving Brownville community live fortune tellers, root doctors, and vendors of magic charms who conduct flourishing businesses.[22a, e, 48] There is a ready market for their wares which are used for the various activities of daily living. Numerous perplexities pertaining to matters of business, luck, and love affairs are thought to be solved by the mere possession of certain charms.[8]

Mattie Sampson,* a robust young Negro woman, told us that she does an active mail order business as representative of the Lucky Heart Company, the Sweet Georgia Brown Company, and the Curio Products Company. She supports herself comfortably by means of selling her credulous neighbors good luck perfumes, roots, lodestones, and similar charms. "Duh chahms an good luck puhfumes an powduhs do deah wuk independent of any additional hep," Mattie said. "Ef anybody believe a puticuluh chahm is wut dey need, well, dat chahm will do duh wuk."

"Mos of muh customuhs depen on special chahms tuh bring em good luck," the young woman continued. "Dey nevuh puhmit deah supply tuh give out but awduh it ovuh an ovuh. I have sevral bes selluhs. One is duh *Mystic Mojo Love Sachet.* Dis is sometimes call *Quick Love Powduh* an is guaranteed tuh make yuh populuh, successful, an happy. Yuh use it tuh attrac a pusson an tuh make dat pusson admyuh an love yuh. A lill uh dis powduh is wone in a bag aroun duh neck aw rubbed on duh body. But ef yuh prefuh, yuh kin sprinkle it in duh dressuh draw aw in duh bottom uh duh shoes.

* *Mattie Sampson, West 32nd Street.*

"*Mystic Mojo Incense* is anudduh one uh muh bes selluhs. On duh box it says dis is duh same incense used by duh Hindus an Arabs an Tuks, an also duh Egyptians, an Chinese. In every box is five diffunt culluhs, each one fuh a diffunt puhpose." From a box which Mattie had on hand we took down the directions: "Work the magic spell now. Just hold *Mystic Mojo* in hand and light match to tip. Perfumed with rare fragrance and exotic sandalwood, myrrh and incense. Price 25¢. Sweet and strong."

Mattie also constantly reorders a product known as *Magnetic Lodestone in Holy Oil.* "Dis is used," she explained "tuh drive away evil spirits an bad luck an tuh bring yuh luck in love, an business, an gamblin games. Den deah's *Five Finguh Grass.* A lot uh duh people heah are sked of witches an spirits visitin em at night. Dey hang *Five Finguh Grass* ovuh deah bed aw doeway tuh protec duh whole house.[11] Some of em use *Black Cat Incense an Powduh.*"

A few blocks from Mattie Sampson lives William Edwards * who follows the diverse trades of root doctor,[48] piano tuner, and watchman at a filling station. For a while the old man stubbornly insisted that, although he had been a popular root doctor in his younger days, he had not treated a patient in years. After a good deal of casual friendly conversation, he at length admitted that he was at present doctoring a man who had malaria. He also admitted that he was treating a cousin for an ailment and said that by the use of roots he had recently cured another patient of kidney trouble.

"Muh roots kin cuo mos any pains," he said earnestly. "I wuks on dogs too. I kin cuo a mad dog in lessn a day ef dey git tuh me in time. I make muh medicine frum King Physics. It grows on duh salts an is bery plentiful neah Montgomery, but yuh hab tuh know how tuh fine it.

"Duh spiduh is bote good and ebil an is useful tuh man.

* *William Edwards, corner West Broad and 32nd Streets.*

I make a medicine out uh duh spiduh[5] by stooin eel skin in lahd wid it. Wen dis is done, I hab a saave dat will stop any kine uh pain. On duh iluns, specially St. Catherine, duh spiduh is hel in high regahd by some uh duh people.[53]

"I make muh medicine out uh King Physic root, an Indian Ash, an Tukish Wine. Wen I wuz a boy I lun many tings frum duh ole people bout herbs dat wuz good fuh diffunt ailments. Deah wuzn so many doctuhs in dem days. We hab tuh fine remedies fuh our sickness an know how tuh cuo snake bite aw cuts an boils, eben female complaints. So I lun wut herbs tuh use fuh deze ailments too.

"I kin cuo any rattlesnake bite in twenty-fo hours. Duh remedy is King Physic, tuhpentine, an wiskey. Attuh duh pizen is kill, gib em plenty sweet milk an ebryting will be all right in twenty-fo hours.

"Duh spiduh web is good fuh stoppin duh blood wen anybody git cut. I make a saave by stooin physic vine leaves an talluh an spiduh tuhgedduh. Dis saave will relieve any bruise aw ole so. It draw all duh pizen out uh duh so.[48a, b]

"Tuh keep ghos away, missus, yuh hab tuh go in duh woods an fine a tree dat wuz strik by lightin, an git some uh duh bahk an put some unduh duh doe step an carry a piece in yuh pocket. No ghos would ebuh bodduh yuh agen. I done dat an ain been bodduh since. Now all yuh hab tuh do tuh keep witches frum ridin yuh is keep a Bible unduh yuh pilluh at night."[12]

Another root doctor * in the section told us that he had been born with a special knowledge of healing and had studied the science of herbs from the time he was a small boy.[48] Some of the herbs he uses in his mixtures are Golden Seal, Yellow Dust, Golden Thread, Hippo Root, Pink Root, Lady Slipper, Yellow Root, Blood Root, Rattlesnake Master, Black Snake Root, and John the Conqueror.

"I know in a dream," he said, "jis wen a patient is comin

* *George W. Little, 737 West 34th Street.*

to consult me an I know head uh time zackly wut kine uh herbs tuh gadduh in awduh tuh cuo im."

He had been born with this power to foretell the future, he asserted.[22a, e] "Outside uh dreams," he went on, "I kin use leaves an coffee grouns an a suttn kine uh seed known as duh sensitive aw jumpin seed. Yuh fine deze seeds at suttn times long duh sho uh duh Wes Indies. Yuh hab tuh keep duh seeds in a closed containuh aw dey will jis disappeah. Tuh tell fawchuns yuh spread duh seeds out fo yuh on duh groun an dey'll moob bout. Dey moob cawdn tuh wut yuh tinkin. Tellin fawchuns is jis a mattuh uh concentratin yuh imagination on suttn tings. Den ebryting will appeah fo yuh." [22b-d]

Conjure is being practiced all the time, the root doctor informed us. "Frawgs an lizuds an sech tings is injected intuh people's bodies an duh people den fall ill an sometime die.[5, 15] Udduh strange tings is happenin, too. Take duh story uh dem people wut fly back tuh Africa. Das all true. Yuh jis hab tuh possess magic knowledge tuh be able tuh cumplish dis.[69c] Not long ago I see a man vanish intuh tin eah by snappin his finguhs. Hab yuh heahd uh duh man wut wuz put in prison in Springfield? He jis flied away frum duh jail an wuz nebuh caught agen.[68b, 69c] Yes, ma'am, I know wut yuh hab tuh hab in awduh tuh fly aw vanish away, but it is mighty hahd tuh git. It's duh bone ub a black cat."

A woman * informant, too, had heard about flying Africans and persons who could disappear at will.[69c] She said also that she had often been ridden by witches. "Dey seem tuh come frum noweah an staht chokin yuh.[69] Witches an root men hab duh same magic powuh."

Relative to the custom of placing food and possessions on a new grave this woman spoke earnestly. "Dis wuz a common ting wen I wuz young. Dey use tuh put duh tings a pusson use las on duh grabe.[47] Dis wuz suppose tuh satisfy

* *Florence Postell, 928 West 51st Street.*

duh spirit an keep it frum followin yuh back tuh duh house. I knowd a uhmun at Burroughs wut use tuh carry food tuh uh daughtuh grabe ebry day.[58] She would take a basket uh cooked food, cake, pies, an wine. Den she would carry dishes too an set out a regluh dinnuh fuh duh daughtuh an uhsef. She say duh daughtuh's spirit meet uh deah an dey dine tuhgedduh."

Another woman * told us that on holidays she carried food to her husband's grave and left it there for the spirit to come and get.[58] "I carry duh kine uh food we use tuh hab tuh eat on duh days he wuz off frum wuk," she said. "I take cooked chicken an cake an pie an cigahs—he like tuh smoke attuh eatin.[58a, b] I do dis cuz I know he will be lookin fuh me tuh bring it.

"Ebuh since I kin membuh I hab heahd bout spirits wanduhin roun at night," [59] she continued. "Muh mothuh nebuh would let us go tuh bed at night widout leabin plenty uh watuh in duh pails fuh duh spirits tuh drink wile yuh sleep. Ef yuh dohn leab no watuh dey wohn leh yuh res good. I tink das wy hags ride some folks,[69] cuz dey dohn leab no watuh. I blieb witches is people dat's sole deah soul tuh duh debil. Dey hab duh powuh tuh change frum deah own shape tuh anyting dey wants tuh be,[68] so dey kin tawment udduh folks. Wen a ghos is roun I kin feel duh hot eah."

We found that belief in supernatural beings such as witches and ghosts was widespread throughout the community.

"Witches is lak folks," one woman said.** "Dey done sell demsefs tuh duh debil an he make em do anyting he wants tuh. Some git a grudge gense yuh an stahts tuh ride yuh.[69] No mattuh wut yuh do, dey kin git in yuh house. Sometime dey come lak a mouse, sometime a rabbit, an sometime eben a roach.[68] I membuh heahin bout a witch wut

---

* *Bessie Reese, 2407 Harden Street.*
** *Emma English, 628 West 36th Street.*

come ebry night lak a rabbit an rode a woman. A man wut knowd duh woman laid a trap fuh duh witch. Duh witch scape frum duh house, but duh dogs track uh down. Wen she see she wuz caught, she beg duh man not tuh do nuttn tuh uh an she wouldn nebuh do no mo witchin."

A Negro preacher * in a near by section said that he had been in the habit of seeing ghosts all his life.[56, 59] "Once wuz jis aftuh muh fathuh died. I saw him all dressed up an weahin a Stetson hat. I called muh mothuh an said, 'Mothuh, heah come Papa.' Wen I tun roun, he wuz gone.

"Aftuh I marry I moob out by duh watuh wuks. A frien uh mine name Arthur Perry die. Some time latuh anothuh frien die. One night I wuz lyin down wen I heah a noise. I look up an deah wuz two men all dressed up in wite, walkin cross dat room. As I watch em dey begin tuh shrink till dey wuzn no bigguhn dawls. Den dey disappeah. I see ghos mos any time, so Ise used to it now."

That he was frequently visited by both witches and ghosts was the assertion of another man.** "Duh witches come in an strangle me," [69] he said, "but duh ghos yuh jis see, an no hahm come frum um. Jis las night attuh I gone tuh bed a ghos come in muh house.[59] I hab tuh git up an run im out. Sometime dey pull duh cubbuh right off muh bed."

The same man said considerable conjuring was being practiced in the neighborhood, but that he kept a careful distance from people who were believed to be able to "do tings tuh yuh." [15]

"Yuh see," he volunteered, "I hab muh leg fix once. Dat wuz back in 1893. Fus muh foot swell up, den muh leg. It wuz so bad I couldn walk. A man tole me tuh go tuh Doctuh Buzzud, a root doctuh.[48] Doctuh Buzzud gimme some root medicine an in no time I wuz all right." [6]

---

* *Harry Higgins, 1810 West Broad Street.*
** *Albert Jenkins, 627 West 36th Street.*

A more recent case of attempted conjure was told us by the woman * who had been the intended victim.[15] We found her living in new quarters where she had hurriedly moved to escape the evil influences directed towards her by the downstairs tenants in her former residence. Stout and middle-aged, she had not yet recovered from her fright at the time she was interviewed. As she talked, her dark eyes rolled wildly and her manner betrayed signs of extreme agitation.

"Dem folks wuz detuhmined tuh git muh spirit. Ef dey do dat, den I go crazy an nobody could hep me. Dey hab a dog trained wut would git unduh muh winduh an bahk twice tuh git me tuh look out. Ise on tuh em an uh stay shut in muh ruhm. Den dey would blow a automobile hawn twice. Sometime dey would beat on a sycamo tree in front uh duh house an call muh name, 'Tressie, Tressie, Tressie, wake up! Yuh gwine tuh sleep alluh time?'

"Dey bun all kine uh powduh unduh muh winduh.[8b] I moob muh bedruhm, but dey fine it out an somehow dey make holes unduh muh bed. Attuh twelve o'clock dey staht bunnin powduh an roots an callin muh name agen. Duh nex mawnin I fine all kines uh tings on muh poach, red peppuh an haiah an some kine uh powduh an some bus eggs.

"One night I see em bunnin some kine uh powduh unduh muh winduh. Dat sho sked me. I run upsteahs and git muh huzbun's gun. Den I stan in duh back uh duh house listenin.

"I heah a voice callin way off. It keep sayin 'Tressie, Tressie,' tryin tuh git me tuh ansuh. I didn say nuttn, cuz ef uh ansuh tuh muh name den muh spirit would be stole. I heah muh name obuh an obuh an it seems dat it go right tru me. I take duh gun an fyuh two shot tru duh flo. Duh voice stop right off. Den somebody call a pleeceman. Wen

* *Tressie Cook, 911 West 38th Street.*

he speak tuh me, I tell im all bout duh root wuk an wy uh fyuhd duh gun. I ax im wouldn he uh done duh same an he say, 'Cose, but dohn do it agen.'

"I bin tuh duh poeleece tuh hep me but dey cuss me out. Once wen dat poeleece show up, duh uhmun wut tryin tuh fix me staht combin uh haiah. She kep it up till duh poeleece jis walk away. Den I went tuh a root doctuh an he tole me duh poeleece caahn do nuttn long as duh uhmun comb uh haiah. He tell me tuh use tuhpentine tuh destroy duh han wut she put down fuh me. Duh uhmun jist keep on wukin gense me an nobody couldn do nuttn tuh stop uh so I know I bettuh moob fo she git muh spirit."

In Brownville we found a man who knew how to make the old time drums. He made one for us out of a hollow log, across the end of which he tightly stretched a goat skin. He fastened the skin to the log by means of a number of wooden pegs. Unlike modern drums, this one was taller than it was wide, measuring about eighteen inches in length and ten inches in diameter.[25]

The drum maker, James Collier,* a middle-aged, intelligent, well-educated Negro (Plate VI), said he had made a number of drums in this primitive manner. Collier told us that he had heard of drums having been used during funeral ceremonies in former years. The mourners beat the drum while on the way to the cemetery; after arriving they marched around the grave in a ring and beat the drum and shouted.[24] "They call it the dead march," explained the man.

"The spirit don't stay in the grave," he went on. "When the funeral procession stahts tuh leave, the spirit leaves the body an follows the people frum the graveyahd. It nevuh stays with the body."[56] A little later he volunteered the additional information, "Fuh the spirit tuh rest in the grave folks have tuh be buried at home. They nevuh feel right ef

* James Collier, 806 West 39th Street.

they buried frum home. The spirit jist wanduh aroun.[1]

"I have seen something I think wuz a ghost. I have no explanation of it, but I think it wuz supuhnatural. I have heard of witchcraft, cunjuh an magic. I believe some of these things happen, and the mo yuh probe intuh them the less yuh know.

"I have heard about a magic hoe that folks put in the gahden. They speak certain words tuh it; then the hoe goes ahead an cultivates the gahden without anyone touching it. They jist tell it tuh do the wuk and it does it." [39]

We questioned Collier again about his personal experiences with supernatural beings and he related the following story:

"Wen I wuz jist a young boy muh family use tuh live in Currytown. Me and muh brothuh use tuh go and see muh aunt who lived in Yamacraw. Tuh get frum our house tuh wheah she lived we had tuh go past a cemetery which wuz in back of the Union Station.

"One time we had been tuh see muh aunt and it got tuh be late. We stahted fuh home. It wuz beginnin of night. Muh brothuh he had rheumatism an he wuz hobblin along on a stick. We stahted along by a fence tuh get tuh West Broad Street an wen we had gone about a hundred yards we saw a lady comin tuhwards us.[59] She wuz very feah, very feah, an she wuz all dressed in black and had on a long black veil. Her dress wuz black silk and rustled as she walked.

"Muh brothuh an I, we were suhprised tuh see the lady all of a sudden, fuh we hadn't noticed her befo. She come up tuh us an she say, 'Are yuh goin roun the fence?' We tell her we wuz an she say, 'Yuh not afraid?' an we say, 'No— we not afraid.'

"The lady wanted tuh walk with us an we all staht walkin along. We had gone a short ways wen all of a sudden we look in the cemetery an we see a little white thing risin up out of the groun. It wuz kinduh hazy an shadowy an it spring up from the groun an streak out tuh meet us on the path ahead. It looked like a lill animal.[54]

"The lady, wen she see the lill white sumpms a comin, she daht out like lightin an she go right tuh meet it. Wen she get tuh it she disappeah right intuh the eah, disappeah right befo our eyes. Muh brothuh fuhgot he wuz crippled, he drop his stick an staht runnin, an I run too. An we nevuh stop runnin, kept right on goin till we got home tuh Currytown. He don't like to speak of it tuhday cause we're not supuhstitious."

Tatemville

◇◇◇◇◇◇◇◇◇◇◇◇◇

EXTENDING SOUTHWEST FROM SAVANNAH OVER A widely scattered area is a section known locally as Tatemville. This settlement is inhabited largely by Negroes, some of whom are survivals of ante-bellum days.

It is interesting to note that a number of these old people in speaking of their fellow-slaves frequently prefix "Golla" to the given name.*

H. H. Miller,** an educated old man of this community, who has acquired considerable wealth, stated, "I knew many of the 'Golla' tribesmen who were brought to this country, when I was a boy. I think some can be found aroun these pahts now."

A palsied old man, William Newkirk,† who said he was born on the Newkirk place, obligingly replied to questions concerning root doctors and conjure, "Well, duh root doctuh wuz all we needed. Dey wuz bettuh dan duh doctuhs now-a-days. Deah wuzn all uh dis yuh cuttin an wen yuh sick, duh root doctuh would make some tea an gib yuh aw sumpm tuh rub wid an das all. Den fo yuh know it, yuh wuz all right.[48a] He would fix tings fuh yuh ef somebody done put sumpm down fuh yuh. Deah wuz many ways tuh wuk it. Sometime he would gib yuh sumpm tuh weah wid yuh aw sumpm tuh take." [6]

Spirits are a reality to Esther Jones,‡ obviously a woman

* See Introduction.
** H. H. Miller 46th and Pearl Streets.
† William Newkirk, Tatemville.
‡ Esther Jones 308 West 46th Street.

of schooling as evinced by her diction. She is a devout member of the Adventist Church, her day of worship coming on Saturday instead of the customary Sunday, a day observed and anticipated by the average Negro.

"Silvia Higgins," Esther testified, "wuz a medium. She talked with spirits all huh life.[56a, b] She used the rapping signal. I myself have seen the work and acts of spirits. I've seen cheahs and tables move about a room. And I've seen a woman and a boy come intuh my yahd and then disappeah, and I know that the woman wuz dead. The boy wuz not dead but wuz not anywheah in this vicinity. Silvia Higgins wuz my mothuh. She has been dead thirty-two yeahs."

One of the most interesting Negroes in this settlement is Tonie Houston,* an old preacher, extremely gracious of manner and eager to be of help.

"I bin yuh in dis town fo dey wuz no big buildings an duh streets wuz all dut an deah wuz no pavement."

"Do you remember any of the people brought over from Africa?" we asked.

"Yas, I know heaps ub um. Deah wuz 'Golla' John Wiley, 'Golla' Jim Bayfield—he wuz bought by Mahse Chahles Lamar, and he sole im to Mr. McMullen. Den deah wuz 'Golla' Jack, 'Golla' Tom, 'Golla' Silvie, 'Golla' Chahles Carr, 'Golla' Bob, Chahlotte, Cain, an Jeanette, an 'Golla' Alice. Dey wuz all bought by Mr. McMullen."

When asked the meaning of so many "Gollas," he replied, "All duh people wut come frum Africa aw obuhseas wuz call 'Golla,' and dey talk wuz call 'Golla' talk." His knowledge of their language, gained by association with the Africans, was scant. Among the words he remembered were *musungo* tobacco, *mulafo* whiskey, and *sisure* chicken. A cow was called *gombay* [25g] and a hog *gulluh*.

To questions regarding the utensils, such as buckets, tubs,

* *Tonie Houston, Tatemville.*

dishes, and tools, of these people, he answered, "Dey would make any ting dey needed. Dey made spoons, trays, buckets. Dey made piggins an mawtuh an pestle from a lawg uh wood. Dey would make wooden cuttuhs fuh meat an vegetubble an would dress some uh dem wid pretty figyuhs." [70d]

For their meetings, he said "Golla" Tom or another would beat the drum signalling them to gather; then all would sing and dance in a circle to the accompaniment of the drum.[23] The drums of death would also sound, summoning to the "settin-up" or wake.[26] "Dey would have some hot drinks," recounted Tonie Houston, "sech as coffee an tea.[37] Den at duh time fuh buryin, duh drum would beat an all would lay flat on duh groun on dey faces befo duh body wuz placed in duh grave. Den all would rise and dance roun duh grave. Wen duh body wuz buried, duh drum would give signal wen all wuz tuh rise aw fall aw tuh dance aw sing." [18]

As to the magic of conjure, he had been well acquainted with a "cunjuh man" who, he said, was a native of Africa and could disappear at will. However, this man, Dick Hamilton, had died three years previously.

There had also been living in Tatemville "Golla" Jones Davis, an African, who, as affirmed by his relative, Solomon Davis, has not been heard of since his departure for his native land, some five or six years ago.

Richard Wright,* bent with age and rheumatism, talked at length about his childhood on the plantation, where he was one of seventy-five children owned by his "Boss." He attested to the skill exhibited in that day by the men in wood carving and the making of farm implements [70d] and by the women in making cloth.

He was staunch in his belief in signs as he declared, "Deah's many tings wut's bad luck. Ef we come in duh house wid our hat on we hab tuh go back an den pull it off an den come in. Wen yuh clean duh house in duh day an

---

* *Richard Wright, Tatemville.*

duh flo git duhty agen by duh night time an yuh sweep duh flo, yuh musn sweep duh dut out duh house, but yuh hab tuh sweep it behine duh doe till mawnin.

" 'Tis bad luck fuh girls tuh wistle. It will suttnly lead tuh misfawchun. Yuh should nevuh put noo bodes on a ole house but yuh should git a ole bode das good tuh men duh place dat yuh hab tuh fix. An nevuh put anudduh ruhm on a house das already buil. It sho mean bad luck, eeduh sickness aw det tuh some uh yuh fambly aw close friens, wen yuh heah duh owl holluh by yuh house.[44] Now yuh kin watch it. I ain see it fail yet."

The custom of spitting on money is a very old one, it seems. This, he explained, will cause it to "stick tuh yuh aw it will draw mo tuh yuh."

Strolling down the sandy road with an ax across his shoulder and a dog at his heels, Jack Waldburg * hastily removed his hat at the sight of us. He is of medium height and slightly bent; his hair and beard are quite gray but his sprightly appearance belies the eighty years he claims.

He greeted us cordially, listened attentively to what we had to say, and answered without hesitation.

"Yes, missis, I bawn an raise in dis paht uh duh country, down at Cherry Hill in Bryan County. But I bin libin roun yuh bout tutty yeahs. Muh gran wuz a African. Das weah he come frum an he name wuz Buck Waldburg. He dahk in culluh an medium high wid strong buil. He hab long haiah. But granmudduh, she from deah, too, an she feah. She duh one wut lun me tuh make medicine frum root.[48b] She a midwife an tell me duh kine tuh use. I dohn make it no mo cuz I ain got a license."

We asked if conjure were practiced by root men.

"No'm, I dohn know nuttn bout cunjuh. Some folks say dey kin wuk it but it bad an I dohn fool wid um.

"Now spirits is diffunt. Deah is good un an bad un.[56a]

* Jack Waldburg, Tatemville.

I caahn see um but uh feels um. Sometime wen folks is comin tuh me I kin tell dey comin fo I see um, an wen yuh die yuh head tun backwud.[57] Soon's yuh die it tun roun.

"Duh folks frum Africa could see um. Dey natchul bawn dat way. An wite dogs! [4c] Dey alluz kin see spirit. Muh brudduh Simon he bawn wid a caul an he see um an play wid um.[4] Dey would climb trees an he climb attuh um so muh mudduh give um some tea made frum caul uh women an bline um tuh um."

We endeavored to gain some information as to the ingredients of this tea but the only explanation was that the concoction was more effective when made from cauls of women.

He could remember nothing as to the use of drums at funerals or other gatherings but his eyes twinkled when we turned the conversation to a culinary line.

"Ma would make ash cake," he recalled. "She would mix duh cawnmeal, den open duh oak ashes an spread in some hickory leaves, den put duh cawnmeal on duh leabes an cubbuh wid mo leabes, den put duh hot ashes an coals on duh top. Wen it done, she take duh bread frum duh ashes an rub it wid a rough clawt aw brush an it would be pretty an brown. Dis," he concluded smacking his lips, "wuz bery fine wid fat meat aw surup."

Justine Singleton * believed firmly in the existence of spirits as verified by her statement. "Yes, wen I wuz sick muh sistuh das dead come tuh me an I knowd dat it wuz huh an she done talk tuh me. She tole me tuh git some weepin willuh an bile it an make a wash fuh muh feet." This, she explained is an excellent remedy for foot ailments. "I done talk tuh duh spirits many times. Sometime I gib em sumpm. I caahn tell yuh no mo now cuz I caahn git muh mine tuhgedduh."

In this locality stands a small one-room structure occu-

* *Justine Singleton, Tatemville.*

pied by an old man and his dog, between whom there is a touching devotion. In addition to other means of livelihood, he follows the profession of root doctor. "I kin cuo any kine uh sickness das put on yuh. An," he added, "I kin tell wut a man want. Soon's uh see im his spirit come tuh me. I lay down an sleep an know wen somebody want me. Deah spirit come an wake me. Many times uh go an fine em lookin fuh me."

This man, whose name is Allen Parker * is unusually adept with his hands, as shown by his skill in mending clocks, watches, and firearms, in making chairs, baskets, piggins, bread trays, spoons and forks,[70d] and in carving figures of such animals as snakes, lizards, frogs, dogs, alligators and rabbits.[50b]

In reference to native Africans, he declared that he had known many of them but that few were left in this vicinity although he thought some might be found around Darien.

It was with difficulty that Rosanna Williams ** was persuaded to talk. She was suspicious and reticent and lived behind tightly locked doors in a house that to all appearance was deserted. After much coaxing she cast aside some of her mistrust and grudgingly responded to our friendly gestures.

"Muh name is Rosanna Williams. Muh pa wuz Lonnon Dennerson. He frum duh ole country. Muh granpa wuz 'Golla' Dennerson, King uh his tribe. Wen muh pa wuz a lill boy, him an muh granpa wuz fool away wid a red hankuhchuh. Dey wuz sole tuh Chahls Grant on one uh duh iluns roun Brunswick. Muh pa wuz six foot tall an on is furud wuz a scah bout dis big." [14] She indicated the end of her forefinger.

We questioned her more closely regarding this mark which

* *Allen Parker, Tatemville.*
** *Rosanna Williams, Tatemville.*

from her description seemed to have been a small scar, oval in shape and slightly raised.

We had been told by her neighbors that she, too, bore a mark, although none of them had seen it.

"Did he mark you too, Rosanna?"

She gave us a piercing look, ignored the question, and continued along another vein. "He eat funny kine uh food. Roas wile locus an mushruhm an tanyan root. It lak elephant-eah an tase like Irish potatuh. He plant mosly benne an rice. I plant a lill benne ebry yeah too. He use tuh beat benne seed in mawtuh an pestle, sometime wid a lill shuguh an sometime wid a lill salt an make a pase. He eat it on bread aw he eat it jis so."

We broached the subject of drums.

"Yes'm, dey use tuh dance tuh drums an dey beat um fuh fewnuls too.

"I wuz too lill tuh membuh anyting wut wuz said bout muh granpa, but muh pa wuk on duh fahm fuh is 'boss.' He make lot uh duh tings dey use. I ain got nuttn wut he had but dis." She brought forth a curious looking tool resembling a can opener with a hook in the end, which, she said, her father had used for extracting teeth. He had also been familiar with various roots and weeds, which he used in the preparation of medicines administered to the sick on the plantation.[48b]

We returned to the subject of the mark, at the mention of which her eyes suddenly narrowed.

"Wut yuh doin? Is yuh gonuh sen me back tuh Liberia?"

When we assured her that we had no such intention she became complacent and even voluble.

"Yes'm, he mahk me," she admitted, "on muh ches."

"What did he do it with? What sort of an instrument did he use?" we asked, vainly trying to conceal our interest.

"I dohn membuh. I wuz too lill."

"But did he tell you why he marked you?" we persisted.

"No'm, he ain say wy. He jis tell me he done it wen Ise lill. I dohn known wut he do it wid an Ise mos grown fo uh know wut it is an Ise duh onlies one he mahk. I duh tomboy uh duh fambly an folluh im roun askin wut duh ole country like."

"Rosanna," we ventured, "would you let us see the scar?"

She hesitated, then cautiously raised her hand to the fastening at the neck of her dress and, baring her chest, allowed us a glimpse of the scar. It appeared to be an irregular circle the size of a fifty-cent piece with faint lines which seemed to run toward the center.[14] Time, however, had obliterated any design or pattern which it might once have had.

White Bluff

◇◇◇◇◇◇◇◇◇◇◇◇◇◇◇

HUGE, MOSS-HUNG OAKS FORM A CANOPY AND CAST filigreed shadows upon the White Bluff Road, which passes directly through the quiet Negro community of White Bluff, eight miles southeast of Savannah.

Winding roads turn from the main highway and terminate in the various sections which form the settlement and which are known as Nicholsonboro, Rose Dhu, Twin Hill, and Cedar Grove. The sections east of the White Bluff Road are on the Vernon River. It is here that many of the inhabitants make their living by catching crab and fish which they sell in the city markets. West of the highway the narrow roads lead through thickly wooded areas of great beauty. Along these roads families have cleared small tracts and built their homes, reserving garden space for flowers and vegetables. In the summer wild crepe myrtle trees, with blossoms as luscious a red as the heart of the watermelon, contrast colorfully with the bright blue paint on the doors and trimmings of some of the houses.

The White Bluff Road, which for two miles forms the main street of the community, passes the houses of other residents set well back from the road. Most of them are small and unpretentious but well kept. At intervals of perhaps half a mile are three rural grocery stores; farther along is a whitewashed church with red and blue glass windows, and at the farthest extremity of the settlement is a similar but larger church.

The inhabitants, of which there are approximately four

hundred, are deeply religious and lay great stress on being "Christian people." Many of the older inhabitants were formerly slaves on a large plantation on St. Catherines Island. After the War between the States many of these Negroes moved to White Bluff, built their homes, reared their families, and have lived to see two generations reach maturity. With all their fervent Christian doctrines the old people have an unwavering faith in many of the beliefs taught them by their grandparents. A few remember their ancestors who were brought from Africa on slave ships.

The younger group seem carefree as they perform their tasks in the cool part of the morning. It is not unusual to see several young men lying on a shady porch resting or happily engaged in a card game as early as ten o'clock on a summer morning. These young people have little faith in the practices of their elders, but they believe profoundly in the power of certain charms to affect luck and love.[8]

Having heard that Sophie Davis was one of the oldest persons in the community, we visited her and found her cordial in her reception. Sophie * does not know her exact age, but was eight at the time of the war. She is very short and very stout with gray hair and a very large smiling face. The day we saw her she wore a cotton print dress with gray predominating. Her sparkling eyes expressed her interest in current happenings of the community, and when she laughed, her eyes became mere slits and her shoulders shook.

Indicating a small bush growing beside the doorway of her little cabin, Sophie told us, "Some uh duh folks heah sho belieb in some queah tings. Yuh see dis lill bush—it call Cherokee an mos uh duh folks yuh plants it at duh doe. It bring um good luck.[34c] Lot uh medicine an cuos is made frum udduh roots and herbs an some uh duh folks uses um wen dey's sick." [48]

We inquired as to the kind of herbs used.

* *Sophie Davis, White Bluff.*

"Duh wite root," pointing to a wild shrub, "dey use fuh stomach troubles. Buttuh root an palmettuh root an May apple, yuh bile tuhgedduh wid a quawt uh watuh till it simmuh down tuh haf uh pint, den yuh add some cawn wisky. Dat a fambly tonic tuh buil yuh up."

Sophie went on to tell us something about the beliefs prevailing in the neighborhood. "Ef some relative is sick, yuh dohn nebuh deah tuh sew on a gahment wut yuh is weahin cuz dat put a spell on duh sick un an dey mos liable tuh die.[49] Deah's anudduh ting too. Yuh sho bettuh not steal tings frum a grabe.[64] I sho know I wouldn. Deah's jis a lot uh udduh tings bout bad luck too. One sho sign is dat ef a pusson sneeze wile dey's eatin long, dat is, dey hab food in dey mout, den dey got tuh put it out lessn dey hab bad luck.[52] Anudduh sign is duh hootin ub a owl." [44]

A strange look of doubt and amusement came into Sophie's eyes at the mention of conjuring. She smiled and slowly shook her head.

"I heahd ub a few cases weah dey say one uh duh neighbuhs cunjuh anudduh,[15] but fuh duh mos paht dey all gits long all right. Das cuz we's all Christians an dohn put no faith much in dem kine uh tings. Dey say dat a powuhful chahm kin be made frum grabeyahd dut[9] fuh cunjuhin puhposes, but duh pusson dat git duh dut mus put some pennies on duh grabe, else he hab trouble hissef. Nebuh let a enemy git any ub yuh haiah wut bin cut off aw yuh nail clippins. Ef he git deze he kin make sumpm dat will cause lot uh trouble.[10] I kin tell yuh sumpm else bout duh haiah too. Ef a bud gits duh haiah, yuh'll hab a headache soon.

"Now Uncle John Bowen on St. Catherines he wuz a root man an one time a man come tuh him tuh git somebody fix. Uncle John he wuz fixin tings tuh linguh um, an duh man sit on duh cheah weah he hab duh cunjuh tings an Uncle John he git so mad he git right up an fix duh cunjuh right now so dat man wut awduh duh fixin die hesef. He fix lot uh people. Deah so much debilment in ole Uncle John Bowen dat finally he eat out hesef till he fix hesef an die."

We asked about the use of drums.

"Yes'm, dey alluz use tuh beat duh drum wen somebody die tuh let duh udduh folks know bout duh det. An at fewnuls too, dey beat it."

Relative to spirits, she replied, "No'm, I caahn see spirits cuz I ain bawn wid a caul. But now Bob Delegal he knows spirits. Down on Blackbeard Ilun, deah wuz a big hawg wut wuz a ebil spirit. Dey call um Blackbeard an dey try an try tuh kill um. So ole Bob Delegal cut up some silbuh an put it in he gun. He aim at duh hawg but he miss um an ole Bob Delegal fall down an couldn speak. Dey carry um home an he nebuh did talk no mo an duh nex day he die."

According to Sophie the old people on St. Catherines would pray at the rising and at the setting of the sun and at the conclusion of their prayers they would say the words "Meena, Mina, Mo." Asked if she knew the meaning of these words, she shook her head negatively.

"Yuh know, Susie Branch, who lib jis cross duh road deah, could tell yuh some uh deze tings too. We wuz chillun tuhgedduh down on St. Catherines Ilun. I gwine call uh."

In a moment Susie * arrived. Tall and thin, she was dressed in a red, green, and blue cotton plaid skirt and a man's shirt with the tail hanging loosely outside. She was very talkative and was enthusiastic in verifying many of the things that Sophie had mentioned.

Susie listened gravely as we inquired about her recollections of the old people in her family. She told us the following story: "Dey steal muh great-great-gran, uh name wuz Sukey, frum off duh beach in Africa wen she wuz a young miss. I dunno wut paht ub Africa she come frum. She alluz say she come frum Africa, duh country weah dey dohn weah no cloze. At duh plantation at St. Catherines she wuz

* *Susie Branch, White Bluff.*

duh seamstress fuh duh slabes. She make mos all dey weah."

When we asked her if she ever heard that dreaming about a snake "meant anything," the old woman replied, "Yes, ma'am, dat mean yuh got a enemy.[51] Not many nights ago I dream bout a snake an uh sho wuz sked wen uh wake up."

They both laughed and Susie leaned over and tapped Sophie on the arm and said, "Oh yes, deah's lots uh dem tings bout babies. Wen dey bawn wid a caul, das sho a sign dey will be bery wise an kin talk wid duh spirits.[4] Ain dasso, Sophie?"

Agreeing, Sophie hastened to add what she had heard about babies born with teeth. "Dey will hab bad luck all deah libes.[66] Dat sho wuk out. Deah wuz one boy bawn dat way wut lib right yuh in Wite Bluff an he wine up by bein in duh chain-gang an dat sho nuff bad luck."

"But dis lill plant heah called 'Cherokee' is spose tuh bring good luck ef yuh plants it by duh front doe step," [34c] said Susie.

In this community as in many others strangers are not allowed to be buried in the local cemetery but in what is known as the "strangers lot," a piece of ground set apart from the cemetery proper. The custom of bringing the dead back to their original home for interment is also prevalent throughout coastal Georgia. The body of a young man who recently died in New York was brought back to White Bluff for burial. Relative to this custom, Susie spoke quietly. "Dey alluz brings um back tuh bury um ef dey kin git duh money, cuz yuh see duh spirit'll jis wanduh roun an nebuh be satisfied lessn it brung back home tuh be buried." [1]

"I know Lunnon Grayson know all bout dem tings too. Yuh tun off tuh duh lef at duh fus road leadin off frum duh highway yuh. Ax anybody den, an dey'll tell yuh wich is his house. He use tuh lib on St. Catherines too, but he come up yuh long fo me an Susie," Sophie said.

Lunnon * remembered a great deal about the old customs. Seated in his front yard under the shade of a crepe myrtle tree, he and Prince Sneed were chatting. Lunnon's hair was snow white and wooly. On his left ear was a gold earring, which he claimed tended to improve his eyesight.[27] When he laughed be bent double and slapped his knees with his hands; at the same time his mouth opened wide, revealing his three remaining teeth. At first he was reluctant to admit that he had heard much about conjuring. He finally admitted, between chuckles, that he had heard about it from his mother and grandmother but vehemently denied any belief in conjure himself. He was serious, however, as he told the following story about Prince Sneed's father-in-law, who was being conjured at the time.

"I lib in White Bluff fuh bout fifty yeahs, an I kin tell yuh many stories I heahd bout cunjuhin an root doctuhs. Somebody heahbouts put an ebil spell on Prince Sneed's fathuh-in-law, Lunnon Milton.[15] He seem tuh git wus an wus an nuttn seem tuh hep him none. Finally he sen fuh a root doctuh an he wuk obuh im but he dohn git no bettuh.[48] He call in eight ub um altuhgedduh, but dey dohn seem able tuh countuhrack dat cunjuh.[6] Duh ole man sick tuh dis day. Maybe some day he fine a root doctuh wut is powful nuff tuh hep him." [48]

As Uncle Lunnon finished his story, Prince Sneed,** a dark man of splendid physique despite his sixty-odd years, added, "It's lak dis. Wen Ise sick, I gonuh see a doctuh right away. Now muh faduh-in-law, he jis keep on wid dem root doctuhs, but he say he ain gittin a bit bettuh."

Prince proved to be an interesting talker, much of his knowledge having been gleaned from conversations by the fireside with his grandfather. The following narrative was still fresh in his memory:

* *London Grayson, White Bluff. Deceased November, 1939.*
** *Prince Sneed, White Bluff.*

"Muh gran say ole man Waldburg down on St. Catherine own some slabes wut wuzn climatize an he wuk um hahd an one day dey wuz hoein in duh fiel an duh dribuh come out an two ub um wuz unuh a tree in duh shade, an duh hoes wuz wukin by demsef. Duh dribuh say 'Wut dis?' an dey say, 'Kum buba yali kum buba tambe, Kum kunka yali kum kunka tambe,' quick like. Den dey rise off duh groun an fly away. Nobody ebuh see um no mo. Some say dey fly back tuh Africa. Muh gran see dat wid he own eye."

He had heard that on Blackbeard Island it was customary in the old days for a group of men to agree upon a location in which to bury their money, whereupon one of them would voluntarily offer his life and be put to death at the hands of the others, thereby enabling his spirit to stand guard and protect the treasure.

"I seen a spirit muhsef once wen I wuz a young man," Prince continued. "It wuz late in duh aftuhnoon. I wuz cookin crab an uh look up an see a man widout a head. I look away, den uh look back tuh weah uh see im, an sho nuff deah he is in plain sight. I rush tuh duh house an staht tuh tell muh fostuh mudduh but she stop me. She dohn wahn me tuh talk bout it. Den duh nex day she ax me wut uh see an fix me sumpm tuh drink an I nebuh did see no mo spirit."

Another woman in the community, Bessie Royal,* in relation to her belief in witchcraft and conjure said, "Lots uh people roun yuh say dat hags ride um at night.[69] None ub um ebuh bodduhed me. Dey say dat duh hags is libe folks wut hab duh powuh tuh change demsefs intuh animals an insecs an any udduh ting dey want tuh be.[68]

"I dohn know how it wuz done but muh faduh wuz cunjuhed [15] by a suttn uhmun dat wuz said to be a hag.[69] He go crazy sometimes an ack lak he wuz sked by sumpm chasin im. He git wus and dey take im tuh a root doctuh. Duh root doctuh say he wuz cunjuhed. He hab us ketch a wite chicken

---

* *Bessie Royal, White Bluff.*

wich he split open wile duh chicken wuz still libe. He place dis chicken, blood an all wile it wuz still wome, on top uh muh faduh head an boun it deah.

"Well, muh faduh git bettuh fuh a wile. Den all at once he hab anudduh attack an he die befo duh doctuh could git tuh im. Attuh dis I belieb in cunjuh mo dan ebuh."

Later that same day we visited a small Negro cabin set deep in the woods some distance from the highway. Here lived Serina Hall,* born eighty-eight years ago on St. Catherines Island and a former slave of Jacob Waldburg. She said that when she was a small child her master had brought the members of her family to Savannah to be employed as house servants.

The old woman at first disclaimed any knowledge of conjure or the existence of supernatural creatures. After a time, however, her attitude changed and she launched into a lengthy discussion of the current beliefs.

"I dohn lak tuh talk bout dem tings," she began, "but I hab tuh belieb wut muh eyes see. I membuh once a man uh knew well got kill. Attuh he wuz buried his spirit use tuh folluh me all duh time. I feel a heat come tuh me, den uh look roun, an deah a shadduh ub a man pass by. I ax duh spirit, 'Wut you want?' Den it leab me lone an I ain seen dat spirit sence." [56, 59]

We asked Serina if she had ever known any conjure workers and she said, "Witches an root men is duh same ting. Dey kin tun demsefs intuh any shape, a insec, a cat, aw a dog, aw any kine uh animal.[68] Dey kin go tru any kine uh hole tuh git at yuh.

"Tuh tun intuh sumpm else dey hab tuh hab duh powuh tuh take off deah skin. I heahd bout somebody watchin a hag take off is skin. He git some salt an peppuh an rub it on duh skin.[69a] Wen duh hag go tuh put is skin back on, duh salt an peppuh bun so he couldn git it on. Duh folks wuz

* Serina Hall, White Bluff.

able tuh ketch im an dey fine it wuz one uh deah neighbuhs. He beg an plead an so dey fuhgib im. Dey nebuh hab no mo hag ridin.[69]

"Muh ma tell me many times bout a man an his wife wut could wuk cunjuh.[48] Anytime dey want tuh dey would fly back tuh Africa an den come back agen tuh duh plantation. Dey come back cuz dey hab some chillun wut didn hab duh powuh tuh fly an hab tuh stay on duh plantation. One uh duh daughtuhs wanted tuh lun tuh fly an wuk cunjuh. Duh faduh tell uh she hab tuh lun duh passwud, den she hab tuh kill a man by cunjuh.[15] Attuh dis den she would hab duh powuh. Duh magic passwud mean sumpm like dis, 'Who loss duh key Branzobo?' "

Pin Point

◇◇◇◇◇◇◇◇◇◇◇◇◇

PIN POINT, A NEGRO COMMUNITY ABOUT NINE MILES southeast of Savannah, is scattered over some twenty or thirty acres on a peninsula overlooking Shipyard Creek. Many of the small wooden cabins are neatly whitewashed and are half hidden by shrubbery and spreading oaks. Flowers and vegetables are planted in the most advantageous sunny spots near the houses and most of the yards are enclosed by picket fences, giving a cozy and pleasant privacy. The lanes, little more than wagon tracks, twist in and out and across the settlement. The informal and haphazard scattering of the houses, with high shrubbery bordering the lanes, gives an effect that is pleasing and unusual.

Pin Point has a church, a pavilion on the tidewater creek, and a crab cannery. The men and women who do not work as domestic servants at the nearby country places find employment in the crab cannery or fish and crab and shrimp for themselves. The life is quiet, soothed by the smell of the salt marsh.

It is only when some great excitement takes place, a stirring religious service, a dance at the community pavilion, a death,[37b, c] or some scandal concerning a neighbor, that quiet Pin Point bestirs itself. Recently, one of the fishermen ventured into the foreign waters of the Ogeechee about ten miles distant and there he was almost devoured by an alligator. All that was left of him, "the ham," was given a burial [2] amid the loud lamentations of his relatives and neighbors.

The people are, almost without exception, black or dark

skinned, proud, upstanding and loyal, suspicious of strangers but generous and trusting to friends (Plate VIII, IX, X). Most of the very old inhabitants have died in the past decade, so that to have reached the age of sixty places a man or woman in the patriarchal class. The grown people between twenty-five and thirty, are still close to the traditions and beliefs in which they have been reared. Firmly believing in the Bible, they still are aware of other beliefs and customs handed down by their parents and grandparents.

A pleasant, intelligent woman * of about forty-five chatted with us. "Cose, det is duh will ub God, but dey do say jis duh same wen a pusson die, 'Maybe somebody fix em' [15] aw 'I sho know dat uhmun wuz rooted.' I ain nebuh bought no powduh muhsef but jis day befo yestuhdy a uhmun frum Tatemville wuz right yuh tuh dis house sellin High John duh Conqueruh fuh fifty cent an she sho say it would bring yuh powuhful good luck, but I ain hab fifty cent.[8]

"Cose, it ain good tuh fool much wid dem tings, but yuh sho hab tuh be keahful not tuh let no enemy git hole uh yuh haiah combins cuz dey say dey sho could fix yuh den." [10] She laughed a little uneasily. "Ef yuh dream ub a snake dassa enemy neahby too, but ef yuh weah a snake skin roun yuh wais, it good fuh wut ail yuh.[50d, e] An ef uh enemy come tuh yuh house an yuh dohn wahn im deah no mo, yuh jis take duh bruhm an sweep out quick attuh im. Den sprinkle a lill salt on duh flo weah his foot track bin an sweep em all out duh doe an he sho wohn come back no mo."

At this point in her narrative a swarm of barefoot children, black and with shining eyes, clustered around us. One and all were eating crabs, biting into the soft part of the body shell or cracking a claw with strong white teeth. Word had evidently just gone out that some excitement was brewing. Strangers had come and were talking to "Miz Minnie." If anything was going on they didn't want to miss it.

* Minnie Dawson, Pin Point.

83

But "Miz Minnie" felt differently. "Go long, yuh chillun. Go long wid yuh crahb an stop lissnin tuh grown folks." Minnie flapped her apron and they scattered like a brood of young chicks.

"Yasm, cose yuh do heah bout cunjuhin." [15] Minnie turned back to us. "Dasso. Dey's alluz talk bout it, an I know ole Lewis McIver (Plate XI) wut libs yuh right now, wut foun a bottle buried in his mattress. He wuz sick an somebody wuz tryin tuh fix im. I seen dat bottle muhsef, wid muh own eyes. Yes, ma'am, I sho seen it. It hab yulluhlak oily lookin stuff in it an deah wuz a piece uh clawt stuck tru wid needles an pins in it." [8] Minnie looked worried at the mere memory. "I seen it fuh sho an dohn nobody know who put it deah. But Lewis is bettuh sence it wuz took out. He say he ain hab neah so much pain.

"Den wen muh ole uncle wuz sick,[15] dey sen fuh a ole uhmun wut know bout cunjuh [48] an she wehn out in duh yahd an dig up a piece uh clawt wadded intuh a ball wid nails in it an she cas it away. I seen dat too. She say somebody plant it deah gense im.

"Dey make mojoes outn anyting but dey do say grabeyahd dut [9] an nails an blood an haiah,[10] dey is impawtant. Cose I know bettuhn belieb all dis," she laughed, "but it make yuh sked an yuh sho full uh worry ef somebody tryin tuh fix yuh." After cogitating on these dangers Minnie smiled, "But ef yuh weahs a silbuh dime tied tuh yuh ankle an yuh step obuh anyting wut put down fuh yuh, duh dime'll sho tun black sudden an quick an den yuh knows it." [12a, c, d]

Pin Point attained a certain measure of fame as the setting of the Bo-Cat murder in 1932. Limerick De Lancy, Pin Point Negro nicknamed Bo-Cat, killed his wife, Catherine, and dropped her corpse into the deep waters near Hell Gate. When the crime was discovered, the fact that it had taken place on Friday, the thirteenth, loomed significant in the consciousness of the small community and in no time inspired a ballad. Attributed to no single author but apparently added to from time to time, the ballad now runs:

On duh thuteent day ub May
Yuh could heah ole Bo-Cat say,
"Git muh deed an policy.
Tun it in duh ashes way."

Den ole Catherine she begin tuh inquyuh.
Didn know ole Bo-Cat had dem in duh fyuh.
It a shame how Bo-Cat done he wife.

Put uh in duh boat,
Dey begin tuh float,
Dey float tuh duh Raccoon Keys.
He knock uh on duh knees.
Catherine holluh, "Wa-Wan-Wa."
Bo-Cat make uh "Na-Nan-Na."
It a shame how Bo-Cat done he wife.

He knock uh in duh bres
An duh oah done duh res.
It a shame how Bo-Cat done he wife.

He knock uh in duh back
An duh oah miss an crack.
It a shame how Bo-Cat done he wife.

Wen Bo-Cat wehn back home
He meet uh daughtuh all alone.
Uh daughtuh say, "Bo-Cat, Bo-Cat,
Weah my mama is?"
Bo-Cat tun right out he head
An he tro uh cross duh bed.
It a shame how Bo-Cat done he wife.

Dey got Bo-Cat in jail
Bout tuh hang im by duh rail
It a shame how Bo-Cat done he wife.

One of the Pin Point women, Margaret Snead,* recalls
vividly the events of the De Lancy crime.

"Wy, duh night fo Catherine De Lanzy wuz kill, she spen
it in town wid me," said Margaret Snead. "Attuh dat night
I didn see uh no mo. People frum duh Pint come inquirin
bout uh but nobody seem tuh know nuttn bout uh weahbouts.
Bout two weeks latuh, a pahty uh wite mens out huntin come
cross duh body at Raccoon Keys. Dis a ilun way beyon
Hell's Gate. Mus be mohn twenny miles frum duh Pint. I
dohn see as how nobody could carry a pusson dat fah jis tuh
murduh em. Anyways, duh body wuz brung tuh duh city,
an at duh unduhtakuh's office people went in tuh see ef dey
could dentify it. Dis a hahd ting tuh do. She bin in duh
watuh fuh days an days fo a high tide wash duh cawpse on
sho. Duh body wuz caught tween two logs weah duh buzzuds went tuh wuk on it.

"I membuh a great big cawn wich she use tuh suffuh wid
but couldn nebuh git rid ub. So I went in an had a look at
duh foot, an sho nuff deah wuz dat cawn jis lak it use tuh be
wen she wuz libe.

"Her ole huzbun, Limbrick De Lanzy, already wuz rested,
an he git sen up fuh life. It wuz Friday, May duh thuteent, dat ole Limbrick carried Catherine off down duh ribbuh an murduh uh. A double bad luck, Friday an duh thuteent,[21] das wy dey make up duh song."

"Was the body buried at Pin Point?" we were interested
to know.

"Yes, it wuz, but we didn hab no settin-up cuz duh body
wuz too fah gone. Dat wuz sad. Ebrybody lub Catherine
an fuh uh tuh die an be buried widout a settin-up aw lettin

* *Margaret Snead, Pin Point.*

anybody view uh face aw lay deah hans on uh [31] wuz sho a pity.[36]

"Ebrybody wuz at duh fewnul. Come frum miles roun tuh pay deah las respecks tuh a po wife murduhed by uh huzbun on Friday duh thuteent.

"Duh body wuz brung frum duh unduhtakuh's pahluh straight tuh Sweet Fiel ub Eden Chuch at duh Pint. Chuch so crowded yuh caahn hahdly see duh coffin up in front. We sing hymns, an den wen duh singin hab die out an yuh could heah jis a lill hummin heah an deah, somebody stan up an say, 'Catherine De Lanzy wuz a sistuh ub duh Lawd.' 'She sho wuz,' somebody else say. 'She wuz a chile ub Jesus an she walk in duh way ub righteousness.'

"Dis staht off duh whole congregation an deah mustuh bin neah a hundud people git up an gib testimony bout Catherine's goodness. Some people cry an scream wen dey tell duh congregation wut a fine uhmun she bin.

"Den duh remains wuz took tuh duh cimiterry neah duh chuch an buried. Duh whole time we sing hymns an sway tuh duh soun uh duh music. Ebrybody tro a hanful uh dut in duh grabe an [28] wen duh grabe digguhs fix duh moun, we put some uh Catherine's tings on duh top. Deah wuz a lill flowuh vase wid duh bottom knock out, an a lamp chimney, an some puhfumery bottles, an duh pitchuh she made ice watuh in jis fo Bo-Cat tuk uh off.[47] Den duh ministuh nounce dat duh fewnul suhmon wuz tuh be preach at duh annyul memorial wen dey pray fuh ebrybody who die durin duh yeah.[42] An den das all an we wehn home."

"Why was Limerick De Lancy called Bo-Cat?" we asked.

"Deah ain no signifcunse tuh dat. I hab a frien dat ebrybody call Friday but [20] uh name is Lula. I hab a cousin name Augus Bond an a son name May Bud simply cuz he wuz bawn in May. One uh muh brothuhs wuz call Baby Head cuz at birth he wuz a tiny baby wid sech a great big head.

"No, I dohn pay much mine tuh names," said Margaret Snead. "But I do pay tention tuh bad luck dates. Look uh po Catherine De Lanzy, depribe ub all duh propuh tings dat come fo burial, cuz it wuz a double bad luck date. Folks at duh Pint do say dat uh spirit nebuh will res in duh grabe." [36]

Sandfly

SANDFLY, ABOUT NINE MILES SOUTHEAST OF SAVAN-
nah, is a scattered Negro community spreading through the
hot pine barrens to the Isle of Hope. There is nothing unusual or outstanding about the sleepy little settlement; its
three hundred inhabitants appear to lead a placid, uneventful existence.

Many of the houses are situated on a side road which leads
to the Isle of Hope. Modern conveniences are lacking, but
the nondescript dwellings are brightened by flower gardens
in the front yards, while small truck gardens occupy the
space to the rear and sides. The more substantial houses of
the more prosperous citizens are set deep in the wooded sections and are reached by means of narrow winding paths
bordered with giant moss-hung oak trees.

Usually life in Sandfly flows along pleasantly and without
serious interruption. Even in the morning men and women
sit around on porches or in yards, sometimes talking, sometimes dozing in the sun. The more industrious are at work
in the gardens or may be seen through doors busily occupied
in washing or ironing clothes. Many of the men are employed as fishermen or day laborers, and the women who
work out are generally engaged as house servants in homes
at near-by Isle of Hope.

At first residents of the community were reluctant to talk
about their superstitions and beliefs and their knowledge of
conjure. Their customary response when first approached
was a laconic, "No, ma'am, I ain got no fait in sech tings as

cunjuh." When pressed for details, however, and when assured that the interviewers' interest was a friendly one, their attitude frequently changed and they talked volubly of queer happenings in the vicinity.

"They jis don't think bout nuthin but cunjuh," said one woman, a newcomer in the neighborhood.* "Yuh heah all the time of folks havin spells put on em an findin cunjuh bags buried in the yahd. All the times some folks are fixin othuhs.[15]

"A woman that lived in Homestead Park jis couldn't seem to have nothin but bad luck. She thought maybe an enemy had cunjuhed uh, so she looked in the yahd an sho nough theah wuz a cunjuh bag. It wuz a queah lookin bundle with a lot of brown clay in it. She destroyed the bag an the bad luck stopped an the evil spirits didn't bothuh uh none."

A small child complained to his parents that he felt snakes moving about in his head.[5, 50] A local doctor diagnosed the illness as ringworm, but this explanation failed to satisfy the parents for the child's own theory of snakes seemed to them much more convincing. One morning, soon after, the mother discovered a large snake crawling about in front of the house. She killed the snake and the next day the inflamed places on the boy's head began to heal. In a few days he was completely cured.**

Professional witch doctors and root doctors [48] ply an active trade and are employed in the more extreme cases, but often the people take matters in their own hands and by means of conjure bags and charms seek to alter their own destinies and those of their neighbors. Retribution brought to bear on an enemy, the favor of a loved one is gained, and luck in business or in games of chance is assured by the possession of some sort of luck charm or powder.[8]

* *Lizzie Jenkins, Sandfly.*
That this informant came from another section of Georgia was reflected in her speech.
** *Ophelia Baker, Baker's Crossing*

In a section of Sandfly known as Baker's Crossing lives Ophelia Baker, better known as Madam Truth, professed fortune teller and clairvoyant. The woman's sober attire and her modern attractive house give little evidence of her profession. When holding a seance, however, her whole appearance undergoes a change; her body becomes tense and jerks spasmodically; her dark eyes roll wildly. Of her ability in her chosen field the medium says, "I advise on business an love affeahs. I tell good an bad nooz comin tuh yuh. Deah's a remedy fuh ebry trouble an I hab dat remedy, fuh a spirit hab brung it tuh me." [22a, e]

Madam Truth, a member of the Holy Sanctified Church of Sandfly, said that all members must undergo a sanctifying process in order to be saved. After this has been accomplished members claim to be able to hear, from a great distance, singing, talking, and the sounding of drums. We were told that the beating of the drums has a special significance, but that was all we could learn on the subject; we were told that this was a secret, divulged only to members.

Members of the church are forbidden to eat certain kinds of fish and also cabbage, lettuce, and other green vegetables. The reason they give is that they have received a warning from the spirits that it is unwise to eat these foods.[65]

The plump, dark-skinned fortune teller said that she had spent her childhood on Skidaway Island. She remembered hearing the drums beaten to tell the people in the nearby settlements of an approaching dance or festival. Her father had been one of those who beat the drum and thumped out a regular message on it, a message that could be heard for miles and was clearly understood by all those who had heard it.[26]

The woman also remembered wakes which had been held on Skidaway. Coffee and sandwiches were served the [37b, c] mourners, each one of whom poured some of the coffee on the ground for the spirit of the deceased.[58b, e]

Another native of Skidaway,* now living in Sandfly, also remembered drum codes being sent out from Skidaway.[26] A member of the Baptist Church, he has never heard drums beaten in the house of praise, but he described with great pride and earnestness the ceremony of a river baptism.

"We gadduh at duh chuch wid duh candidates who comes all dressed ready fuh baptism in long wite robes. Duh deacons range duh folks in line, two by two. Den duh mahch tuh duh ribbuh begin, duh pastuh an duh deacons leadin duh way. Dis is a solemn time, an duh candidates an deah friens an relatives all rejoice. As we mahch we sing. Some uh duh songs we sing is *I'm Gwine Down tuh duh Ribbuh ub Jawdan* an *Oh, Who Will Come an Go Wid Me?*

"Wen we git tuh duh ribbuh some uh duh folks is so happy an dey scream an jump roun so much dat some uh duh udduhs hab tuh hole em. Duh candidates is led intuh duh watuh, one by one, an baptize. Attuh duh baptizin dey change deah cloze an we all go tuh duh chuch fuh duh communion services."

Here, as in many other sections, a silver coin is frequently worn on the ankle to insure good luck [8] and to give warning by turning black at any effort by an enemy to conjure the wearer.[12a, c, d] In regard to this custom of wearing a coin one woman who is married to a man "wid duh powuh tuh see tings" [22a, e] said, "Duh folks roun yuh use tuh weah five dolluh gole pieces on deah ankle, but hahd times jis nachly make dem gole pieces jump off." **

The same woman told that when she and her husband first moved to Sandfly several years ago, a neighbor employed a conjure man to put a spell on them to drive them away.

"I membuh wen deze folks cross duh way wuz cunjuhin us, an strikin roun, I went tuh duh sto an change a dolluh bill fuh one of deze silvuh dolluhs. It wuz roun an shiny as yuh

---

* *John Bivens, Baker's Crossing.*
** *Lee Baynes, Sandfly.*

please. I carry it in muh pocketbook an duh nex day it tun
black an I know fuh sho dey wuz tryin tuh cunjuh us." [15]

Repeated efforts were made to conjure the newcomers.
At first bottles filled with a queer oily substance were buried
around the house. When these failed in effect a more powerful charm was compounded, and a few days later the intended victim discovered buried in her back yard what she
described as "a bottle neck down in duh groun. It wuz filled
wid some kine of funny lookin oil."

"I know dis wuz a cunjuh," she said. "I call muh huzbun
an show it tuh im. He git plenty mad an say he gonuh
settle mattuhs once and fuh all wid dis cunjuh man. He
wait fuh im by duh lane an wen he come long, he grab im an
shake im an tell im he know all bout wut he bin doin. He tell
im he bettuh stop tryin tuh cunjuh us, fuh he know bout
cunjuh his ownsef an he tell im all duh tings dat he done.
Wen duh cunjuh man heah dis, he fall down on is knees an
beg muh huzbun tuh fuhgib im. He tell im bout all sawts
uh magic dat he wukd on udduh folks in duh neighbuhood.
He promise not tuh do no mo uh dis an muh huzbun let
im go."

We were told of another woman who, as a result of conjure,[15] fell mysteriously ill and felt snakes running up and
down her left side under the skin.[5, 50] Medical care did not
help the case and she is now, according to report, "jis wastin
away an no one caahn do nuttn." *

Graveyard dirt is often employed in the making of conjure bags.[8, 9] If possible this must be taken from the grave
of a murdered person and some money must be left in exchange. Not very long ago when a man was arrested for
murder, his friends, wishing to save him, went to the grave
of the murdered man, secured some dirt, and left three pennies on the grave. A man, lingering in the vicinity, stole the
money and shortly thereafter spent it in the neighborhood

* Lee Baynes, Sandfly.

store. As one neighbor put it "duh han come widin an inch uh wukin." Although the defendant was not acquitted, he was sentenced to a mere two or three years, and there was some speculation as to whether or not the theft of the money had been what kept him from going entirely free.* [64]

A woman, suspecting that someone was attempting to conjure her daughter,[15] dug up the ground around her house until she found the evil charm. Of this case our informant says, "It wuz two balls of graveyahd dut,[9] all wrapped up in a clawt. Dey tuk it roun an show it tuh ebrybody. It wuz up at duh poolruhm all spread out on duh pool table, an folks stop in all duh time tuh xamine it. Duh girl dat wuz cunjuhed buy a han [6] frum a root man an duh spirits dohn bodduh uh none." **

People in the community believe that extremely powerful charms can be made from the dust from people's foot tracks.[7] There is a constant dread that someone will secure this dust, and zealous care is taken to prevent this. We were told, "A ole uhmun who libed heah-a-bouts wuz so sked dat somebody would fix uh dat she alluz carried a rake wid uh. Down duh road she would go, rakin up uh foot-steps in back of uh, so dat nobody could git dat dus an fix uh." †

Another resident who neglected these precautions said she became very ill, due to the fact that someone had manufactured a charm from the dust left by her foot tracks. As her condition became more aggravated she at length consulted a root doctor. He sold her a counter charm [6] and soon the mysterious illness disappeared.‡

Death, especially if violent or unexpected, is attributed to witchcraft or conjure.[15] One woman voiced the sentiment of many of the community when she said, "Theah ain't supposed tuh be no sech thing as nachul death yuh in Sandfly.

* *Lee Baynes, Sandfly.*
** *Ibid.*
† *Ellie Davis, Sandfly.*
‡ *Lizzie Jenkins, Sandfly.*

Wen a pusson dies some one have fix im sho. Bout a yeah ago an ole woman went fuh a walk right down this road yuh. She went up on a hill cross frum yuh weah she live an the nex mawnin she wuz foun dead theah. Mos folks said she wuz cunjuhed that night, though theah wuz some wut did say she have haht trouble. Jis a week aw so ago the brothuh of a neighbuh die right sudden an folks said he wuz cunjuhed too." * 15

In regard to death we found a rigid observance of customs that were prevalent also in the other communities. For example, one Negro's body had been shipped back from New York City in order that it might be buried in Sandfly. Otherwise, we were told, the spirit of the deceased would have found no rest, but instead would have roamed the countryside.[1] Here, too, was observed the practice of placing broken bits of pottery and possessions last used by the dead person on the grave for the purpose of supplying the needs of the spirit.[47]

In Sandfly there is a ready market for love powders and charms.** This field has been highly commercialized and representatives of different corporations frequently visit Sandfly selling such articles as *Adam and Eve Root, Lucky Mojo Love Drops, Black Cat Ashes,* and *Courting Powder.*[8] Apparently the women resort to the use of the love charms more frequently than the men, and their reason for doing so was described by one woman as being "so dat dey kin rule duh men." †

Old and young entertain a firm belief in the existence of witches and spirits. The witches may come in a variety of shapes, appearing as a person either male or female, an animal, or sometimes as an insect.[68] When questioned regarding the apparitions, one person said, "A witch ride muh sistuh mos every night.[69] He come singin a lill song. I

* *Lizzie Jenkins, Sandfly.*
** *Ibid.*
† *Lee Baynes, Sandfly.*

heah uh movin bout an moanin an in duh mawnin she is jis bout wone out an uh haiah is all tangled. Sometime she wake up an drive him away, but some nights he come back two aw three times an ride uh. In duh mawnin she jis too tied tuh go tuh wuk.*

"Deah wuz a ole woman in Savannah dat dey say wuz a witch. One night a ole man wake up an foun dis witch ridin im.[69] He say it look lak a bug.[68] He ketch it an break off duh leg at duh joint. Duh nex mawnin he go an see duh ole woman an sho nuff she have uh han all tie up wid a bandage. Dey tell me bout uh an I go see uh. Uh finguh wuz right off at duh joint."

Spirits of the dead often wander along the dark road-ways,[56, 59] and frequently some belated stroller runs screaming in terror, declaring that he is being pursued.** The spirits may appear as misshapen men or women, as sheep, dogs, and cats.[54, 55] A spirit need not always assume the same appearance but may change form entirely each time.†

The following story was told by a woman in the community:

"I sho believe in spirits. I have seen em wid muh own eyes. One evenin jis as it wuz gittn dusty I wuz goin in tuh town tuh see duh dressmakuh. I walk tuh duh cah tracks an deah sittin on a rail wuz a lill tiny man, bout long as dis. I nevuh seen sech a lill man.[54b, 55] He wuz so lill he ain good fuh nuthin. I look at im hahd. On his head wuz a lill tin lamp wut gleamed in duh dahk. He wuz kine of an Indian culluh. He wuz a grown man fuh sho fuh he hab a lill mustache. I holluh fuh a man tuh come out an see wut I foun, but wen he git deah duh lill man hab disappeah. Jis den duh cah blowed an I hab tuh leab.

"Wen I gits home dat night, it wuz real dahk. I ain goin tuh walk dat dahk road by mysef an I holluh fuh every man

* Lee Baynes, Sandfly.
** Ibid.
† Ibid.

I knowd dat live neahby. I make em all walk home wid me, but deah wuzn no signs of duh lill man.

"Attuh dat lots of folks say dey see im. Wen duh moon is noo an deah is a drizzle, he come walkin along wid his lill lamp. He take all kine uh shapes. Sometime he's a man an sometime he's a animal.[54] Dey say he's comin roun cuz deah's buried treasure neah yuh." * [61]

Here in this little Negro community there seem to be few phases of life left untouched by superstitious fears. As one woman aptly expressed it—"Everything that happen is cause by cunjuh an magic. They jis dohn leave nuthin tuh Gawd." **

* *Lee Baynes, Sandfly.*
** *Lizzie Jenkins, Sandfly.*

Grimball's Point

◇◇◇◇◇◇◇◇◇◇◇◇◇◇◇◇◇◇◇◇◇

GRIMBALL'S POINT, LYING AT THE NORTHWESTERN end of the Isle of Hope on the marshes and creeks that run from the wide Skidaway River, is one of the characteristic spots of Savannah's rural landscape. The lowland spreads grassy flats against the horizon; the squawks of marsh hen rise from the long reeds on Grimball's Creek; all the year round a familiar sight is the Negro fisherman sitting patiently in his small bateau or trudging with his plump catch up an old oak-shaded shell road.

A few white residents maintain comfortable summer homes at Grimball's Point, but the settlers scattered on the southern part of the point are Negroes, former slaves and descendants of slaves who once worked the great plantations on the Isle of Hope and other near-by islands. Some of the inhabitants are employed on Grimball's Point hunting preserve, while others are farmers or fishermen. Their abodes are frame bungalows with front porches or little shacks of one or two rooms, but most of the dwellings are surrounded by sun-dappled yards, fenced with boards or chicken wire. Each has its backyard pump as there is no running water.

Of the ten Negro families on the point, young and old believe in signs and auguries. "Catfish Tom" William, Habersham Gibson, and Solomon Gibson professed to know that "some signs sho do wuk." Thomas Tuten, who has spent his fifty-eight years on the island, warned us that "yuh sho has tuh watch people cuz dey kin do yuh." Aging Aunt Cinda Smith, employed on the old Wiley place, is given the respect of all the settlers as one who can read signs and interpret dreams.

Solomon Gibson's wife, Mary Liza,* a slender black woman of about forty, came to the island from Skidaway upon her marriage. She was an amiable person, not at all disinclined to an interview.

"I kin cook and wash an ion an make baskets an do anyting roun duh house," she said. "Yes, I belieb in many signs. Yuh musn sweep out duh doe aftuh dahk an it bad luck tuh split a tree wen yuh's walkin. Deah's two signs uh det. Ef duh dog holluhs aw a owl holluhs,[44b] somebody is gonuh die. I lun all dis frum duh ole people an I know it's true."

Bruurs Butler,** well past three score and ten, worked for "Capm Wiley" for nearly thirty years and is still an able field hand. He owns his small house, which is equipped with electricity and a radio.

"I wuz bawn on DeRenne place," he told us, "an my mothuh an fathuh wuz owned by Mistuh DeRenne. My fathuh wuz a second sergeant in the Confederate Ahmy. None of us lef duh plantation aftuh duh waw. I wuk crops fuh Mistuh DeRenne till I wuz a young man."

We asked if there had been any Gullah Negroes on the Isle of Hope in the old days and he nodded.

"Use tuh be many 'Golla' people roun yuh but dey all died out. Dey tell me them people could do all kine uh curious tings. Dey could make fahm tools wuk fuh um jis by talkin tuh um.[39a] An," he added soberly, "some of um could disappeah at will.[69c] Wist! And dey'd be done gone.

"Yuh askin me bout signs? Well," he appeared amused, "yuh'll fine that ef yuh believe sumpm is bad luck an yuh look fuh bad luck, yuh gonuh fine bad luck. Deah's some signs that come frum Gawd, though, and these is unfailin. Lak dreams an foewahnin not tuh do dis aw dat." [22a]

---

* *Mary Liza Gibson, Grimball's Point.*
** *Bruurs Butler, Grimball's Point.*

One of the oldest of the residents is white-haired F. J. Jackson * who remembers his childhood days on "Massuh George Wiley plantation" when many freed Negroes stayed on to work in the cotton fields. Years have weakened his once sturdy frame and slowed down both thought and gesture, but the light of humor still gleams in his dimmed eyes. We found Jackson in the kitchen of his comfortable frame bungalow, a new house built to replace a little old shanty that was burned down. He was making a casting net, his twisted old fingers still deft with the cords. He conversed like one glad of congenial company.

"Does I membuh ole times?" he repeated in answer to our question. "Yes, I dohn git away frum dis place much now an uh jis sit roun an tink ub a long time ago. Deah wuzn no automobiles an duh only way tuh git tuh Savannah wuz by duh mule an caht aw git in duh road wid yuh foots. Not many uh duh people still livin wut come long wid me. Dey's bout gone. Me an ole man Bruurs Butluh's bout duh onlies ones lef uh duh fus settluhs.

"Yes, I membuhs duh plantation days. Massuh George wuz a slave dealuh fo duh waw, an he tuk us all, muh grandaddy, Lewis Hargray, an muh maw, an muh daddy—I name attuh him. Massuh George use tuh buy an sell but he wuz a good man an lot uh his slaves stay wid im on duh fahm attuh freedom. Dat big house in duh ben uh duh road wuz weah he lib, an dey still got duh ball an chain an duh banjo table in duh house now.

"Wen I lef duh fahm an moob tuh duh pint, ain but five wite families yuh. Ain no roadn nuttn, jis woods. I done a lot uh huntin an fishin. Deah wuz plenty uh deahs roun yuh.

"I use tuh go back tuh duh fahm on Satdy night fuh duh big times. Dey hab wut yuh call shouts. Wut kine uh music did us hab?" Jackson's aged eyes twinkled. "We use

* F. J. Jackson, Grimball's Point. Deceased July, 1940.

drum an fife an we made duh drum frum holluh beehive lawg.[25b] I tell yuh how we done it. Yuh cut duh lawg an tak a deah hide an stretch obuh duh hole. Den yuh cut a hoop ban dat could lock roun duh lawg. Den yuh cut strips uh deah hide an make bans tuh hole duh head cuvvuh tight. How yuh make duh fife? Well, yuh jis cut reed cane.

"Lots uh udduh tings we make our ownsef," said the old man. "All duh fishin cawd made out uh deah hide, and we make mos uh duh house needs sech as cheahs an tables, baskets an buckets an stools, an sometime spoons an beds and cubbuds. Oh, deah's much I caahn tell off han."

Jackson's wife, who was not many years past middle age, came in about this time, greeted us, and sat down to listen.

"Wut dis bout signs?" Jackson laughed. "Sho I knows a few. Deah's some dat foetell wut comin. Wen yuh see duh hawgs bring straw in deah mouf, it's a sho sign wintuh goin tuh be cole. Ef duh roostuh come in duh doe an crow an den go out, it's sho sign uh sorruh in dat house. Duh owl is a true messenjuh uh det,[44] an wen yuh see a bunch uh crows flock up, yuh jis watch out fuh a fewnul. Deah's many signs an wunduhs. Duh Bible tell us so. I had a buckeye fuh many yeahs dat keep off bad luck. I use tuh have a hawse shoe ovuh duh doe uh duh ole house wut bun down,[11a] but I ain put one on dis un yet.

"Rootn?" he shook his head disdainfully. "I seen duh root man say he tak wuhrums an pins an tings out uh people, but I belieb it's some trick. I ain got no fait in dat stuff."

"But I have," put in his wife.* "Muh brothuh-in-law wuz fixed by his wife.[15] Not muh sistuh but anothuh woman. He tun intuh a invalid an laid down helpless fuh twenny-five yeahs. None uh the medical doctuhs couldn hep im, an sevral root doctuhs wuz called in.[48a] One of um said nuthin couldn be done fuh im cuz the pusson that put im in this fix wuz dead an theah wuzn nobody tuh throw it back tuh. So

* Della Jackson, Grimball's Point.

he had tuh linguh on till finally it reached his haht an he died."

Jackson scratched his bristly chin and smiled sheepishly. "I do belieb in some rootn," he said, "but uh didn wannuh talk too fas. I seen a root man tak is bag an in it wuz needles an pins an grabeyahd dut an sulphuh an rusty nails, an he made it *crawl*.[48e]

"But nuttn evuh done me hahm," he went on in his gentle voice. "I alluz got wut I want all deze yeahs. Cuz yuh know wy? I hab a black cat bone."

We had heard of the potency of the black cat bone. Other Negroes had told us that it could ward off conjure, cure sickness, or even give its possessor the power to fly. Thus far, however, we had met no one who had acquired so miraculous a charm.

"How did you get the bone?" we excitedly queried. We summoned up visions of Jackson creeping in the dead of night to some lonely spot near a cemetery and shooting a black cat between its glowing green eyes. The actual facts proved far different.

"Wen I wuz a young man," said Jackson, "I ketched a big black cat. Den I made a big fyuh in duh yahd an put on a pot uh watuh an let it come tuh a bile. Den I tied duh black cat up an put im in duh watuh alibe an put a weight obuh duh pot tuh keep im in and uh let im bile tuh pieces. Den I strain duh stoo an separate duh bones an I shut muh eyes an pull duh bones tru muh mouf till uh got duh right one. All deze yeahs I kep dat bone an nuttn ebuh do me no ebil."

Wilmington Island

◇◇◇◇◇◇◇◇◇◇◇◇◇◇◇◇◇◇◇◇◇◇◇◇

UNCLE JACK TATTNALL* AND UNCLE ROBERT PINCK-
ney ** are river men. For many years they have earned a
frugal living by casting for shrimp or crabbing or fishing in
the Wilmington River. Apparently they are in little fear of
the elements. Winter or summer, at whatever hour of the
day or night the tide is "right," they are on the water in
their bateaux.

Many of the Wilmington Island Negroes depend upon the
river for their livelihood. In leisure hours, here as in other
sections, skillful fingers carve or weave to pass the time away.
We were fortunate in being shown a walking stick (Plate
IIb) carved some years before by an old fisherman of the
island.† The delicately detailed figure of a human being
formed a third of the stick, with hair, features, fingers, and
shoes carefully executed. The narrow thin figure stood
stiffly gowned in a garment edged with a saw-tooth design.

For some time we had been anxious to obtain interviews
with Uncle Jack and Uncle Robert, who were among the
oldest inhabitants of Wilmington Island, in order that we
might learn something regarding beliefs and customs that
had been handed down to them. Until the present time, we
had met with little success.

A barbecue to be held in the side yard of Celia Small, one
of the islanders, at last gave us the long hoped for opportunity of meeting a number of the residents at one time.

* *Jack Tattnall, Wilmington Island.*
** *Robert Pinckney, Thunderbolt.*
† *Property of Edward A. Sieg, 128 West Jones Street, Savannah.*

When we arrived, it was just getting dark. Black masses of trees were outlined against the sky. To the south a shining river curved into shadows. A little wind blowing up from the marsh tasted of salt.

The party was in full swing. Small groups clustered about the open fire, chatting amiably and tending the juicy pork which was slowly roasting on a grill. The light of the fire lit up the shiny black faces and touched here and there on a bright blouse or turban.

Uncle Jack, tall, bony-framed and lanky, had worn his usual workaday clothes to the party. His kindly, near-sighted eyes shone with excitement. Uncle Robert, small and spry, had dressed up in honor of the occasion. He was conspicuously proud of his derby hat, neatly brushed and cleaned. It was about two sizes too large and came down to Uncle Robert's ears at the sides and to his eyebrows in front, but, almost new, it gave the old man a certain air of assurance and seemed to make him forget that his brown suit was faded and well worn.

When the opening merriment had somewhat subsided, the crackling of pork fat and the smell of hot yams drew the party around the fire where Uncle Jack and Uncle Robert were exchanging reminiscences of old times. For the most part the others listened, occasionally interjecting a sentence or two.

We asked how long the old men had lived on the island and Uncle Jack answered, "All muh life I lib right yuh on Wilmington Ilun. Bawn yuh an nebuh want tuh lib no place else. I got ebryting I want right yuh."

Uncle Robert, who was eighty-one, about ten years older than Uncle Jack, said that he had come to the island from Clinch County just before the War between the States.

The long journey undertaken so many years ago had made a vivid impression on him. With a far-away expression in his eyes, the old man told us about that trip.

104

"We come in a wagon hitch up tuh a double team uh hawse. We pile ebryting in duh wagon, all duh pots and pans an beddn. Duh women ride in duh wagon an duh men trudge longside.

"It take us days an days tuh come frum Clinch County tuh yuh. We cross tree ribbuhs. We git tuh one ribbuh wut take us a half day tuh git obuh. Wen night come, we sleep in duh houses long duh road wut duh folks desuhted. I membuh one time we stay at a house wut dohn hab no flo. Jis walls an a roof. We put duh beddn right down on duh groun an sleep deah.

"We done sell tuh Mistuh Barnard. Yuh know duh Barnards, missus? Mis Barnard come outn a Barstow. Dey lib yuh, too. Well, wen we git tuh Wilmington Ilun, deah wuz jis a few houses on duh ilun. Deah wuz still some folks yuh wut hab come frum Africa. I recollect dat one gang uh slabes wuz brung frum Liberia. Dat wuz fo I git yuh. Duh las gang wuz brung attuh I git yuh an dey come ovuh frum Africa an dey stop an add tuh um at Santo Domingo.

"Yuhs heahd bout dat lot, ain't yuh? Big boat try tuh creep up duh Savannah Ribbuh, but dey chase um out tuh open sea an dey keep chasin um till wen dat boat git way an kin lan dem slabes, it way down tuh Jekyll Ilun. Den attuh dey git um deah, dey steal some ub um back an carry um up yuh tuh Hutchinson Ilun. I tink dasso, missus.

"I membuh doze Africans wen dey fus come couldn walk on duh groun bery good. Dey hab lill clumpy feet an dey ain weah no shoes needuh."

We asked if Uncle Robert had ever heard the Africans say how they had been captured and he nodded. "Yes'm, I heahs um talk bout dat many times. Dey say duh wite mens git um tuh come on ship an dey fool um wid all kine uh pretty tings. Den dey lock um in duh hatch an wen dey git out, dey way out on duh open sea."

Did Uncle Robert remember any particular words that the African people had used?

"Ole man Pompey he say, 'skinskon' ebrytime he git mad. Wen he wuz bery mad he alluz say dat. But nobody know wut he mean. He call a watuhmelon a 'balonga.'

"I membuh duh African mens use tuh all duh time make lill clay images. Sometime dey lak mens an sometime lak animal. Once dey make a big un. Dey put a speah in he han an walk roun im an say he wuz duh chief. But dat clay got too much ribbuh mud in um an he ain las long. Sometime dey try tuh make duh image out uh wood, but seem lak duh tool ain right, so mos times dey's ub clay." [41g, 70c, e]

We questioned the old man about any other recollections he might have concerning African people and he added, "Doze Africans alluz call one anudduh 'countryman.' Dey know ef dey come frum duh same tribe by duh mahk dey hab.[14] Some hab a long mahk an some hab a roun un. Udduhs weah eahring in duh eah. Some weahs it in duh lef eah an doze frum anudduh tribe weahs it in duh right eah.

"Deah's two Africans buried on duh ilun right now. Lonnie Green an his brudduh, dey buried right neah duh Indian mouns. Jack Pinckney yuh, he bury um."

At this point Uncle Jack and Uncle Robert engaged in an animated discussion of the types of funerals which had been held in those early days.

Uncle Jack said, "Wen a pusson die, we beat duh drum tuh let ebrybody know bout duh det.[26] Den dey come tuh duh wake an sit up wid duh body."

Uncle Robert added, "Wen one uh doze Africans die, it wuz bery sad. Wen a man's countryman die, he sit right wid um all night. Den in duh mawnin he go out an pray tuh duh sun. Yuh know, missus, doze Africans ain got no Christianity. Dey ain hab no regluh religion. Dey jis pray tuh duh sun an moon an sometime tuh a big stah. Attuh dey pray, dey come in an put deah han on duh frien an say good-bye.[30, 31] Den dey go home."

"We beat duh drum agen at duh fewnul." [24]   This from Uncle Jack. "We call it duh dead mahch. Jis a long slow beat. Boom-boom-boom. Beat duh drum. Den stop. Den beat it agen."

We wanted to know what the drums looked like and the two men took turns in supplying the information.

Uncle Robert spoke first. "Duh ole drums wut duh Afri-cans make wuz make out ub a skin uh some kine uh animal stretch obuh a holluh lawg. Dey didn eben take duh haiah off duh skin. Jis put it on datta way." [25]

Here Uncle Jack spoke up, "Ain so long sence dey stop makin drums. Wen I wuz a young man, we use tuh make um. Dey wuz fo-cawnuhed sometimes an wuz cubbuh wid a skin. Dey wuz bout fo feet high. At duh fewnul wen we beat duh drum we mahch roun duh grabe in a ring."

We asked if any of them knew any spider stories. There was some hesitancy; then they all said, "No'm."

Celia Small,* a slim, middle-aged Negro woman, listened intently, nodding her head. We asked Celia if she had heard of them.

"Yes'm, muh granma she speak ub em many time an say dey's wicked." Celia laughed slyly. "She say dey talk bout um mung duh mens."

We asked if the spider had a name, like Brer Rabbit.

"No'm, he ain got no name. Lease, I ain nebuh heahd it. Only time I knows yuh call a spiduh wen yuh say, 'An Nancy got um,' an das wen he ketch duh fly.[53] Duh spiduh is wicked. Hab tuh be bery keahful bout um. He drop right down out uh duh sky on yuh."

"What about the spider stories?" we persisted.

Celia looked at us warningly. She laughed softly.

* Celia Small, Wilmington Island.

"Spiduh stories mus be bad. Caahn git duh mens tuh tell um tuh dis day. Dey jis say dey ain know nuttn bout um. Dey ain want tuh tell um tuh duh ladies."

Gene,* Uncle Jack's stalwart son, who had for the most part stood quietly at the fringe of the little group and had volunteered no information at all, now contributed, "Doze spiduh stories ain nuttn but duhty jokes. Dat's all dey is. Yuh call a duhty joke 'An Nancy story.' Ain no stories tuh tell duh ladies." [33]

A sudden silence followed and we asked if any of the group had heard of flying Africans. Uncle Jack's face brightened. "Long as I kin membuh, missus, I been heahin bout dat. Lots uh slabes wut wuz brung obuh frum Africa could fly. Deah wuz a crowd ub um wukin in duh fiel. Dey dohn lak it heah an dey tink dey go back tuh Africa. One by one dey fly up in duh eah an all fly off an gone back tuh Africa."

As the old man was talking, the others nodded in agreement and mumbled that they too had heard of "folks wut could fly." Peter McQueen,** small and middle-aged, said, "Deah's folks wut kin fly eben now. Folks is alluz complainin bout bein rid by witches.[69]

There was again a murmur of agreement and we were able to catch snatches of conversation dealing with people in the neighborhood who had been ridden by witches.

Celia Small told us, "Dey's mosly folks yuh know. Jis change deah shape at night an come in duh house an ride yuh." [68]

"Now das sumpm reel," approved Uncle Robert. "I bin rid lots uh time by witches. Jis sit on yuh ches an ride yuh. Yuh wake up an feel lak yuh smudduhin. Ef yuh kin git duh succulation an tro um off, it all right."

The talk of witches suggested other apparitions and we

* Gene Tattnall, Wilmington Island.
** Peter McQueen, Wilmington Island.

were informed that a variety of spirits were said to be seen on the island. These, it seemed, took different sizes and shapes and frequently appeared to the local residents.[54, 55, 59]

"Sometimes," said Celia, "doze spirits put spells on yuh, fix yuh."

"Spirits ain duh only ones," added Peter McQueen. "Folks kin wuk wid cunjuh too.[15] Ain dasso, Uncle Robert?"

"Dasso," Uncle Robert nodded sagely. "Muh own brudduh wuz cunjuhed. He hab a spell put on um. He hab fits all duh time—hydrophobical fits—act lak he crazy. Nuttn we do hep im, an attuh a few yeahs he die."

"Only ting yuh kin do tuh keep frum bein cunjuhed is tuh carry a han," said Peter. "Mos folks tote a han wid um."[8, 12, a, c, d]

"Plenty folks kin fix yuh wid a han dey make deysef," said another voice.

"What are the charms made of?" we wanted to know.

"Haiah," "Nails,"[10] "Frum duh cloze" were the various responses and Celia enlarged on this information. "Ef yuh hab a enemy, nebuh let um git a piece uh yuh cloze. An yuh bun yuh haiah an yuh nail parins. Dey kin sho make powuhful han frum deze."

We inquired if many persons made a profession of this, and Peter informed us, "Sometimes dey git um frum a root doctuh."[8c, d, 48]

"Duh root doctuh kin hep yuh too," added Uncle Robert. "Dey is powful smaht. I use tuh heah tell ub a root man name Smaht McCall.[6, 48] Ef yuh git in any trouble, yuh jis go see um an he git yuh out ub it. Deah wuz a man wut got rested. He wuz plenty skeah bout wut would happen tuh um. He go see Smaht McCall an Smaht say not tuh worry cuz he would hep um. Duh day uh duh trial come an wen dey try duh case, a buzzud fly in duh cote house winduh.[68b] He fly roun. Den he light on duh jedge desk. Well,

109

suh, wid dat buzzud deah duh jedge jis couldn do nuttn. He jis had tuh pick up an go. Duh case wuz dismissed."

"Tell bout wut Smaht McCall done tuh Doctuh Rogers," requested Uncle Jack.

"Well, Doctuh Rogers, he wuz a regluh doctuh an sometime duh folks would go tuh see um wen dey git sick stead ub goin tuh Smaht McCall. Smaht, he git mad. He say he fix dis Doctuh Rogers. He put a spell on duh hawse. Wen Doctuh Rogers go out nex time an git in he carriage, duh hawse run right intuh a tree an Doctuh Rogers git kill." [15]

As an afterthought he finished with, "Sometime deze root doctuhs is smahtuhn duh regluh doctuhs. Long time ago a doctuh tell me I hab tuh stop eatin meat. He say it ain good fuh me an ef uh eat it, I git sickn die. I bin eatin it ebuh sence an Ise still alibe. Dat doctuh bin dead fuh yeahs. Mos deze root doctuhs knows plenty; dey know nuff tuh lib."

There were a number of palmetto trees in the section and we asked if any of the people had ever heard of eating palmetto cabbage.

"Yes'm," they answered.

"Palmettuh cabbages is good eatin."

"Yuh kin jis cut it up an eat it raw an yuh kin cook it up wid fat meat," Uncle Robert told us.

"Yuh kin make good palm wine outuh duh berries," volunteered Peter McQueen.[45]

Various members of the party asked Peter McQueen to tell one of the numerous stories about Brer Rabbit and Brer Wolf. Peter pondered for a minute; then he started:

"Bruh Rabbit and Bruh Wolf wuz alluz tryin tuh git duh bes uh one anudduh. Now Bruh Wolf he own a hoe an it wuk fuh crop all by itsef.[39] Bruh Wolf jis say, 'Swish,' tuh it. Den he sit down in duh fiel an duh hoe do all duh wuk.

"Bruh Rabbit he wahn dat hoe. He hide behine bush an watch how duh wolf make it wuk. One day wen duh wolf way, Bruh Rabbit he steal duh hoe. He go tuh he own fiel an he stan duh hoe up an he say, 'Swish.' Duh hoe staht tuh wuk. It wuk and it wuk. Fo long duh crop is done finish. Den rabbit want hoe tuh stop, an he call out an he call out but hoe keep right on wukin. Bruh Rabbit dohn know wut wud tuh say tuh stop it. Pretty soon duh hoe cut down all Bruh Rabbit wintuh crop an still it keep on wukkin an wukkin. Bruh Rabbit wring he hans. Ebryting he hab is gone. Jis den Bruh Wolf come long an he laugh an he laugh out loud wen he see how Bruh Rabbit steal he hoe an how it done ruin all duh crop. Bruh Rabbit he keep callin out, 'Swish, swish,' an duh hoe go fastuhn fastuh. Wen he see Bruh Wolf, he ax um tuh make duh hoe stop. Bruh Wolf wohn say nuttn uhtall cuz he mad dat Bruh Rabbit steal he hoe. Den attuh a time he say, 'Slow, boy,' an duh hoe he stop wukkin. Den Bruh Wolf he pick up he hoe an carry um home."

By this time it had grown late, and the figures about the fire were shadows. From the direction of the marshes the wind was blowing more sharply and it was time to go home. Uncle Jack came up to say goodbye to us and said that he was going to spend the night on the river, shrimping. When we expressed surprise, he laughed and said that this was his usual custom.

Uncle Robert nodded in agreement. "We's at home in duh ribbuh," he said. "Bin out deah so many yeahs. Ain nuttn tuh be feahed ub."

Sunbury

❖❖❖❖❖❖❖❖❖❖

OUR CAR CAME TO AN ABRUPT STOP IN THE SANDY
road before the board fence which enclosed a small group of
weather-beaten clapboard houses. We called to a young
Negro girl who lounged in a doorway and she came forward
to see what we wanted. Almost simultaneously there appeared from the other houses scattered about the clearing a
number of other persons.

Two women about thirty-five years old and nine or ten
small children all approached the fence. At first they were
rather wary, but their attitude gradually turned to friendli-
ness and they hung over the high board fence, talking and
laughing in great good humor. Elizabeth Roberts,* the
young girl whom we had first seen, appeared to be the leader
of the group.

We were interested to know if these people had river baptisms any more. "Duh Sunbury Baptis Church an duh
Palmyra Baptis Church both hab baptizins," Elizabeth told
us. "Cose it depend on how many folks wants tuh leab duh
Presbyterian Church an jine duh Baptis. Mos ub us is already baptize."

"Where do they hold the baptisms?" we inquired.

The group all pointed in the direction of the river.
"Right obuh deah in duh Sunbury Ribbuh," they chorused.

Elizabeth again took the initiative. "All duh candidates
is robed in wite," she explained. "Duh preachuh come frum

* *Elizabeth Roberts, Sunbury.*

112

Savannah an he is dressed in a long robe. He walk long an duh folks all mahch behine im. Dey goes down tuh duh ribbuh an sing as dey go. Dey alluz hab duh baptizin wen duh tide is goin out so duh watuh will wash duh sins away. Attuh dey all gits tuh duh ribbuh, dey stop an duh preachuh ast duh candidates tuh step fawwud. One by one he dip em in duh watuh an dey is buried in baptism. Wen dey is all baptize, duh preachuh pray tuh duh ribbuh an [63] ast dat all sins be taken away. Den all duh folks sing an shout an praise duh Lawd."

The little group leaning on the railing nodded in agreement and as if in memory of the ceremony their bodies swayed rhythmically. As we listened and watched we could almost see the white robed procession winding to the river bank; we could almost hear the chanting of the converts as their sins were washed away.

The conversation turned to burial customs in the section and the women told us that "settin-ups" were still held for those who died.

"We all sit wid duh body an sing an pray an keep duh spirit company," said one of them.

Another added, "At duh fewnul we sing an we puts our hands on duh cawpse tuh say goodbye. It bad luck not tuh do dis." [31]

We had heard in other communities that in case of death away from home the body is brought back to its native town for burial. This custom is also prevalent in Sunbury, we learned.

"Ebrybody wannuh be buried in deah own town," [1] Elizabeth said. "An we nebuh bury strainjuhs wid our own folks. Ef a strainjuh die yuh, we bury em in duh strainjuh's lot." [3]

Emma Stevens,* tall and slim, a baby in her arms and several small children gathered about her, spoke up, "Yuh got

* *Emma Stevens, Sunbury.*

113

tuh be plenty keahful bout duh spirits. Duh spirit is hungry
jis lak duh pusson. Yuh hab tuh put food in duh ruhm fuh
duh spirit tuh come eat." [58]

"Dat is duh truth," agreed young Elizabeth. "Ef duh
spirit is hungry, it will sho come back an hant yuh." [58f]

This talk of spirits started us on a new train of thought
and we were curious to learn of the local theories regarding
ghosts and witches.

"Duh spirit nebuh go in duh groun wid duh body," [56] volunteered Emma. "It jis wanduh roun. Dey come out wen
duh moon is noo."

Mary Stevens,* whose short, stocky figure was clad in
bright pink and who wore a sailor hat perched rakishly on
her head, stated, "Duh spirits is ebryweah. Dey peah mosly
at duh fus dahk an in duh middle night."

Young Elizabeth, too, had something to say about spirits.
"I sees em all duh time," she said. "Dey dohn hurt yuh none,
jis walk long wid yuh an talk. Some hab duh head on an
some hab duh head off." [59a]

From ghosts and shadows of the night the discussion followed its natural course to even darker powers, such as conjure, evil roots, and counter charms. The little group
glanced slyly at one another. It was in lowered tones that
they volunteered remarks on this subject.

"We do heah bout folks rootin each udduh all duh time.[15]
Yuh sho hab tuh be keahful. Some folks weahs a dime aw a
penny tied on duh ankle an wen it tun black, dey knows somebody is tryin tuh root em." [12a, c, d]

"What are the conjures made of?" we wanted to know.

"Dey make em uh haiah an nails an frum lots uh tings,"
we were told.[10]

Elizabeth said, "Duh heabiest root I ebuh heard bout wuz
a cunjuh made uh some funny oily stuff in a bottle. Duh
enemy ketch duh pusson's spirit in dat bottle an dat wuz a

* Mary Stevens, Sunbury.

powuhful spell.[8]   Duh man fell sick an had tuh go tuh a root doctuh [48] fo he git cuod."

"Yuh sho hab bad luck ef yuh do a lot uh tings," warned one of the women. "Nobody ebuh carry a hoe aw a rake tru duh house. Das a bad sign."

"It's bad luck tuh carry wood on yuh shoulduh tru duh house," was added to this information.

"But it ain bad luck ef you weahs a Lucky Haht," interposed Emma.

"And what is a Lucky Heart," we inquired.

"It's fuh good luck. All duh people roun yuh carries Lucky Hahts and Lucky Mojoes an sech tings." [8]

Respecting harvest festivals one of the women said, "I hab heah tell how dey dohn do dat no mo." [38]

"We do git tuhgedduh an hab dance an pahties an big suppuhs," stated another. Her eyes sparkled at the pleasant memory. "We does duh Snake Hip an duh Buzzud Lope."

The others chorused, "An addalas dance we did duh Fish Tail an duh Fish Bone an duh Camel Walk." [17]

All efforts failed to persuade the women to describe these dances. Evidently thinking of the antics of their neighbors at the recent dance they laughed repeatedly, shaking their heads and nudging one another but refusing to be cajoled into a demonstration.

After learning that we wished to record the old customs as far back as possible, the women suggested that we visit Uncle Jonah,* who was the great grandfather of Elizabeth. In answer to repeated halloos the old man came trudging down the road. As he drew nearer the car, we could see that he was a spry, erect little figure, clad in a blue chambray shirt and a pair of dark trousers. Although he carried a gnarled stick for support, he appeared to move with considerable rapidity. His salutation was, "Dis is Uncle Jonah, duh man wut swalluh duh whale."

* "Uncle Jonah," Sunbury.

Uncle Jonah told us that he was eighty-seven years of age and that he had been born on a plantation on Harris Neck. He had remained there until after the time "uh duh big raid," he said and he had been in Sunbury for a period of about sixty years.

When asked if he could remember any of the slaves who had come from Africa, a faraway expression came into his eyes. Finally he offered, "Yes'm, I membuh two. Ole man Ben an Sally dey bote come frum Africa. Dey sho use tuh use some funny wuds. Wen it would tunduh, dey would alluz say it wuz 'maulin a bumba.' "

Uncle Jonah tried to recall some of the African stories he had heard in his youth. He knit his brows in deep thought. After a time he said, "I membuh heahin bout a boatload uh Nigguhs wut wuz bring frum Africa. Dey wuz kep hid in duh cabin till dey git tuh Sunbury. Wen dey let um out an dey see dey wuzn in Africa, dey jis take wing an fly back home. Cose now, ma'am, I didn see dis but I heah bout it many times."

Another story that the old man told us was as follows: "Deah wuz two countrymen wut bote come frum Africa libin on duh plantation. One ub dem die an dey bury um widout duh udduh knowin bout it. Pretty soon he lun bout how he frien die an he make um dig um up. He say he wannuh say a few wuds tuh um. Dey dig up duh man an he speak tuh um an den put um back in duh grabe. It wuz all right attuh he say goodbye." [30]

"Uncle Jonah," we asked, "do you remember much conjuring in those days?"

The white head nodded slowly. "Yes'm, deah sho wuz cunjuhin, but deah's mo cunjuhin [15] in deze days dan deah wuz in doze. I heah bout it all duh time roun yuh."

Our interview concluded, we set out in search of Siras Bowen, who, we had been told, carved wooden tombstones.[70a, h] We rode down the sandy, tree-lined road until we came to the

Sunbury Baptist Church, a white frame building set back from the highway against a background of verdant spreading trees. The Bowen family burial ground was to the right of the church and here we discovered that Siras' skill in wood carving was manifested in many unusual markers.

These were wooden images (Plate XII) set on graves that were close together. One resembled a large bird; another represented a snake writhing upon a stand; and the third was the figure of a man, round and pole-like of body, with a head that resembled a ball and rudely sculptured features.[41e] Another Bowen marker was of clay painted yellow; in its surface was roughly cut the outline of an open hand with a small mirror glittering in the palm.

Most of the graves were decorated with possessions of the departed persons.[47] There were many glasses, bottles, and vases, most of which had been turned a shimmering purple from long exposure to the sun. For a time we wandered through the little cemetery, reading the inscriptions on the various tombstones.

The same day we visited another cabin on the dirt road leading back from Sunbury Bluff. We had already driven past the little two-room shack, painted green, its dark roof patched in many places, when our attention was attracted by a stout, middle-aged woman who was sitting on the porch idly playing with a long, dangerous looking knife. At once we reversed the gears and rolled backward to a stop. Near the woman was seated the husky figure of a young girl. She wore but one garment, a faded green dress which hung raggedly to about the knee. Beneath the skirt were large muscular legs that were twisted about the rungs of the chair. Long, staring yellow eyes looked out at us with disturbing, unblinking fixity. The girl's hair stood out stiffly in a number of tight little braids. She was slowly, laboriously stringing weights on a fish net.

The older woman spoke at first in a grudging, reserved

manner. The girl continued her work on the fish net, occasionally glancing at us with that impenetrable expression.

After much persuasion we gained the older woman's confidence and she spoke to us freely. She, too, attended the baptisms held by members of the two churches and also remembered various "settin-ups" she had gone to. She told us that food was usually prepared for the watchers.

"Bread an coffee," she said, "das wut dey gie yuh at a settin-up."

"We thought they ate chicken," we remarked.

"No, dey dohn hab no chicken. Jis bread an coffee."

The subject of food led us to inquire if she knew of any persons who refused to eat certain things.

"Muh huzbun wohn nebuh eat chicken. Ain nebuh eat it sence he wuz bawn, an needuh his mudduh befo him." [65]

"Why is that? Doesn't he like it?"

"Ain no mine wedduh he lak it aw ain lak it. He jis wohn eat it. Lots uh folks say deah's some food wut dey dohn eat. I nebuh eat rabbit. An none uh muh folks wouldn eat it needuh. Dey say it wuz no good tuh eat."

The conversation drifted on until the talk of food brought to the woman's mind gala occasions at which she had feasted and danced in her youth.

"We use tuh dance all duh time tuh duh drums," she said. "We would dance roun an roun in a succle an clap our hans an sing. Dey would hab duh dances obuh on St. Catherine Ilun."

"How would you know when they were going to hold a dance?"

"Dey beat duh drums on St. Catherine.[26] Den dey heah it at Harris Neck an folks deah tell all ub us yuh bout duh dance. We all go obuh tuh St. Catherine in a boat an dance an dance till mos daylight."

When the talk finally turned to roots and other potent

elements of conjure, we were told of a recent incident in the neighborhood.[15]

"I sees dis wid muh own eyes," asserted the story-teller. "Deah wuz a ole man roun yuh wut wuz cunjuhed an hab lots uh trouble wid his eyes. He dig roun his yahd tuh see ef any dose is buried deah. Attuh a time he fine a dawl baby buried unduh duh doe step.[8] Its two finguhs wuz stuck in its eye. Duh man tro duh dawl in duh ribbuh an duh trouble disappeah."

She said that she knew of no other recent case of conjure, but it appeared that both women had had experiences with witches. We were informed that it was a common occurrence for "folks tuh hab witches ride um at night."[69] The girl contributed little to the conversation, but occasionally nodded her head in agreement when the older woman made a statement. Only once did she speak, and then it was to issue a brief sharp rebuke to a very small child who was scampering naked about the yard.

After a time the older woman, too, sank into a heavy, unresponsive silence. When she answered our queries at all, it was with a flat, "No, ma'am, I ain nebuh heahd uh dat," or an exasperating, "Wut, ma'am?"

We left the two women as dusk was falling. Looking back, we saw the older woman again slowly waving the knife and the girl still in the same almost motionless pose, her slow methodical work on the fish net continuing.

119

Harris Neck

◇◇◇◇◇◇◇◇◇◇◇◇◇◇◇◇◇

TURNING OFF FROM THE COASTAL HIGHWAY NEAR
Riceboro a tree-shaded dirt road leads to Harris Neck, a remote little settlement connected to the mainland by a causeway and located about forty-eight miles south of Savannah.
Narrow, rutted roads curve and turn unexpectedly through
the densely wooded area. Set singly or in little clusters of
two or three and sometimes almost hidden by the trees and
foliage are the houses of the inhabitants. There is a peaceful
atmosphere about the entire island; life flows along in a
smoothly gliding stream; the people seem satisfied for the
most part with a simple, uneventful scheme of existence.

The first house we stopped at was that of Ed Thorpe,* a
familiar and well liked character in the section. A small,
neatly inscribed placard placed near the gate bore the
owner's name. The attractive house was set well back from
the road in a large grove of oak trees. A whitewashed fence
protected the property.

The old man, who was eighty-three years old, was working
in the side yard adjoining the house. His broad, erect
shoulders and his bright alert eyes made him appear to be
much younger than his actual age. He told us proudly that
he had lived in this particular house for twenty-five years.
Then he apologized because his present circumstances prevented him from having the house and fence repainted.

We discussed native Africans and Ed Thorpe remembered that his grandmother had come from Africa.

* *Ed Thorpe, Harris Neck.*

"She come frum Africa an uh name wuz Patience Spaulding," he began. "She tell me dat in Africa she use tuh eat wile tings. I membuh she use tuh go out in duh woods roun yuh an bring back some kine uh weed wut she cook. She call it 'lam quato.' It look lak pokeberry tuh me.

"She say all duh people in Africa loves red. Das how dey ketch um. I mean duh folks wut bring um yuh as slabes. Dey put up a red clawt weah dey would see it. Wen dey git close tuh duh boat, dey grab um an bring um yuh. She say das duh way dey ketch huh.

"Wen muh gran pray, she kneel down on duh flo. She bow uh head down tree time an she say 'Ameen, Ameen, Ameen.'

"Muh gran say deah wuz lots uh cunjuh in Africa. Deah wuz some men wut could make a pot bile widout fyuh an deah wuz some wut could fly.[48, 69c] She tell me dat deah wuz witches wut rode folks.[69] Dey could take off deah skins an hang um up an go out as cats.[68] Wen dey come back duh nex mawnin, dey would put on duh skins. Deah is folks roun heah tuhday wut says dey caahn sleep nights cuz duh witches ride um.

"Folks say duh road tuh Maringo is hanted.[59] I use tuh lib at Maringo some time back, but I nebuh did see no spirits. Once I tink I see one. Wen I git closuh, it tun out tuh be a big dog."[54]

Later that day we stopped at a neat whitewashed cottage and talked for a while with Isaac Basden,* a blind basket-maker [70a] about sixty years of age. The old man had learned his trade during his youth before he had gone blind and now supported himself comfortably in this manner.

We found him sitting in the front room, surrounded by his work. A number of finished baskets were also in evidence. They varied widely in size and shape and were all of the coil type.[70i] Many were fanners, while there were also a number

* *Isaac Basden, Harris Neck.*

of large round baskets, about twenty inches in diameter, with matching covers that fitted well down over the rim. Isaac used bulrushes and grasses for his material and worked with a sure deft touch that insured sturdy construction.

He remembered that drums had been used for a variety of purposes during his youth. He said, "I use tuh dance tuh duh drum.[23] I recall wen dey beat duh drum tuh call duh people on Harris Neck tuhgedduh fuh a dance aw fewnul.[26] Cose, dey hab a diffunt beat wen dey call um tuh a settin-up aw fewnul frum duh one dey use tuh call um tuh a dance. Deah wuz two kine uh drum. One dey call duh kittle drum, an one wuz duh bass drum. It stan bout two an a half foot high. Dey use tuh alluz hab a settin-up wen somebody die. Wen folks would go tuh duh settin-up, dey would gib um bread an coffee.[37b, c]

"Dey still hole ribbuh baptisms yuh. Dey git tuh duh ribbuh an attuh dey pray an sing up on duh bank, duh preachuh take duh candidates down in duh ribbuh. Fo he baptize each ub um, he say a prayuh tuh duh ribbuh an ax fuh all duh sins tuh be wash away."[63]

Remembering what we had been told about the haunted road to Maringo, we questioned Isaac and he said, "Yes'm, I hab heah bout duh hanted road tuh Maringo on duh Young Man Road. Lots uh folks say deah is spirits roun deah.[59] Wen yuh try tuh pass duh fawk in duh road, duh spirits stop yuh sometime an wohn let yuh by. Some uh duh spirits mus be good, fuh Ise heahd one story bout a man who wuz passin by an all ub a sudden his hawse jis stop shawt in his tracks. Jis wouldn go anudduh step. Duh man try an try, but he couldn make duh hawse moob. Den he see a spirit come long an it take hole ub duh hawse bridle an lead him long. Duh hawse go right long. Den duh spirit disappeah. I hab heahd lots uh stories bout dat road but uh nebuh see nuttn muhsef."

Our next interview was an unusually delightful one. Sitting on the front porch of Liza Basden's * small, compactly constructed brown house, we listened to her comments about the prevailing beliefs and customs. The scene before us was restful. The garden planted at the sides and front of the house was enclosed by a low wire fence. Within this enclosure a number of dogs and chickens scuttled about. At a short distance from the house stood an iron pump and an immense rusted iron pot, probably used in the past for boiling clothes. On all sides as far as the eye could see were vast stretches of green land, shaded by massive-trunked, moss-draped trees and covered with an abundance of semi-tropical foliage and underbrush. Here and there could be glimpsed the slanting roofs of neighboring houses.

When we first arrived Liza, a pretty golden-skinned, rather heavy-set woman about eighty years of age, and a small black grandchild were the only occupants of the porch. She told us she had recently come home from a visit to children in the North. Presently her husband and a daughter approached without speaking and sat down unobtrusively in a corner. For the most part they listened to the conversation, contributing only an occasional remark.

"I wuz bawn with a caul," Liza told us, pausing in her task of peeling and eating figs from the pan that she held in her lap. "That means I see ghos.[4] Least I could see em till aftuh I stop havin chillun. Then I stop seein em.

"Three of my chillun they bawn with cauls too. They wuz always skedduh than othuhs. They wuz always fraid of the dahk an nevuh lak tuh go off by themselfs. I nevuh know jis wut they see."

"What did the ghost that you saw look like?" we inquired.

A reflective expression crossed Liza's round pleasant face and she nodded her gray head with its neatly pinned braids.

"They peah jis as nachral as anybody. Most of em ain got no heads. Jis go right along down the path.[59] One time

* *Liza Basden, Harris Neck.*

I see a man go right down that path theah. I go out tuh
see who he wuz an all of a sudden he disappeah. Theah
wuzn't no foot tracks aw nuthin. I nevuh see im no mo. I
think maybe he wuz gahdin buried treasure.[61]

"Anothuh time I look out in the yahd an theah wuz a
hawg jis a eatin up the cawn.[54b] That wuz the biggest hawg
I evuh did see. He stand theah an keep eatin an eatin. I
run an tell muh huzbun an he drop wut he wuz doin an come
runnin. Wen we git theah, the hawg done disappeah.
Theah wuzn't no sign of im an the cawn wuz all right theah.
It didn't look lak anybody bin eatin on it uhtall.

"Then one time I see a crowd of cows in the field.[54b]
Theah wuz a big bull in the middle. They wuz jis a cuttin
down the cawn. Theah wuz a big empty space weah they
have already eat. I run tuh weah muh brothuh wuz an tell
im tuh come quick. We run weah the cows wuz but wen we
git theah, they have all vanished. They wuz all gone. Theah
wuz no tracks an all the cawn wuz grown back. All of a sudden I feel a terrible pain. I could hahdly git tuh the house.
That's the way it is bout the spirits. Ef yuh tell yuh see em
an they disappeah an no one else can see em, then it cause
yuh tuh git sick."

After a while Liza remembered an incident that had been
related to her by her grandfather and she told us, "Muh
gran, he see a deah come down the bluff. He run quick an
jump on his back. The deah run all aroun the woods. He
teah an scratch an try tuh shake muh gran off. He couldn
do it. Finally he run intuh the rivuh. Muh gran jump off
an make it tuh the sho. He wuz so tired he wuz mos dead."

Was there no protection against the visits of these creatures from the spirit world, we wanted to know. All of the
little group assembled on the porch shook their heads and
mumbled a reply.

"Yes'm, mos of the folks carry sumpm fuh pruhtection," [8] said Liza. "These keep othuh folks frum wukin cun-

juh on em too. They's made of haiah, an nails,[10] an grave-yahd dut,[9] sometimes from pieces of cloth an string. They tie em all up in a lill bag. Some of em weahs it roun the wrist, some of em weahs it roun the neck,[11b] an some weahs a dime on the ankle. Then ef somebody put down cunjuh fuh em it tun black an [12a, c, d] they git anothuh one tuh wawd off the evil.[6] Some of em has a frizzled chicken in the yahd. People do say they kin dig up cunjuh an keep it frum wukin gense yuh.[13a]

"Yuh heah all the time bout folks wut is cunjuhed. They gits crippled up an ef they dohn do nuthin bout it, some of em dies." [15]

We asked if river baptisms were still held in the section and Liza answered, "Yes'm, they hole the baptisms right down yonduh in the rivuh. They always hole em on the ebb tide; that's so the sins be washed away. All the pruhcession mahch down tuh the rivuh. The preachuh leads the way. Fus the preachuh stan on the bank an pray. Then he take the candidates one by one an dip em in the watuh. Then he make a prayuh fuh the rivuh tuh wash away the sins.[63] I call that prayuh 'the matrinal.' "

Liza was unable to explain just what this term meant, but she said it was always applied to the prayer to the river. She told us, too, that "settin-ups" were held for those who died and that the mourners sat up all night with the body and sang and prayed. "In the ole days they always use tuh beat the drum at the funeral an they still does it tuhday. As they take the body tuh the graveyahd, they beat the drum as they move long.[24] They put the body in the grave. Then they mahch roun an sing an beat the drum."

We had been told that several midwives rendered services to those residing in the section. We asked Liza about this and she told us, "Anna Johnson, she's my sistuh. She's a midwife an she tends tuh lots of folks roun heah. Those midwifes sho knows wut tuh do.[48] They use a shahp knife aw sizzuhs tuh cut the pain. Once wen I wuz in pain a midwife put a peah of sizzuhs unduh muh pilluh. All of a sudden the pain stop right quick. The pain wuz cut right off." [12b]

Josephine Stephens,* one of the older residents of the island, lived a short distance from Liza Basden. Her house was set back several hundred yards from the highway in the midst of a large field. There was no pathway and in order to get to the house we had to cut directly through the field. As we neared the gate at the front of the house a tall gaunt woman, who we learned was Josephine's daughter, ran to meet us. It appeared that the mother had been ill for some time past and the younger woman had been caring for her.

As we talked with Josephine, the daughter stood in an adjoining room, ironing clothes. She stopped every now and then to take part in the conversation. The two women were utterly different types. Josephine, dressed becomingly in a blue and white checked gingham outfit, was the antebellum type of Negro. The daughter, tall, thin and dashing, and probably in her forties, represented a more modern era. She had on a blue checked sport shirt, a white skirt upon the surface of which was the dim outline of the trade name of a flour mill, and a pair of shiny black satin bedroom slippers. Her two front teeth were gold and shone and sparkled as she talked. Two large gold hoop earrings dangled beneath her close cropped straightened hair.

"I bin wukin ovuh at St. Simon," she explained to us. "Befo that I had a good job up Nawth. My mothuh git sick tho, an she need me tuh take keah of huh. That's why I come heah an stay. She gittin tuh be long in yeahs an caahn do so well by uhsef."

The mother did not know exactly how old she was but said she had been about fourteen at the close of the War between the States. We questioned her about her recollections of

* *Josephine Stephens, Harris Neck.*

early days, but her memory was rather clouded. She answered pleasantly, however, and when she was not talking to us mumbled softly to herself.

"I do know dat folks bawn wid a caul kin see spirits," [4] she admitted. "Plenty uh folks roun yuh say duh spirits peah tuh um." [59]

When we inquired about drums being beaten at funerals, she shook her head stubbornly and refused to say anything on the subject.

The daughter, overhearing the conversation, paused in her task of ironing, and said, "Yes'm. Dasso. They beats the drum tuhday at the fewnul.[24] Specially ef yuh blongs tuh a awganization, they goes right along in the fewnul pruhcession an beats the drum as they mahch. I remembuh heahin bout in the ole days they beat out messages on the drum.[26] Let the folks know wen sumpm wuz bout tuh happen. Wen they give a dance ovuh on St. Catherine, they beat the drum tuh let the folks heah know bout it."

At a funeral, the bottles and dishes and other possessions belonging to the departed person were left on the grave, the women informed us. "The spirit need these," [47] the younger woman explained, "jis lak wen they's live. Evrybody mahch roun the grave in a succle an shout an pray."

We inquired if some people in the section were afraid to eat certain foods. Once more Josephine shook her head in negation.

The obliging daughter who listened intently to everything that was said again interceded. "I do heah bout that. Theah is some folks wut caahn eat suttn foods. They say it's bad luck an they nevuh do eat it. Right now theah's lots of foods wut some folks dohn eat." [65]

At this point in the conversation the older woman brightened and told us about the harvest festivals held during plantation days.

"We hab big feas. Ebrybody bring some ub duh fus

crops. We all gib tanks fuh duh crop an we dance an sing." [38]

Shortly after this she again fell to mumbling and muttering unintelligibly and seemed unwilling to be drawn again into the conversation. She did confide in us that she had lived in her house for over fifty-eight years and she proudly displayed her immaculate blue outfit which she said her daughter had recently purchased for her. As it was growing late and we had other interviews to obtain in the vicinity, we concluded our visit. The two women urged us to return soon. Setting out again to make an uncertain jagged path across the field, we looked back and saw Josephine, a rather tragic tall figure huddled at the end of the porch. The daughter waved gaily. Her gold earrings glinted in the sun.

When we found Anna Johnson,* she was standing in the front yard of Ed Thorpe's talking with a tall middle-aged woman who, we later learned, was Rosa Sallins,** her niece and Liza Basden's daughter.

The two women walked over to the car and greeted us. We inquired about the various methods the midwife employed and she said, "Tuh cut a pain yuh use a shahp instrument, lak a knife, aw a peah of sizzuhs. Yuh put it unduh duh pilluh on duh bed. Duh pusson who is sick musn see yuh do it aw it wohn wuk. Sometime yuh use a smoothin ion. Dat cut duh pain too." [12b]

Rosa, who had been rather impatiently waiting an opportunity to speak, now offered, "Lots ub duh chillun bawn wid a caul. Ef dey is bawn wid a caul, dey kin see spirits." [4]

The midwife looked solemn. "Folks hab tuh be mighty keahful wen duh chile is bawn lak dat. Ef dey dohn do sumpm bout it, duh chile will be hanted all its life. It'll alluz be fraid uh ghos." [59]

* *Anna Johnson, Harris Neck.*
** *Rosa Sallins, Harris Neck.*

"What can be done so that the child won't be haunted?" we asked.

"Dey dry duh caul an make a tea out ub it an hab duh chile drink it.[8] Den all duh ebil will disappeah. Duh chile will see ghos, but dey will nebuh hahm um an he wohn be afraid ub um."

Rosa exposed her large white teeth in a broad smile. "I wuz bawn wid teet. Had two front teet wen I wuz bawn." [66]

Neither Rosa nor the midwife knew the significance of this unusual occurrence, though both women thought it was probably a good luck sign.

Anna was reminded of some old remedies that she had found beneficial to teething babies. "Yuh take a alligatuh tusk an clean it an shine it an hang it roun duh neck uh duh chile," she explained. "Den yuh kin take duh foot ub a groun mole. I fuhgits wich one it is. Wich is it, Rosa?"

"Dohn mattuh wich one it is jis so long its duh foefoot."

"Yuh dry it, put it in a sack made out ub a new piece uh clawt an hang it roun duh baby's neck.[8, 12] Sho heps wid duh teethin. I knows plenty bout cuos lak dat," she concluded. "I ain lak deze root folks, dough, das alluz fixin people."

Rosa agreed with her aunt. "Sho is plenty rootin yuh. It goin on all duh time. Deah's plenty uh root people wut is alluz wukin gense folks." [15]

"Dey git a grudge gense yuh an put down sumpm fuh yuh," supplemented Anna, "an pretty soon yuh dohn know yuh ownsef."

"Sometime dey put it in yuh food," this from Rosa again. "Ef yuh got a enemy, yuh dohn dare eat wut yuh lak. Nebuh know wen deah's sumpm in duh food, an ef deah is, yuh sho wohn las. Cose ef yuh weahs a han, it'll wahn yuh an keep duh cunjuh frum wukkin.[12a, c, d] Lots uh folks carries some kine uh chahm all duh time." [8]

"Some uh our folks yuh keep frizzle chicken. Dey dig up

cunjuh wut is laid down fuh yuh an let yuh know wen some-body is aftuh yuh." [13a]

The midwife told us that she had recently returned to Harris Neck, after having lived for many years in Way-cross. We asked her which community she preferred and she said, "I lak it in Waycross, missus. Duh two places jis ain nuttn lak. Tings is sho diffunt yuh. Duh folks jis dohn ack duh same. Yuh wouldn even know dey wuz human. Soon as I kin Ise goin back tuh Waycross. I jis dohn lak it heah."

The conversation turned to drums and in regard to this subject Rosa spoke up emphatically. "Yes'm, I membuh bout how some time back dey use tuh beat out messages on duh drum.[26] Dat wuz tuh let us know wen deah wuz tuh be a dance aw a frolic. Wen dey hab a dance obuh on St. Catherines, dey beat duh drum tuh tell us bout it. Duh soun would carry obuh duh watuh an we would heah it plain as anyting. Den duh folks heah beat duh drum tuh let em know bout it in udduh settlements."

The women also spoke of drums in connection with death customs. They told us that they were still beaten by those in the procession accompanying the body to the grave.[24]

"Ebrybody put duh hans on duh body tuh say good-bye," [31] Rosa told us.

"Yuh speak tuh duh pusson, too, an tell um a las mes-sage," said Anna.

"Yuh put dishes an bottles an all duh pretty pieces wut dey lak on duh grabe.[47] Yuh alluz break deze tings fo yuh put um down." [47a]

We wanted to know the reason for doing this, for we had been informed on other occasions that it was done so that no one would be tempted to steal.

Rosa, however, stated an entirely different motive.

"Yuh break duh dishes so dat duh chain will be broke. Yuh see, duh one pusson is dead an ef yuh dohn break duh tings, den duh udduhs in duh fambly will die too. Dey will folluh right long. Folks alluz hab two fewnuls. We hab one wen dey die an den once a yeah we hab a suhvice fuh ebrybody wut died durin duh yeah.⁴² Duh preachuh say a prayuh fuhrum all."

From this source we obtained added verification of the fact that river baptisms were still held.

"We alluz baptize on duh ebb tide," said Rosa. "Duh watuh washes duh sin away. Duh preachuh pray up on duh bank an den wen he baptize duh candidate, he pray tuh duh ribbuh tuh take away duh sins." ⁶³

Later in the conversation the women recalled harvest festivals ³⁸ that had been held many years before. "Dat wuz alluz a big time." Anna's rather somber face lit up at the remembrance of the festive occasion. "Ebrybody bring some ub duh fus crop tuh duh chuch an we prepeahs a big feas. We pray an gib tanks fuh duh crop an pray fuh duh nex yeah. We all eat an sing an dance. One uh duh dances call duh Buzzud Lope.¹⁷ We still dance dat tuhday."

Rosa told us proudly that she was a granddaughter of Katherine Basden who had been recognized as a leader among the Negroes in the section.

"Me an muh brudduh wuz muh granmudduh's favorites," she said. "She alluz said she lak us bettuhn all duh udduh chillun. Wen I wuz only bout twelve yeahs ole, she tell me wen I grow up I would take huh place an carry on duh wuk she wuz doin."

Moving her powerful shoulders in rhythm and clapping her hands together, the woman sang us a song that her grandmother had crooned to new-born babies as she held them in her arms. The words were, for the most part, indistinguishable. Over and over we caught one repeated phrase, "nikki yimi, nikki yimi."

"Muh granmudduh wuz took very sick. She knew she wuz gonuh die. Dat wuz jis wen muh oldes chile wuz bawn.

Muh granmudduh jis refuse tuh die fo she seen me an duh baby. She say she hab tuh see us fo she die. Ebry day she ax fuhrus. She git weakuh an weakuh but she jis wohn die. Wen duh baby wuz a few days ole, I git dress an go tuh see uh. Fus I wuz fraid tuh bring duh baby intuh duh sick ruhm fuh dey say it bad luck fuh somebody bout tuh die tuh look at a baby. Sometime duh baby die too. I tell dis tuh muh gran an she laugh at me an tell me she ain gonuh take duh baby wid uh. Den I bring duh baby in an she sing tuh uh an hole uh in uh ahms. She tell me she wuz gonuh die now an dat I wuz tuh continue uh wuk wid duh folks yuh. Right attuh dat she die."

For a while longer the woman chatted on in a friendly manner, discussing various incidents that had taken place in the neighborhood. In parting they presented us graciously with some fresh figs from the garden and asked us to visit them again whenever we returned to the settlement.

Pine Barren Near Eulonia

◇◇◇◇◇◇◇◇◇◇◇◇◇◇◇◇◇◇◇◇◇◇◇◇◇◇◇◇◇◇◇◇◇◇

AFTER THE MUDDY RUTS THROUGH THE PINE clearing had ended, there was no road, and the car jerked and bounded about among the pine trees. The soft brown needles made better traveling than the boggy wagon tracks that were behind us, but our method of procedure was rather bewildering, for there was no mark by which to retrace our tracks. As we went deeper into the pine woods there was no sign of habitation.

Our driver,* who had offered to help us when our car had stuck in the bog, was a six-foot, shiny black Negro, strong necked and lithe, with a twelve-inch hunting knife strapped to his hip. We had never seen him before, nor the smaller Negro beside him on the front seat. In the back seat we were concerned with our feet, which rested precariously among loose cartridge shells. We feared that a sudden jolt from a pine stump might make us stamp down on the shells and explode them.

Suddenly we came upon a reed and paling fence higher than the head of a tall man. There was nothing to be seen over the top of it, no sign of occupation. We drove around to the side where, protected by some feathery bushes, a small opening hardly distinguishable from the palings led into an enclosure. Scattered without plan about a smooth sand clearing were three or four small unpainted wooden cabins, two connected by a narrow board walk just above the ground. Other smaller structures, sheds, and work tables were placed

* Reuben Taylor, Eulonia.

helter-skelter about the enclosure. There was some wire fencing, but dogs, cats, chickens, a litter of very young puppies, and an old rooster roamed at will. Sunning themselves against a cabin wall were two old women, and from the windows of another cabin popped the heads of three curious younger women. An open door suddenly gave forth several children, smiling and scantily clad, shining eyes and surprised faces upturned to the strangers.

The two elderly women rose and came forward to greet us. Our guide explained our mission and inquired as to the whereabouts of Uncle Ben Washington, with whom we wished to talk. Aunt Sarah,* who was Uncle Ben's wife, explained that her husband had gone to work in the woods early that morning.

A glance at the dense forest surrounding the little clearing convinced us that Uncle Ben would be unlikely to hear the halloos with which our guides were attempting to summon him.

Just as we were about to abandon the venture a unique figure appeared inside the fence and Reuben Taylor, the older of our guides, exclaimed, "Deah's Uncle Ben now." Uncle Ben ** appeared in a long frock coat and high felt hat, carrying a walking stick. It was difficult to understand how he could have worked in such a costume. He seemed young for the eighty-five years he claimed, for he moved about with considerable agility.

As he drew nearer, Aunt Sarah went forward to greet him and the two old people came toward us together. When we again explained about the information we were seeking, Uncle Ben said with grave courtesy that he was glad to have visitors.

Thinking of the precarious journey that lay behind us and wondering how far from the main road this little settlement

* Sarah Washington, in the pine woods about five miles from Eulonia.
** Ben Washington, in the pine woods about five miles from Eulonia.

might be, we asked Uncle Ben how often he went to town. He shook his head slowly. "We dohn nebuh go tuh duh road," he said. "We got ebryting we needs right yuh."

Aunt Sarah nodded her gray head in agreement. "Seems lak we libed yuh fuh mos ub our libes," she stated simply. "We built deze houses wen we fus come yuh. All duh chillun wuz raise yuh an we nebuh take up no time wid duh folks on duh outside. Nebuh did set no sto by mixin wid strainjuhs an sech doins."

Incredible as it seemed, they were speaking the truth. For half a century they had lived in this isolated spot, only a few miles from a frequently traversed highway.

Despite their evident liking for solitude the old couple were not averse to answering our questions. "Is there much conjure and magic around here, Uncle Ben?" we asked.

"I heah tell uh tings lak dat," he answered and looked up with a sly quizzical smile. "Ise heahd bout bein cunjuhed an I know fuh true deah's sech tings as magic." Uncle Ben chuckled, "Ef yuh ebuh see a cross mahk in duh road, yuh nebuh walk obuh it. Das real magic. Yuh hab tuh go roun it. It's put deah by a enemy an ef yuh walks cross it, duh ebil spell will cause yuh hahm.[15] Duh cross is a magic sign an hab tuh do wid duh spirits."

"Ef dat happens," said Aunt Sarah, "reckon bout duh only ting yuh could do would be tuh see a root doctuh.[48] He gib yuh sumpm wut cuos yuh."[6]

Uncle Ben turned to us. "Lots uh folks carry hans all duh time an dis bring em luck an keep duh ebil spirits away."[8, 12a, c, d]

The old man seemed unable to describe these good luck charms, but he was more successful in describing the charms used in conjuring an enemy.

"Dey is made mosly frum haiah aw nails an lots uh times duh dus frum yuh foot track," he said.[7]

Aunt Sarah's face darkened. "Ain nobody git my haiah"

she declared. "I buns it so nobody kin wuk hahm wid it." [10]

Young Reuben spoke up. "Ef yuh weahs a silvuh coin, it brings yuh good luck," he stated doggedly. "An ef any body cunjuh yuh aw wuk gense yuh, duh money tun black an yuh know yuh hab tuh do sumpm bout it fo duh cunjuh wuks." [12a, c, d]

"Did you ever see anyone who was conjured?" we asked. All three nodded solemnly.

Uncle Ben spoke first. "Dey's mosly all crippled up an caahn moob bout. Ef dey dohn do nuttn, duh cunjuh gits wus an dey dies." [15]

"Folks wut is cunjuhed hab snakes in em an sometimes frawgs.[5] Yuh kin see em moobin roun in deah bodies," volunteered Reuben. "Wen dey visit duh root doctuh [48] an he wuks obuh em, den dey's jis as good as noo."

"Some folks roun bout say dey sees spirits," added Uncle Ben. "Dey calls em plat-eye, cuz dey hab jis one big eye hangin out in front.[62] I dohn fool roun wid sech tings fuh dey's sho bad luck."

"In some places the people told us that dead people's spirits returned to earth. Is that true here?" we asked.

Aunt Sarah speculated. She wagged her black-bonneted head until her brass earrings jangled. Finally she offered, "I dohn guess yuh be bodduh much by duh spirits ef yuh gib em a good fewnul [36] an put duh tings wut belong tuh em on top uh duh grave." [47]

Uncle Ben helped with this explanation. "Yuh puts all duh tings wut dey use las, lak duh dishes an duh medicine bottle. Duh spirits need deze same as duh man. Den duh spirit res an dohn wanduh bout."

Aunt Sarah said that they went to set-ups and that in the old days, after the mourners had arrived, a chicken was killed.[35, 37b, c] Neither Aunt Sarah nor Uncle Ben, however, knew the reason for this.

Catching sight of a few crudely made farm implements

propped up against one of the buildings, we recalled a belief prevailing in most of the Negro communities already visited.

"Does a hoe possess magic qualities?" we wanted to know.

Uncle Ben and Reuben glanced at each other, then muttered in unison, "Yes'm, duh hoe is magic sho nuff."

From Reuben we received the additional statement, "Ef yuh carry duh hoe tru duh house, it sho mean bad luck."

Uncle Ben's contribution was, "I heah lots uh tings bout duh hoe. I heah tell bout how it jis stan right up in duh fiel by itsef an wuk fuh yuh widout nobody techin it—das ef yuh kin wuk it right." [39]

When we asked about the music played at dances and at church services, Uncle Ben explained to us, "Some yeahs back at duh dances dey would alluz beat duh drums an shake some kine uh bones wut dey make frum cow's ribs. All duh folks would keep time wid deah hans an feet an dance tuh duh music." [23]

Apparently the memory of similar affairs was pleasant to Reuben, the young guide, for his eyes gleamed and his white teeth flashed in a sudden smile. "Fo I wuz married," he said, "I use tuh go tuh dances an picnics all duh time. Dey would hab only duh drums fuh music an dey would beat on em an duh folks would dance roun in a ring tuh duh toon."

As it was growing dark, we were forced to end our visit to this interesting settlement. Reuben led the way back to the car and we plunged again into the pine forest.

Going back over the trail we commiserated with Reuben, who apparently made the trip frequently. "I comes tuh see em mos ebry day. Yuh see, Ise married tuh deah baby girl," he confided.

137

Possum Point

◇◇◇◇◇◇◇◇◇◇◇◇◇◇◇◇◇

A WINDING TREE-SHADED DIRT ROAD LEADS FROM Darien up the Altamaha to the Negro community of Possum Point. The freshets in the section rise in the rainy season and the road is often flooded. On either side the trees are mirrored in the shallow water which surrounds them. In the spring against the fresh green of the trees and foliage there is the soft color of wild honeysuckle and Cherokee Rose. Through the thickly-massed trees the sun filters dimly; a misty, unreal atmosphere overhangs the entire scene.

Set back from the roadway are occasional small dwelling places, with boards turned dun-colored from age and exposure. Neatly tended vegetable and flower gardens stretch out to the front and sides of the houses. The owners can be found industriously working in the gardens, sitting on the porches, or gathered in little groups along the road. Here and there small bridges span the road, and at each of these a number of persons are often seen leisurely fishing, their long bamboo poles forming graceful arcs from the bank to the water.

We had been told that Alec Anderson was an old man and one who would be able to enlighten us regarding the beliefs prevalent in that section. We stopped a few times to inquire where he lived. After continuing for several miles, the road turned to the right. It swerved again a short distance later and continued in a narrow, uneven pathway through the woods. This section was but sparsely settled and we glimpsed a cabin only now and then.

At length we came upon a neatly kept house enclosed by a wire fence set back from the road. In the distance we could see a bent and stocky figure trudging toward us along the road and this we thought might be Alec. At one side of the house was a garden; at the other side the sprawling branches of an old oak tree shaded an iron pump and an ancient black iron pot used for boiling clothes. Chickens scuttled about the yard and a small black puppy, dozing in the sun, awoke at our approach.

On the porch a group of Negroes were seated. A plump, elderly woman, a young girl and two small children watched with interest as we approached.

The older woman was Rachel,* Alec Anderson's wife (Plate XIV). She scarcely appeared to be the seventy-three years she admitted. Her round good-natured face was framed with a number of tight little gray braids on top of which perched a small brown felt hat. Her green blouse and red skirt were worn but clean and her bare brown feet peeped out from under the voluminous skirt. The younger woman was reticent but friendly, and the two children watched the proceedings with wide-eyed concern.

The man we had noticed walking down the road turned in at the gateway, and as we had surmised this was Alec (Plate XIII).** He was clad in a pair of faded and torn blue overalls and a battered felt hat. Thick-lensed brown glasses did not entirely hide amiable, intelligent eyes. With profound courtesy the old man greeted us and started in to chat in a pleasant, unselfconscious manner.

"Cose yuh do heah bout cunjuh," he told us. "But I nebuh bodduh much wid dat kine uh ting. Deah's plenty uh folks wut does belieb in it an I hab heah uh strange tings happenin tuh some folks wut hab spells put on um." [15]

Here Rachel interrupted. "I alluz bun muh haiah com-

* Rachel Anderson, Possum Point.
** Alec Anderson, Possum Point.

bins cuz das wut mos folks make cunjuh outuh.[10] Ef dey git
yuh haiah, yuh hab to do any ting dey wahn yuh tuh."

Alec stated solemnly, "Some folks is alluz sayin dat spirits
is bodduhin um.[59] Nebuh hab trouble wid um muhsef."

This was explained by Rachel who said that they knew a
horse-shoe was an excellent remedy for "keeping duh hant
away." [8]

"Witches come in at night an ride yuh too," [69] said Alec.
"Jis ride duh folks till some ub um gits so po dey jis pass
way."

We asked if they had ever heard that a frizzled chicken
could dig up conjure laid down for a victim and they both
nodded in affirmation.

"Chicken kin sho dig up cunjuh.[13a] Alluz hab heah uh
dat," they echoed.

Alec told us that he had been born three years before freedom. He dwelt for a time on those long-past days and recol-
lected some of the customs that had been prevalent then.

"Use tuh alluz beat duh drum at fewnuls. Right attuh
duh pusson die, dey beat um tuh tell duh udduhs bout duh
fewnul. Dey beat a long beat. Den dey stop. Den dey
beat anudduh long beat. Ebrybody know dat dis mean
somebody die. Dey beat duh drum in duh nex settlement
tuh let duh folks in duh nex place heah." [26]

We had previously been told of a similar means of communication employed by the people in this section in former
years. At various points large metal discs were hung on
trees and posts. On these messages had been beaten out and
relayed from place to place. In this manner the people were
informed of dances, picnics, meetings, wakes, and other such
gatherings.[26]

The old couple went on to describe what took place at a
wake.

"Wen dey fix duh cawpse, dey put pennies on duh eyes an

dey put salt on duh stomach tuh keep it frum purgin. Ebrybody put duh hands on um tuh say good-bye.[31]

"On duh way tuh duh grabe dey beat duh drum as dey is mahchin long.[24] Wen duh body is put in duh grabe, ebrybody shout roun duh grabe in a succle, singin an prayin. Each one trow a hanful uh dut in duh grabe." [28]

The conversation shifted to topics of a more cheerful nature and Rachel told us that in former years at harvest time, they had been in the habit of holding "crop suppuhs." [38]

Her face creased itself into a delightful grin and her eyes shone as she told us, "Dat sho wuz a big time. We hab a big feas. All night we shouts an in duh mawnin right at sunrise we pray an bow low tuh duh sun. Muh great-gran—she name Peggy—I membuh she pray ebry day, at sunrise, at noon, an at sunset. She kneel down wen she pray an at duh en she bow low tree times, facin duh sun."

Alec's thoughts in the meantime had turned to more trivial affairs. He went on to tell us about the various dances that are popular at the present-day social affairs.

"Cose we do duh Buzzud Lope," [17] he began. "Ebrybody knows dat. Den we alluz does anudduh dance. We calls it 'Come Down tuh duh Myuh.' We dance roun an shake duh han an fiddle duh foot. One ub us kneel down in duh middle uh duh succle. Den we all call out an rise an shout roun, an we all fling duh foot agen."

In answer to our question about river baptisms the old people informed us that they are still held in the section. Alec described these. "We all sing an pray an duh preachuh pray tuh duh Lord. Cose duh candidate caahn be save less he reely want tuh be. Duh preachuh an duh candidates goes down in duh watuh. Den duh preachuh make a prayuh tuh duh ribbuh an duh ribbuh washes duh sin away." [63]

It is bad luck to eat certain types of food, Rachel told us. This belief had never influenced Rachel or Alec but they had known of people who were "fuhbid tuh eat eel fish mong udduh tings." [65]

Our visit was such a pleasant one that we stayed for a while longer to talk. The household was an unusually contented and peaceful one. The old couple were apparently satisfied with a simple scheme of existence although Alec did venture the usual remark regarding his old-age pension. "Sho would lak tuh hab it, missus. Mebbe yuh kin git dem gubment folks tuh see dat I gits it."

When we were about ready to leave, a middle-aged daughter, who had been lingering at the gateway, came up and joined the group. She confided that she had been married to one man for thirty years, but that he had died and she had recently remarried. This second marriage was evidently not so successful, for she said, "Dis huzbun ain lak duh fus one. He's triflin an ain sech a good providuh. Wen I loss duh fus huzbun, I sho loss ebryting."

At that time Rachel and Alec had been married for fifty-seven years and during all this period there had been few differences or unpleasant happenings. As Alec escorted us to the car he told us of his high regard for his wife, assuring us in conclusion, "I ain nebuh had no trouble wid uh. Ain so much as tech uh wid a pocket hankuhchuh sence I done bin had uh."

A little later we went to visit Susan Maxwell,* who was sitting on the porch of her house when we drove up. She was about ninety-two years old and, having been ill recently, was snugly wrapped up in a variety of garments.

The house, she told us, was about one hundred years old. A hall ran from the front to the back part, and from the back porch a passage led to a lean-to kitchen. A barn near the house was about to collapse from age and lack of repair. In the yard a black ox lay chained under a tree and a large

* *Susan Maxwell, Possum Point.*

hollowed-out log set on legs served as a watering trough for the ox.

Susan told us about the death of her mother, Rachel La Conte, who had come from Liberty County. "She die right in dis house. Dey measure uh wid a string. Dey beat duh drum tuh tell ebrybody bout duh settin-up.[26] We all set up wid duh body. We hab a big wash pot full uh coffee an hab a big sack uh soda crackuh fuh duh folks.[37b, c] Ebrybody place dey han bery light on uh eahs an on uh nose an den dey say, 'Dohn call me. I ain ready fuh tuh go yit.' [30, 31]

"We bury uh by tawch light attuh dahk. Ebrybody mahch roun duh grabe in a succle. Ebry night attuh duh fewnul I put food on duh poach fuh duh spirit tuh come git it.[56, 58]

"In duh ole days dey beat duh drum tuh call duh people tuh duh fewnul.[24] Dey beat it slow—boom—boom—boom. Wen dey wannuh stuhrup duh folks fuh a dance aw frolic, dey beats duh drum fas. Den dey knows it ain fuh no fewnul an dat it's fuh a good time. Duh people neahby, wen dey heahs it, beats deah drum an das how dey sends a message so udduh folks gits it.[26]

"I kin membuh two kine uh drum. Deah wuz duh lill kittle drum. Hit wuz bout fifteen inches cross an tree an a half foot high. Dat wuz duh drum dey beat fuh a settin-up."

Susan, too, gave us a description of the river baptisms. "Dey baptize in duh watuh down at duh landin. All duh candidates is dressed in wite. Dey all confess deah sins an say dey want tuh be save.

"We all mahch long in a line an sing an pray. Wen we git tuh duh ribbuh bank, we stop an duh preachuh say a long prayuh tuh duh Lawd. Den duh preachuh take duh candidates one by one and dey go down in duh ribbuh. Duh preachuh he say a prayuh tuh duh ribbuh. Dey alluz baptize on duh ebb tide cuz duh ribbuh is spose tuh wash duh sins away.[63] All duh folks sing a song called *All Muh Sins Done Wash Away*."

There were several white chickens wandering about the yard and Susan told us that her principal reason for keeping them was that they possessed the power to dig up conjure.[13]

We asked the old woman if she had ever known any Africans, and she said, "I know one man. He name Primus O'Neal. He come frum Africa an he talk funny talk. He call a pot a 'jam.' I membuh he say, 'Lemme cook sumpm fuh nyam.' He mean sumpm fuh tuh eat."

It later developed that this same Primus O'Neal was the grandfather of Rosa Grant * whom we found living in a small gray cottage on the Townsend Road. Rosa was sixty-five years old, with copper-colored skin and rather aquiline features.

We asked about her grandfather and she told us some of the things of which she had heard him speak.

"He tell me dey nebuh hab tuh plant in Africa. Dey gadduh wile okra an palmettuh cabbage fuh food frum duh forres. He tell bout a wine call 'figlin watuh' dat dey drink in Africa. But he nebuh say jis how dey make it.

"Muh gran come frum Africa too. Huh name wuz Ryna. I membuh wen I wuz a chile seein muh gran Ryna pray. Ebry mawnin at sun-up she kneel on duh flo in uh ruhm an bow obuh an tech uh head tuh duh flo tree time. Den she say a prayuh. I dohn membuh jis wut she say, but one wud she say use tuh make us chillun laugh. I membuh it wuz 'ashamnegad.' Wen she finish prayin she say 'Ameen, ameen, ameen.'

"She talk plenty bout cunjuh.[15] Say dat wen a pusson bin made tuh swell up frum a ebil spell, dey got tuh hab somebody tuh pray an drag fuhrum. Ef yuh hab a pain aw

* *Rosa Grant, Townsend Road, Possum Point.*

a misery in duh leg aw ahm, yuh kill a black chicken an split it open an slap it weah duh pain is an dat will cuo duh pain.

"She tell me dat in Africa she lib in a palmettuh house. She say dey kill animals wid a bow an arruh. Some dey use fuh food an some dey kill fuh skin. All duh people keep deah finguh nail long so dey could grab tings tuh eat off duh trees an bushes. Eben attuh she come tuh dis country, she keep uh nail long fuh a long time. Wen she staht cuttin um, she alluz bun duh pieces an she bun duh combins frum uh haiah too. She say it dangerous tuh let anybody git um. Dey make cunjuh gense yuh.[10] She say in Africa dey plant berries an pumpkin an dey had tuh plant um ebry seben yeahs or dey die.

"Friday wuz duh day she call huh prayuh day. Den she use tuh make bread. Wen she mix it up, she put duh dough in a wet bag an bake it in duh ashes.

"She tell me bout duh hahves time wen duh folks stay up all night an shout. At sun-up dey all sing an pray and say dey live bettuh an be mo tankful duh nex yeah." [38]

"Was your 'gran' grown up when she came from Africa?"

"No'm, she wuz jis a leedle ting. She say dat duh way she happen tuh come frum Africa wuz dat dey wuzn use tuh seein anyting red. One day dey see a boat wid a red piece uh clawt flyin on it. Wen dey go up close tuh see it, dey wuz caught. Huh mothuh, Theresa, wuz caught too an dey wuz brought tuh dis country. Attuh dey bin yuh a wile, duh mothuh git to weah she caahn stan it an she wannuh go back tuh Africa. One day muh gran Ryna wuz standin wid uh in duh fiel. Theresa tun roun—so—" here Rosa made two quick swings with her skirt. "She stretch uh ahms out—so —an rise right up an fly right back tuh Africa.[69c] Muh gran say she wuz standin right deah wen it happen. She alluz wish dat uh mothuh had teach uh how tuh fly. She try an try doin duh same way but she ain nebuh fly. She say she guess she jis wuzn bawn wid duh powuh."

145

Darien

❖❖❖❖❖❖❖❖❖❖

THE NEGROES OF THE DARIEN SECTION, MANY OF whom live in small scattered communities outside the town, are proud of their Darien ancestry. When the younger people migrate to larger communities, it is a common thing to hear them say proudly, "My people come frum Darien."

One of the most typical settlements is opposite the Todd Grant Negro School. A few houses are clustered about the knoll facing the school building, and more dilapidated board shacks are scattered over the little hill. At the top is Aunty Jane Lewis' cabin, surrounded by small sheds and fenced patches of ground where chickens and a goat are kept from wandering too far. At the north a few cypress trees straggle off to the wood. A sturdy bush provides the sunny drying ground for the gourds that later will be used as water dippers.

Aunty Jane * claims that she is one hundred and fifteen years old, and to see the small bent woman with the deeply lined black skin and filmy eyes is to believe her claim. Her voice is high pitched, with the thin timbre of extreme age, but she still moves with sudden agile gestures. During our conversation she hopped up from the steps and began to do the Buzzard Lope [17] to illustrate her story.

"I belong tuh Robert Toodle wut lib in Nawt Calina an he sole me down yuh wen Ise twenty-one. I ain membuh much bout Nawt Calina but uh membuhs plenty bout duh ole days yuh, cuz I bin yuh neah bout a hunnud yeahs. I be-

* *Jane Lewis, Darien.*

146

longs tuh Huger Barrett an Ise one uh duh bes fiel hans on Picayune Plantation."

We interrupted the old woman's reminiscences about plantation days to question her about funeral customs.

"We didn alluz hab too much time fuh big fewnul in dem days cuz deah wuz wuk tuh be done an ef yuh ain do yuh wuk, yuh git whipped. Lots uh time dey jis dig a hole in duh groun an put duh body in it, but wenebuh we kin, we hab a settin-up."

We asked Aunty Jane if they used to provide plenty of food for the mourners.

"Yes'm, dey sho did hab regluh feastes in dem days, but tuhday, at mos settin-ups, yuh dohn git nuttn but coffee an bread.[37b, c] Den dey would cook a regluh meal an dey would kill a chicken in front uh duh doe, wring he neck an cook um fuh duh feas.[35c] Den wen we all finish, we take wut victuals lef an put it in a dish by duh chimley an das fuh duh sperrit tuh hab a las good meal.[58] We cubbuh up duh dish an deah's many a time Ise heah dat sperrit lif um. We ain preach duh suhmon wen we bury um but we waits a wile so's all duh relations kin come."

"Is it bad luck to steal from a grave?" we wanted to know.

"Bad luck?" repeated Aunty Jane. "Sho it bad luck. Dem dishes an bottles wut put on duh grabe is fuh duh sperrit an it ain fuh nobody tuh tech um.[64] Das fuh duh sperrit tuh feel at home.[47] Wen he die fah off, we bring um home tuh bury um, dohn leh no strainjuh be bury wid um. Yuh gib people wut ain belong tuh yuh anudduh piece uh groun tuh be bury in.[3] We alluz hab two fewnul fuh duh pusson. We hab duh regluh fewnul wen yuh die. Den once a yeah we hab one big preachin fuh ebrybody wut die dat yeah." [42]

Aunty Jane looked up slyly when we asked her if she believed in conjure.

"I ain belieb in um muhsef but deah's plenty wut do. Ise had Ellen Hammond libin wid me. She die las yeah. She sho

147

wuz alluz fixin cunjuh.[15] She tie up ebryting in sacks. She git a lill foot track dus,[7] a lill haiah combins, an nail parin,[10] an she tie um up wid a lill rag. Cose, I dohn belieb in dis an wen she die, I bun um. Ef yuh hab any trouble wid snakes,[50] yuh ketch um an bun um wid duh trash. Den all duh whole kingdom uh snakes will leab yuh lone." [50]

We next questioned Aunty Jane about signs.

"Yes'm, I knows plenty uh signs but my head so full uh-rum I dohn know wich tuh tell yuh. Some ub um I beliebs an some ub um I ain belieb. Wen yuh go on a journey an yuh hattuh tun back, yuh make a cross mahk on duh dut an spit on it, an it sho bad luck tuh bring a hoe in duh house."

The subject of drums was then brought up.

"I ain heah um beat duh drums in my chuch," Aunty Jane said. "But I sho is heah plenty uh drum beat. We use tuh alluz dance tuh duh drums. We dance roun in a succle an we hab drum an we hab goad rattle an we beat tin pan tuh-gedduh.[23] Some time dey hab sto-bought drum, but Alex Harris, he muh son, he make um. He lib up duh ribbuh."

Aunty Jane gave us a description of how the drums were made.

"Yuh kill a coon an yuh skin um an yuh tack duh skin up side duh house tuh dry an yuh stretch um good till um tight an smood. Den yuh stretch um obuh duh en ub a holluh tree trunk.[25] Sometime dey is big drum wut stan as high as dis." She raised her hand about three feet from the ground.

We asked Aunty Jane what trees they used. Did they use oak?

"No, ma'am, it ain good tuh use oak ef yuh kin hep it. It too hahd. Yuh take a good cypress aw ceduh wut eat out on duh inside an yuh take um an scoop um out an stretch duh skin obuh duh ens. Sometime yuh kin fine a holly wut'll do. Alex, he make drum up tuh two yeah ago an we sho hab big time doin duh dances wile dey beat duh drums. Wene-buh we happy aw wannuh celebrate, we dance." At this point Aunty Jane rose to give us an exhibition of two dances, the Buzzard Lope and the Snake Hip.[17]

Across the highway from Aunty Jane's settlement, about one mile north of Darien, back of a turpentine still, is an irregular settlement of small houses, most of which are enclosed by high dilapidated paling fences. Here Wallace Quarterman * occupied a cabin with his daughter, Abby Gibson. Wallace was old but with a clear mind, and he enjoyed a high standing in his community. We felt that he would know about the old beliefs and customs.

We left the highway on a narrow dirt road, little more than a path through the bush, and after much winding in and out we came upon a street of Negro cabins with their enclosed yards, vegetable patches, and tumbled down sheds. Wallace was sitting on the porch of Abby's house. Lizzie Sanders volunteered to be our guide and paid a visit to Wallace along with us.

We asked him how old he was and where he was born.

"Ise bawn July 14, 1844. Now figguh dat out fuh yuhsef, missus. Ise bawn at Sout Hampton, Libuty County, an I belong tuh Roswell King, but he done die long bout sometime in duh fifties an Ise sole fuh debt tuh Cunl Fred Waring on Skidaway Ilun. Ise bin bout fifteen wen I sen tuh Skidaway."

For a long time we had wanted to establish some connection with Skidaway Island that reached back before the War between the States. We questioned Wallace about the church on Skidaway.

"We sho did hab big time goin tuh chuch in doze days. Not many uh deze Nigguhs kin shout tuhday duh way us could den. Yuh needs a drum fuh shoutin."

We asked if they shouted to a drum then.

"We sho did. We beat a drum at duh chuch an we beat a drum on duh way tuh duh grabeyahd tuh bury um. We

* Wallace Quarterman, Darien. Deceased autumn, 1938.

149

walks in a long line moanin an we beats duh drum all duh way." [24]

We inquired about the making of drums and the kinds of drums.

"We makes drums out uh sheep hide but we gottuh dry um an stretch duh skin obuh. Some makes it out uh holluh lawgs wid skin obuh duh en an some ub um is as long as tree feet." [25]

We asked the old man if he remembered any slaves that were real Africans.

"Sho I membuhs lots ub um. Ain I sees plenty ub um? I membuhs one boatload uh seben aw eight wut come down frum Savannah. Dat wuz jis a lill befo duh waw. Robbie McQueen wuz African an Katie an ole man Jacob King, dey's all African. I membuhs um all. Ole man King he lib till he ole, lib till I hep bury um. But yuh caahn unduhstan much wut deze people say. Dey caahn unduhstan yo talk an you caahn unduhstan dey talk. Dey go 'quack, quack, quack,' jis as fas as a hawse kin run, an muh pa say, 'Ain no good tuh lissen tuh um.' Dey git long all right but yuh know dey wuz a lot ub um wut ain stay down yuh."

Did he mean the Ibos * on St. Simons who walked into the water?

"No, ma'am, I ain mean dem. Ain yuh heah bout um? Well, at dat time Mr. Blue he wuz duh obuhseeuh an Mr. Blue put um in duh fiel, but he couldn do nuttn wid um. Dey gabble, gabble, gabble, an nobody couldn unduhstan um an dey didn know how tuh wuk right. Mr. Blue he go down one mawnin wid a long whip fuh tuh whip um good."

"Mr. Blue was a hard overseer?" we asked.

"No, ma'am, he ain hahd, he jis caahn make um unduh-stan. Dey's foolish actin. He got tuh whip um, Mr. Blue, he ain hab no choice. Anyways, he whip um good an dey

---

* *A group of slaves from the Ibo tribe refused to submit to slavery. Led by their chief and singing tribal songs, they walked into the water and were drowned at a point on Dunbar Creek later named Ebo (Ibo) Landing.*

gits tuhgedduh an stick duh hoe in duh fiel an den say
'quack, quack, quack,' an dey riz up in duh sky an tun hesef
intuh buzzuds an fly right back tuh Africa." [68b, 69c]

At this, we exclaimed and showed our astonishment.

"Wut, you ain heah bout um? Ebrybody know bout um.
Dey sho lef duh hoe stannin in duh fiel an dey riz right up
an fly right back tuh Africa."

Had Wallace actually seen this happen, we asked.

"No, ma'am, I ain seen um. I bin tuh Skidaway, but I
knowd plenty wut did see um, plenty wut wuz right deah in
duh fiel wid um an seen duh hoe wut dey lef stickin up attuh
dey done fly way."

This story of the flying Africans seemed to be a familiar
one, for it was later repeated to us by William Rogers,* who
lived about a mile from Darien on the Cowhorn Road. We
had been told that he had been a cabinet maker in his youth
and still spent much of his spare time in the carving of a
variety of objects. The old man was evidently well known
in the vicinity, for upon inquiry neighbors quickly directed
us to his house.

Because a short time ago a fire had destroyed Rogers'
home and most of his possessions, we found him living in an
unfinished cottage which was as yet unpainted except for the
bluish-green trimming on all the window facings. In spite
of the apparent newness of the house, there was a pleasant
homelike atmosphere about it. Proof of Rogers' skill was
demonstrated in scroll-work which decorated the porch and
in a cupboard and fine square chimney in the dining room
which the old man and his wife were building.

Rogers, who was seventy-two years old, was small of stat-
ure with copper-colored skin and alert black eyes. His manner was affable and friendly despite the fact that a recently
suffered paralytic stroke had partially deprived him of the
use of his hands. He told us that his grandmother had been

* William Rogers, Cowhorn Road, Darien.

one-quarter Indian. While we were on the subject of In-dians, he remembered a rusty part of an old Indian gun which he had found in the vicinity. Displaying this, he ex-plained in detail how the trigger struck a piece of flint, thereby igniting the powder.

We inquired about his wood carving and he showed us some of the wooden figures about which we had been told. One of these, a spoon of cedar, was about a foot in length and had the roughly-sculptured head of a man on its handle (Plate IIc).[41e] The head was square in shape, the features were only slightly raised, and the eyes were nail heads.[41c] Another item was a frog [41i] which, with eyes of brass nail heads, crouched on a block of wood (Plate IVc). The frog and the stand had been carved from a solid piece of wood [70f, h] and lightly varnished.

As we left, the old man promised us, "Wen I gits muh hans back intuh use, I hopes tuh cahve a cane wid a gatuh on it lak duh ones I made long ago. Wen I do, I sho sen it tuh yuh."

We had no idea that we would hear from him again, but a few months later he wrote us that he had made a stick especially for us. This proved to be of stout cedar carved with a large alligator and topped with the bust of a Negro man cut all in one with the body of the stick and painted black to signify his race (Plate IVa). The smooth, almost square, protruding skull of the figure, its small, high-set ears, broad mouth, blue bead eyes driven in by minute steel nailheads, and little short arms with four-fingered hands are all noteworthy points. The alligator's eyes are also blue beads driven in by nailheads.

After leaving William Rogers, we retraced our way back over the winding dirt roadway into Darien and from the town we drove eastward through a residential section. The houses here were substantial and attractive, surrounded by trim lawns, and the thoroughfare was shaded by old moss-hung trees. After a distance the road narrowed; for a time there were no houses in sight; then we came to the Low Bluff community. Negro cabins dotted the landscape and the settlement terminated at a grassy bluff where stood the last small house.

We were looking for Priscilla McCullough * and the obliging neighbors directed us to her house. It stood to the left of the roadway, a queer haphazard little dwelling place that looked like something out of a fairy tale. It was a tumble-down house, painted white, its roof patched with pieces of loose roofing which overlapped one another and hung down some distance in the front. An irregular fence made alternately of board and wire surrounded it. The tiny porch was crowded with old pieces of furniture and miscellaneous items, including half of a tattered screen which hung at one side. Near the house a second building leaned at such a precarious angle that it could be expected to tumble over momentarily.

We made our way down the little dirt walk and into the house and there in the center of the room sat Priscilla. She was sewing on a mattress which almost filled the small space. Even the bizarre exterior had not prepared us for the appearance of the inside of the house. Here again there was so much crowded together that it took a while before separate articles could be clearly seen. Jumbled closely around Priscilla was a mass of furniture, each article of which was in turn almost hidden by a burden of clothing, dishes, bottles, pictures, and items too numerous to mention.

Priscilla adjusted her eyeglasses which were tied on with a shoestring and told us something of her early life. She said she had been "bawn tree yeahs fo freedom in Sumtuh, Sout Calina." As quite a young woman she had moved to

* Priscilla McCullough, near Darien.

153

Georgia but still retained many pleasant recollections of the days of her early youth. She had heard of many African customs and went on to tell us some of these.

"I heahd many time bout how in Africa wen a girl dohn ack jis lak dey should, dey drum uh out uh town. Dey jis beat duh drum, an call uh name on duh drum an duh drum say bout all duh tings she done.[26] Dey drum an mahch long an take duh girl right out uh town.

"Girls hab tuh be keahful den. Dey caahn be so triflin lak some ub em is now. In Africa dey gits punished. Sometime wen dey bin bad, dey put um on duh banjo. Dat wuz in dis country."

This being "put on duh banjo" was unintelligible to us and we asked for an explanation.

"Wen dey play dat night, dey sing bout dat girl an dey tell all bout uh. Das puttin uh on duh banjo. Den ebrybody know an dat girl sho bettuh change uh ways."

The story of flying Africans was a familiar one to the old woman and she said that her mother had often told her the following incident which was supposed to have taken place on a plantation during slavery times.

"Duh slabes wuz out in duh fiel wukin. All ub a sudden dey git tuhgedduh an staht tuh moob roun in a ring. Roun dey go fastuhnfastuh. Den one by one dey riz up an take wing an fly lak a bud.[68b, 69c] Duh obuhseeuh heah duh noise an he come out an he see duh slabes riz up in duh eah an fly back tuh Africa. He run an he ketch duh las one by duh foot jis as he wuz bout tuh fly off. I dohn know ef he wuz neah nuff tuh pull um back down an keep um frum goin off."

As we left, Priscilla accompanied us down the walk to the gateway. She was reluctant to see us go and until the last minute regaled us with a variety of stories.

We had learned that an elderly Negro named Lawrence Baker * lived out on the Ridge Road near the Ridgeway

* Lawrence Baker, the Ridge Road, near Darien.

Club. We followed the road for about two miles and came
finally to a signpost directing us to turn right in order to
reach the club. This section in former times had been occupied by extensive plantation holdings. Most of these
estates had been deserted for years and now and then we saw
a house, once evidently charming but now in a dilapidated
and crumbling condition.

Through an old gateway to what had once been a prosperous estate we rode past acres now weed-grown and neglected. At last we came upon a one story white plantation
house. Inside blinds were at all of the French windows and
the wide floor boards gave indication that the house had
probably been standing for about one hundred years.

The man for whom we were looking was plowing in a field
at the rear. Baker's rugged build and his keen intellect
made it difficult to believe that he was in his late seventies.
For years he had acted as caretaker of the club and often
lived in the plantation house, as it had been unoccupied for
some time.

He had heard of the custom of beating drums to warn
people of a recent death. He said, "Dey use tuh alluz beat
duh drum aw blow duh hawn wen somebody die.[24] Dey beat
two licks on duh drum, den dey stop, den dey beat tree licks.
Wen yuh beat dat, yuh know somebody done die.[24, 26] Lots
uh duh drums wuz home-made. Dey wuz made out uh goat
skin aw coon skin wut stretch out obuh hoops.[25] Deah wuz
tree sizes uh drums. Deah wuz duh big barrel drum. It
wuz highuhn it wuz cross. Den deah wuz a lill drum frum
twelve tuh fifteen inches wide an bout eighteen inches high.
Duh udduh drum wuz duh medium size, kine uh in between
duh udduh two. Duh big drum wuz duh one dey beat at duh
wake. Dey use drums at dances an meetins, too.

"Wen we hab a fewnul, we all mahch roun duh grabe in a
ring. We shout an pray."

We wanted to know if river baptisms were always held

during an ebb tide and Lawrence hastened to assure us, "Yes'm, dey alluz hole duh baptism on a high ebb tide. Das so duh tide will carry duh sin out." [63]

Had the old man ever known any people who had been named for the days of the week?

"I knowd one man name Fridy, one dat wuz name Satdy an anudduh he name wuz Toosdy. Guess dey name um dataway cuz dey wuz bawn on doze days." [20]

Baker told us that many people in the section refused to eat certain foods, believing bad luck would follow if they ate them.

"Deah's lots dataway now," he commented. "Lots uh folks dohn eat some food cuz ef dey did dey say it would bring bad luck on duh parents. Some dohn eat rice, some dohn eat egg, an some dohn eat chicken.[65]

"Muh gran, she Rachel Grant, she use tuh tell me bout lot uh deze tings. I membuh she use tuh pray ebry day at sunrise, at middle day and den at sunset. She alluz face duh sun an wen she finish prayin she alluz bow tuh duh sun. She tell me bout duh slabes wut could fly too. Ef dey didn lak it on duh plantation, dey jis take wing an fly right back tuh Africa.

"Muh gran say dey use tuh eat wid oystuh shells. Use um fuh spoons. Wen dey go tuh shoot duh gun, dey ketch duh fyuh wid a rag an flint."

We asked him if he had ever heard of a hoe that worked by itself and he told us that he had often heard this story regarding the hoe [39] and that he had also heard many tales about a magic rail splitting wood without anyone touching it.

Suddenly the quiet of the afternoon was shattered by a high reed-like whistling sound. It continued for quite a time, then stopped as abruptly as it had started. Was it a person or an animal? It was impossible for us to tell.

"Das a spiduh, missus," Baker explained. "It come roun

yuh all duh time an wistle jis lak a pusson. I dohn fool wid
no spiduh. Dey is bad luck. All duh time dey drop down
right out ub a tree.

"I know deah is spirits an ghos cuz I kin see um.[59]   Yuh
hab tuh be bawn wid a caul tuh be able tuh see duh spirits.[4]

"Some uh duh folks is rid so much by witches dat attuh a
time dey git tin an po an jis die.[69]   Wen a witch come in duh
house, it hang up duh skin behine duh doe an ef yuh put
salt on duh skin, duh witch caahn put it on agen. Benne
seed is bad fuh duh witch too an keep um way.

"Witches take all kine uh shape. Sometime dey lak animal, sometime lak bud.[68]   In Harris Neck deah wuz a big
buzzud wut use tuh light on duh fence ebry time dey would
be milkin duh cows. Wen duh buzzud would fly off, one uh
duh milk buckets would alluz be dry.[69c]   Dis happen ebry
day. Dey would shoot at duh bud but nobody could ebuh
hit it. One man he take a dime an he quawtuh it; den he put
it in duh gun. Duh nex day wen duh buzzud light, he shoot
at it an he hit it in duh wing. It fly off an go down a chim-
bley ub a house. Wen duh men go in duh house, dey fine
a ole uhmun wid uh ahm broke. Dey know den she wuz a
witch. I know deah wuz some talk bout bunnin uh up, but
I dohn tink dey do it.

"Ebry night I sit on dis poach heah." He pointed to the
back porch of the white house. "I kin see duh spirits goin
by. Deah is a whole crowd uh lill wite tings. Dey is goin
obuh deah tuh duh spring. Some is lak chillun; some is lak
grown folks. Dey jis go cross duh fiel tuh duh mahble steps
uh duh ole gahden an down duh steps tuh duh fountn. I ain
nebuh bodduh um an dey ain nebuh do me no hahm."

Sapelo Island

◇◇◇◇◇◇◇◇◇◇◇◇◇◇

SAPELO ISLAND IS ONE OF THE CHAIN OF "GOLDEN Isles" lying along the Georgia Coast. The word Sapelo was derived from "Zapala," the name used by the Indians when the island was a favorite hunting ground for the tribes that had given up much of the mainland to the Spaniards and later to the English. Among the landmarks that recall colorful historical episodes are Indian mounds, tabby ruins of colonial days, and the remains of a house built by Jean Berard Mocquet, Marquis de Montalet, a French Royalist who immigrated to Georgia from Santo Domingo about 1797.

Plantation life flourished on Sapelo in the early nineteenth century. Here Thomas Spalding conducted one of the most extensive agricultural enterprises in the coastal section. The "big house" on the south end of the island was a spacious tabby mansion, so strongly constructed that the original walls are still standing and form the nucleus of the present dwelling. The island, with the exception of a number of Negro homesteads, is now the property of Richard Reynolds of Winston-Salem, North Carolina, but, although many improvements and changes have been made, much of the atmosphere of the early days has been preserved.

Industrial activity is concentrated in the central portion of Sapelo, where there is a sawmill that gives employment to many of the islanders. Nearby are the company houses, a post office, and a store. Several Negro churches and a dance hall are located elsewhere on the island.

Small Negro settlements are scattered at the north end of Sapelo and are reached by winding roads that cut through the tropical woodlands and brush. The Negroes are descendants of the slaves of the plantation era. Many lead an easy, carefree life which consists chiefly of fishing, crabbing, and cultivating a small patch of garden, while others engage in regular employment at the sawmill or in the company offices.

Living an isolated island existence, these Negroes have preserved many customs and beliefs of their ancestors, as well as the dialect of the older coastal Negro. An old oxcart (Plate XVI) jogging along a tree shaded road is a familar sight, and under the guidance of a Negro boy named Julius we discovered instances of crude wooden implements in common usage. The many Negroes interviewed gave a graphic picture of survival elements that have persisted since the days when slave ships brought their ancestors to the new country.

One of the oldest inhabititants is Katie Brown (Plate XV),* whose grandmother, Margaret, was a daughter of Belali Mohomet, the Mohammedan slave driver of Thomas Spalding. Katie, sunning herself on the back steps of her small house, was disposed to be gracious to us. Shaking her head at the size of the shoes brought to her as an incentive to conversation, she relented at the sight of some pipe tobacco and began to talk:

"I dunno bout drums at chuches. Use tuh hab um long time ago, but not now on duh ilun,—leas I ain heah um. Hahves time wuz time fuh drums. Den dey hab big times.[38] Wen hahves in, dey hab big gadderin. Dey beat drum, rattle dry goad wid seed in um, an beat big flat tin plates.[23, 25] Dey shout an moob roun in succle an look lak mahch goin tuh heabm. Hahves festival, dey call it."

In response to our query about "set-ups" Katie replied,

* *Katie Brown, Sapelo Island.*

"Yes'm, we hab set-ups wid duh dead, but I ain know bout killin chicken. At duh fewnul, dey kills hawg an hab [40] plenty tuh eat.[37b, c] Duh reason fuh dis is so dat sperrit hab plenty at duh las. Wen fewnul pruhcession gits tuh grabeyahd, dey stops. I ain know wy dey do it but dey stops at duh gate, and dey ax leab tuh come in. Deah ain nobody at duh gate, but dey alluz ax jis duh same. Dey say, 'Fambly, we come tuh put our brudduh away in mudduh dus. Please leh us go tru gate.' " [60]

About conjure, however, the old woman was not very communicative. "I ain know bout cunjuh," she said. "I heahs bout spells on people, but I ain see um. Now shadduhs, I see um. One night comin down duh road, I git tuh place weah road tun, an I heah sumpm behine me runnin long close tuh groun. He got big long tus, dis long, an he tongue hangin out. He pas close tuh me, an he look a me. I see um good. He got long tick haiah lak Noofounlan. Deah ain nebuh bin dog lak um on ilun. He mus be shadduh.[54]

"Den one night, I come frum chuch wid huzbun. We gits tuh tun, I heahs sumpm agen. I looks, an deah is sumpm look lak man. Huzbun he ain see um. Den I heahs a stompin, an sumpm come by so close tuh me I kin mos tech um, an he tun tuh spotted ox. 'Budge,' I calls um wen dey changes lak dat. Dat spotted ox go gallopin off, an I say tuh huzbun, 'Yuh ain see um?' He say, 'Wut?' I say, 'Da spotted ox wut go pas down duh road an out in da fiel?' He say, 'I ain see nuttn.' Das wen I luns dat wen yuh see um, yuh musn talk bout um.

"No'm, I dunno no animal stories. I heah um, but I fuhgits. I know bout lizzud an rabbit, dough. Yuh ain know bout lizzud an rabbit? Well, lizzud, he wuk hahd. He hab sode wut he cut crop wid, an it wuk by itsef an it cut so fine, nuttn lef.[39] Lizzud he speak wuds tuh it—it do all duh wuk. Now, rabbit, he smaht. He ain got no sode lak lizzud got an he wahn one. He hide behine bush, an he watch da sode wuk fuh lizzud, an he wahn it bad. One day wen lizzud not at home, rabbit, he sneak up, an he steal lizzud sode. He laf tuh hesef cuz he got da sode. He take da sode tuh he fiel an he staht it tuh wuk. He tink he know duh wuds dat lizzud say tuh sode, an he call, 'Go-ee-tell.' Sode staht wukin. Pretty soon, sode finish duh crop, an rabbit wahn um tuh stop. Sode comin too close tuh noo wintuh crop wut rabbit got tuh hab fuh lib on. So rabbit he yell, 'Go-ee-tell' in loud voice, and sode he wuk all duh fastuh. He cut down ebryting rabbit hab an ain leab nuttn. Lizzud who bin hidin in bush, he laf an he laf tuh he sef at rabbit, cuz rabbit tink hesef so smaht wen he steal sode an now he ain got nuttn tuh eat all wintuh. Rabbit he see lizzud, an he call, 'Stop dis sode.' Lizzud he say, 'It my sode.' Rabbit he say, 'Dasso. It yuh sode, but stop it. It cut down ebryting uh got.' Lizzud say, 'Sode wuk fastuh ebry time he heah 'Go-ee-tell.' " Den lizzud he staht laffin an he calls out loud, 'Go-ee-pom,' an sode stop. Lizzud den go out an pick up sode an tak um home."

Knowing that Katie was a descendant of Belali, we asked her if she knew anything of him. She nodded and answered, "Belali Mohomet? Yes'm, I knows bout Belali. He wife Phoebe. He hab plenty daughtuhs, Magret, Bentoo, Chaalut, Medina, Yaruba, Fatima, an Hestuh.

"Magret an uh daughtuh Cotto use tuh say dat Belali an he wife Phoebe pray on duh bead. Dey wuz bery puhticluh bout duh time dey pray an dey bery regluh bout duh hour. Wen duh sun come up, wen it straight obuh head an wen it set, das duh time dey pray. Dey bow tuh duh sun an hab lill mat tuh kneel on. Duh beads is on a long string. Belali he pull bead an he say, 'Belambi, Hakabara, Mahamadu.' Phoebe she say, 'Ameen, Ameen.'

"Magret she say Phoebe he wife, but maybe he hab mone one wife. I spects das bery possible. He come obuh wid all he daughtuhs grown. He whole fambly wuz mos grown up.

Hestuh she Shad's gran. Yuh knows Shad? Bentoo she duh younges. Magret she my gran."

We asked if Belali Mohomet had been related to Belali Sullivan on St. Simons.

"I ain know bout St. Simon but Cotto use tuh talk bout cousin Belali Sullivan.

"Yes'm, I membuh muh gran too. Belali he frum Africa but muh gran she come by Bahamas. She speak funny wuds we didn know. She say 'mosojo' an sometime 'sojo' wen she mean pot. Fuh watuh she say 'deloe' an fuh fyuh she say 'diffy.' She tell us, 'Tak sojo off diffy.'

"Wen sumpm done she say, 'Bim-boga-rum.' Yuh tell uh sumpm wut is a suhprise lak somebody die, den she say, 'Ma-foo-bey, ma-foo-bey.'

"She ain tie uh head up lak I does, but she weah a loose wite clawt da she trow obuh uh head lak veil an it hang loose on uh shoulduh. I ain know wy she weah it dataway, but I tink she ain lak a tight ting roun uh head.

"She make funny flat cake she call 'saraka.' She make um same day ebry yeah, an it big day. Wen dey finish, she call us in, all duh chillun, an put in hans lill flat cake an we eats it. Yes'm, I membuh how she make it. She wash rice, an po off all duh watuh. She let wet rice sit all night, an in mawnin rice is all swell. She tak dat rice an put it in wooden mawtuh, an beat it tuh paste wid wooden pestle. She add honey, sometime shuguh, an make it in flat cake wid uh hans. 'Saraka' she call um."

Before the cabin stood a crudely constructed wooden mortar made many years before by Katie's husband and used originally for the pounding of rice. A deep basin-like aperture had been hewn out of the center of a log which was about three feet long and from eighteen to twenty inches wide.[43]

Across the dusty road from Katie Brown's another narrow wooden gate opened into a field where a winding path led to the small cabin of Julia Grovernor,* called Juno by the island Negroes. Julia, very black, tall and gaunt, was slightly hostile and suspicious and disinclined to talk. Even the pipe tobacco, potent in most cases, she indifferently dropped.

"No'm, I ain know nuttn. Ise feeble-minded. I bin weak in head sence I small chile. No'm, I ain know nuttn bout witches. I ain know nuttn bout root doctuhs. No'm, I ain nebuh heah uh cunjuh. No'm, I ain know nuttn bout spells. No'm, I ain kin tuh Katie Brown."

This refusal to answer except in the negative seemed to continue indefinitely. Finally, however, after innumerable slow, quiet, good-humored questions that showed no resentment at her hostility, she became friendly in a reserved and superior way. It was soon evident that this sullen, reticent woman, though hostile to outside invasion, was not feeble-minded, but on the contrary sharp-witted, with a dry sense of humor.

"Muh gran, she Hannah. Uncle Calina muh gran too; dey bote Ibos. Yes'm, I membuh muh gran Hannah. She marry Calina an hab twenny-one chillun. Yes'm, she tell us how she brung yuh.

"Hannah, she wid huh ahnt who wuz diggin peanuts in duh fiel, wid uh baby strop on uh back. Out uh duh brush two wite mens come an spit in huh ahnt eye. She blinded an wen she wipe uh eye, duh wite mens done loose duh baby frum huh back, an took Hannah too. Dey led um intuh duh woods, weah deah wuz udduh chillun dey done ketched an tie up in sacks. Duh baby an Hannah wuz tie up in sacks lak duh udduhs an Hannah nebuh saw huh ahnt agen an nebuh saw duh baby agen. Wen she wuz let out uh duh sack, she wuz on boat an nebuh saw Africa agen."

* Julia Grovernor, Sapelo Island. Deceased winter, 1938.

A back path from Julia's house led to the house of her sister, Katie,* who had a regal and impressive bearing. She, too, had a hostile and taciturn manner.

"No'm, Ise younguh dan Juno. I dohn membuh nuttn uh doze times. No'm, I ain heah tell uh cunjuh. I dohn know bout witch doctuhs. I dohn know spells. No'm, I dohn know none uh dis yuh askin. Yes'm, I nuss Hannah an Calina wen deys ole, but I young chile, an I dohn membuh nuttn bout um. No'm, I cahn unnuhstan um; dey talks a funny talk. I cahn unnuhstan um."

In the afternoon we went to see Phoebe Gilbert,** another descendant of the Ibos, Calina and Hannah. Phoebe, black, buxom, and comely, lived in a comfortable cottage in Shell Hammock. Obviously embarrassed at being the center of a rapidly increasing crowd of Negro listeners, she evaded most questions. Our visit did not prove entirely unsatisfactory, however, for after considerable humorous chatting Phoebe rewarded our efforts by giving a vivid description of how her grandfather, Calina, was captured and brought here from Africa.

"Belali Smith muh gran. I ain know bout Belali Mohomet. Yes'm, I membuh muh gran. She Hannah. Yes'm, muh gran Calina, too. Dey's Ibos. Muh gran Calina tell me how he got heah. He say he playin on beach in Africa, an big boat neah duh beach. He say, duh mens on boat take down flag, an put up big piece uh red flannel, an all chillun dey git close tuh watuh edge tuh see flannel an see wut doin. Den duh mens comes off boat an ketch um, an wen duh ole folks come in frum duh fiels dey ain no chillun in village. Dey's all on boat. Den dey brings um yuh."

Cuffy [20a] Wilson,† sitting in the clean-swept yard which surrounded his whitewashed house, told us about the much-discussed experience of a neighbor of his. This dealt with

* *Katie Grovernor, Sapelo Island.*
** *Phoebe Gilbert, Sapelo Island.*
† *Cuffy Wilson, Sapelo Island.*

the current belief concerning the necessity of asking leave to enter the graveyard.

"Grant Johnson, he wannuh cut some wood an he git obuh duh fence uh duh cimiterry," he explained to us. "He didn ax leab uh nobody.[60] He wuz a cuttin duh wood down as fas as he could wen all ub a sudden he see a big black dog wut [54] come attuh im. Dat wuz a shadduh an he ain lose no time in jumpin obuh duh fence.

"Wen yuh hab a fewnul eben today, yuh hab tuh ax leab tuh entuh duh cimiterry gate. Duh spirit ain gonuh let yuh in lessn yuh ask leab ub it."

We visited Nero Jones,* an elderly Negro who lived on his sixty-five-acre tract of land with a daughter, Henrietta. Sitting beneath the protecting shade of an arbor which overlooked a peanut field, the old man was busily engaged in shucking a large basket of the nuts.

He, too, remembered having seen harvest dances. "We use tuh hab big time at hahves," [38] he began. "We pray an sing duh night tru. Wen duh sun riz we go out an dance. We hab big beatin uh drums an sometimes we dry duh goads an leab duh seed in um. Dey make good rattle.[23, 25]

"I membuh Uncle Calina an An Hannah well. Dey mighty ole an dey bun up in duh house. Day talk lot uh funny talk tuh each udduh an dey is mighty puhticuluh bout prayin. Dey pray on duh bead. Duh ole man he say 'Ameela' and An Hannah she say 'Hakabara.' "

Later we drove slowly over the flat grass-lands to Hog Hammock, another Negro community at the south end of Sapelo. The red-legged herons winging their way against the vivid blue of the sky, the dense foliage rimming the edges of the inland marshes, clumps of feathery bush, all contributed to the tropical beauty of the island.

At Hog Hammock we visited Shad Hall (Plate XVII),**

---

* *Nero Jones, Sapelo Island.*
** *Shad Hall, Sapelo Island.*

another Belali Mohomet descendant, who came to the door of his neat cottage clad in blue denim. Delighted to have visitors, Shad was eager for conversation. With a few polite words of thanks for the pipe tobacco, he began to talk of the old days.

"Muh gran wuz Hestuh, Belali's daughtuh. She tell me Belali wuz coal black, wid duh small feechuhs we hab, an he wuz bery tall. She say Belali an all he fambly come on same boat frum Africa. Belali hab plenty daughtuhs, Medina, Yaruba, Fatima, Bentoo, Hestuh, Magret, and Chaalut.

"Ole Belali Smith wuz muh uncle. His son wuz George Smith's gran. He wuz muh gran Hestuh's son an muh mudduh Sally's brudduh. Hestuh an all ub um sho pray on duh bead. Dey weah duh string uh beads on duh wais. Sometime duh string on duh neck. Dey pray at sun-up and face duh sun on duh knees an bow tuh it tree times, kneelin on a lill mat."

We asked Shad if he had ever heard his grandmother say anything about Africa. Had she ever mentioned what sort of house they lived in or what food was generally eaten? Shad nodded eagerly, and from the steady flow of talk that followed it was evident that he had heard much of the land of his ancestors.

"Muh gran Hestuh say she kin membuh duh house she lib in in Africa. She say it wuz cubbuh wid palmettuh an grass fuh roof, an duh walls wuz made uh mud. Dey make duh walls by takin up hanfuls uh mud an puttin it on sumpm firm, sticks put crossways so. I membuh some pots and cups dat she hab made uh clay. She brung deze frum Africa. She membuh wut dey eat in Africa too. Dey eat yam an shuguh cane an peanut an bananas. Dey eat okra too. Yes'm, das right, dey calls it gumbo. Dey dohn hab tuh wuk hahd wid plantin deah. Jis go in woods an dig, an git big yam. Dey eat udduh roots too. Dey ain no flo tuh house. Dey sleep on hahd groun inside house. House wuz neah lill ilun weah dey ketch parrot and sell um."

"Do you remember any special kinds of food that your grandmother used to prepare?" we asked.

Shad, after pondering briefly, said, "She make strange cake, fus ub ebry munt. She call it 'saraka.' She make it out uh meal an honey. She put meal in bilin watuh an take it right out. Den she mix it wid honey, and make it in flat cakes. Sometime she make it out uh rice. Duh cake made, she call us all in an deah she hab great big fannuh full an she gib us each cake. Den we all stands roun table, and she says, 'Ameen, Ameen, Ameen,' an we all eats cake."

We asked Shad what sort of animals his grandmother remembered seeing in Africa, and he said, "She say lion is duh mos powful uh beas. She say lion git up tree jis lak cat. Yuh come long unduh tree, an lion he reach down wid great paws an grab yuh—so. Snakes, dey big, too. Dey wrap deah tail roun tree an lean obuh an reach yuh, too."

Shad furnished us additional information regarding "set-ups." "Yes'm, Gran Hestuh tell me uh set-ups. Dey kill a wite chicken wen dey hab set-ups tuh keep duh spirits way. She say a wite chicken is duh only ting dat will keep duh spirits way an she alluz keep wite chicken fuh dat in yahd.[35] Lak dis. Hestuh, she hab frien an frien die. Ebry ebenin friens spirit come back an call tuh Hestuh.[56] Hestuh knowd ef she keep it up, she die too. Hestuh den kills wite chicken, tro it out uh doze, an shut doe quick. Wen she tro it out, she say, 'Heah, spirit, moob away—dohn come back no mo.' I dunno wut she do wid duh blood an fedduhs.

"Yes'm, I heah tell uh witches, but I ain see um. I know eel skin tie roun neck bring good luck an cuo yuh ef yuh sick. Yes'm, I see um bury sack unduh doe step tuh [11] pruhtec house; I see um tie rag tuh gate tuh pruhtec too.[11b, c] I ain know snake-skin bring good luck, but eel-skin, yes'm.

167

"Yuh ain heah so much bout cunjuh on dis ilun, but deah's a few wut does a mighty lot uh talkin. Nellie Dixon, she lib right obuh deah in dem trees, she alluz talkin bout roots. She say somebody go tru duh yahd an drap a root fuhrum. She tote a sack roun uh neck tuh gahd um." [8, 12a, c, d]

When asked to whom he had belonged during slavery he answered, "Muh fus massuh Montally. He ole massuh. Young massuh wuz Massuh Tom Spalding. Den I belongs tuh Mike Spalding; dat befo freedom. Sometime duh ole folks call duh missus 'maduba' an duh massuh 'mahaba.' Yes'm I bin big man wen freedom come."

Shad remembered that during his childhood he had often witnessed harvest festivals and dances.

"Hahves time dey hab big time. It come once a yeah an dey pray an dey sing all night long till duh fus cock crow. Den dey staht tuh dance an tuh bow tuh duh sun as it riz in duh sky. Dey dance roun in a succle an sing an shout. Sho is a big time.[38]

"Wen yuh hab a buryin, yuh alluz hab tuh ask leab tuh duh grabeyahd. Dey do dat tuh dis day. Yuh say, 'Fambly, please let us lay yuh brudduh in mudduh dus.' " [60]

The story which Cuffy Wilson had already told us about Grant Johnson's having been chased from the graveyard by a shadow was also verified from this source. Shad told us, "Grant Johnson he go deah one time tuh cut wood widout askin leab. He busy cuttin wood wen all ub a sudden he see big black dog comin tuh um wid one paw raise an red eye an big grinnin teet.[54] Grant he ain lose no time in gittin way. Dat dog wuz shadduh wut come attuh um.

"Duh ole folks use tuh tell dat story bout duh hoe wut could wuk by itsef. It stan right up in duh fiel widout nobody holdin tuh it.[39] Das ef yuh knowd how tuh wuk it. Doze Africans knowd how tuh make dat hoe wuk an dey knowd how tuh wuk roots.

"Doze folks could fly too. Dey tell me deah's a lot ub um wut wuz bring heah an dey ain much good. Duh massuh wuz fixin tuh tie um up tuh whip um. Dey say, 'Massuh, yuh ain gwine lick me,' an wid dat dey runs down tuh duh ribbuh. Duh obuhseeuh he sho tought he ketch um wen dey git tuh duh ribbuh. But fo he could git tuh um, dey riz up in duh eah an fly way. Dey fly right back tuh Africa. I tink dat happen on Butler Ilun.

"I use tuh heah lots ub animal stories, but it bin so long I mos fuhgit bout um. I ain heah much bout duh spiduh cep he is bery wicked an he shahp. He kin spin he tread an riz right up in duh eah widout nuttn tuh hep um. He see a fly an begin tuh spin roun an roun um till he ketch um in he web. Den he caahn git way an An Nancy got um. Das wut duh chillun say tuh dis day wen dey see a spiduh ketch a fly —An Nancy got um.' " [53]

On Sunday evening Julius drove us through black swamp and bush to the church at Silver Bluff (Plate XVIII). The little white frame building with yellow light from oil lamps shining through the windows made the night suddenly come alive. Negro men and boys were moving about outside in the darkness and a few were gathered on the steps. All the women and children were inside.

Escorted by Julius and a deacon we went into the church and took our places on the second from the front middle bench. The pulpit stood on the raised platform on which most of the light was concentrated. The men and boys came in. The church was filled with a tense quietness.

The preacher came from behind the platform and stood silently behind the pulpit desk, looking dramatically over his congregation. He was tall and spare, with brown skin, narrow face, and a thin pointed beard, a Mohammedan looking Negro. He wore a black skull cap, which we learned later was not ritualistic but was worn to protect his head from the draught. This was Preacher Little who, we were afterwards told, was an itinerant preacher, not a native to the island but a type native to the district.

His text, read in a loud, commanding voice, was "You ah the salt of the earth; but if the salt has lost its savory, wherewith shall it be salt; it is then no good and should be trompled intuh earth." The exposition of this pronouncement was awaited with breathless interest.

The sermon that followed, however, was in no way connected with the text. Preacher Little divided his sermon into three parts and lectured his congregation on "straying frum duh paat." What he said was not really coherent. Words stood out, phrases rang in our ears, quotations from the Bible resounded at random but that was the beginning and the end. The impelling element was the sound of Preacher Little's voice.

In each part he began slowly, quietly, persuading and reasoning with his congregation. His voice would carry a pleading question to them and they would answer, "Huh." [29] As he progressed, the quiet reasoning diminished; he shouted to his listeners. The "Huh—Huh's" became loud, guttural, vibrating grunts that echoed through the little building. Regular stamping of the feet began; the vibration penetrated into every corner. It was impossible not to think of the beating of the drum. The regular rhythmic, swelling noise was deafening. It meant agreement with Preacher Little. It urged him on to greater heights until his shouting voice not only seemed to fill the church but to reverberate from wall to wall. This climax was reached three times, at the end of each of the three parts of the sermon. Each time it seemed to act as a great emotional purge to the listeners and leave them happily exhausted.

When the sermon ended, spirituals were sung under the able direction of a young Negro named George Smith.* The

* George Smith, Sapelo Island and Brunswick.

singing was enhanced by the fervor and the earnest simplicity with which it was presented. Shining countenances raised heavenward, voices lifted exultantly, and feet beating rhythmically in accompaniment, the congregation entered wholeheartedly into the singing and seemed oblivious of everything else.

The next day on the boat returning to the mainland, Smith, young and well educated, tried to remember some of the tales told him when he was a boy. They were mostly the better known ones, except the Fox and the Rabbit, which concerned the Fox thriftily planting sweet potatoes and the Rabbit digging them up.

Prevalent beliefs covered wider ground. If an owl hoots on top of the house or near the house, it is supposed to be a sign of death.[44] A counteractive is to throw salt on the fire, burn an old shoe, or turn pockets wrong side out. If a rooster comes upon the porch and starts crowing, it is a sign of death in the house.[13b] It is also considered bad luck to start on a journey and have to turn back. The method employed to ward off disaster is to draw a cross where you turned back and spit on it. We were told that most of the island Negroes believed in root doctors, but that they imported them from the mainland. There were none on the island.

Smith admitted that he knew very little about the Negroes' belief in spirits. He did know that if a person had something that the spirit wanted very badly that person would be haunted by the spirit.

A frizzled chicken is known as a wise chicken and is used to find lost articles. If something has been buried and its place forgotten, a frizzled chicken can, according to the islanders, find the place and scratch up the lost article.[13a]

Smith remembered hearing the older Negroes tell of having watches on certain definite occasions when they sat up all night waiting for sunrise. When the sun at last appeared

171

over the horizon, they would start a sun-dance and bow to the sun.

Death watches he knew nothing about, except present-day customs. However, he did say that the snake known as the coach-whip was sometimes wrapped around the neck of a person supposedly dead and its tail put in the person's mouth to see if he were still breathing.

We questioned young Smith about the festivals that the other Negroes had described and he told us that during the harvesting season various celebrations are still held.[38]

The boat neared the mainland. Our trip was over. As we bade goodbye to our guide, we cast a look of farewell at the dim outline of the tropical island. On the journey homeward impressions received during our stay on Sapelo crowded against one another in disturbing sequence. Innumerable memories assailed us. Faintly the echo of shouting rose and fell in the distance. The measured chanting of voices and the pounding of feet seemed to follow us across the water.

St. Simons Island

◇◇◇◇◇◇◇◇◇◇◇◇◇◇◇◇◇◇◇◇

ST. SIMONS, ONE OF THE LARGER COASTAL ISLANDS, lies off the Georgia coast not far from Brunswick on the mainland. For about fifteen years it has been connected by causeway and bridge to the Coastal Highway. St. Simons has always had a considerable Negro population, owing to the fact that from early times many large plantations as well as smaller settlements flourished on the island. This has given the Negroes considerable contact with white people and of late years with the rather sophisticated type of tourist. Fearing that the old customs would have been forgotten, we had little hope of good field work here.

However, we had not worked half a day in the north end settlements of the island before we were happily surprised. Around Harrington and Frederica there still live many old Negroes who remember the customs and beliefs told them by their parents and grandparents. Most of them are intelligent, reticent, and proud. Not easy of approach but with good manners, they responded to the request to help record the traditional beliefs of their forefathers. Once they had realized the object of our conversation, they talked freely and graciously, and several were outstanding for their keen comprehension.

We went to see Catherine Wing,* who lives at the corner of the Harrington Road and the main Frederica Highway. Her comfortable frame house was set in the midst of a flower garden and her washtubs were conveniently placed under a

* *Catherine Wing, St. Simons Island.*

173

grape arbor and spreading live oaks. On the side road stood three stately pine trees from which hung silvery festoons of Spanish moss. Catherine was black, small, and lively at sixty-nine.

"Ise bawn in Meridian," she said, "but Ise lib mos muh life heah. Muh people belong tuh duh Atwoods uh Darien an tings heah on duh ilun is pretty much duh way dey wuz deah. Some tings is changed wut hadduh change, lak wen we hab a fewnul duh unduhtakuh come an git duh body an dey dohn lak yuh tuh hab no settin-up. In duh ole days we would sing an make prayuh all night an dey would come an measure duh body wid a string tuh make duh coffin tuh bury em in. Dey use tuh alluz sen yuh home tuh bury[1] ef dey could git duh money but dey ain eben alluz do dat no mo. Dey nebuh use tuh bury no strainjuhs in duh buryin[3] groun but heah dat ain kep strick needuh."

We asked about the dances and festivals of her youth.

"We use tuh hab big times duh fus hahves,[38] an duh fus ting wut growed we take tuh duh chuch so as ebrybody could hab a piece ub it. We pray obuh it an shout. Wen we hab a dance, we use tuh shout in a ring. We ain hab wut yuh call a propuh dance tuhday.

"One uh duh dances wuz call duh Buzzud Lope.[17] It's a long time sence we done it, but I still membuh it. We ain hab much music in doze days but dey use a drum tuh call duh people tuhgedduh wen dey gonuh hab games aw meetin.[26] It sho bin a long time sence I tought bout dem days."

Catherine told us that Ryna Johnson, who lived about a mile down the Harrington Road, was one of the oldest people on the island. Leaving the main highway, we followed the narrow, less traversed side road. It was a heavily wooded section. We viewed the massive-trunked hoary oak trees through a misty curtain of hanging moss. The fences along the road were covered with honeysuckle and wild grape. Shortly before we arrived at our destination, the road divided to give way to a growth of towering oaks; then it joined again, resuming its winding trail through the quiet, shadowed countryside.

The little settlement now known as Harrington was formerly the property of the Demere family. A little less than a mile north of this settlement was Harrington Hall, home of Raymond Demere, who came to this country with Oglethorpe after serving ten years under Lord Harrington at Gibraltar.

To the left of the road was a small unpainted store operated by Ryna Johnson's daughter with whom she lived. Various advertisements on the front of the small building gave splashes of color to the green of trees and foliage.

Set back from the store was Ryna's house, surrounded by an expanse of short grass upon which a horse was grazing. The house was weathered with age, as were the vertical boards of the fence that enclosed the garden; here and there in the fence a new unpainted board, regardless of length, had replaced an old, and the top presented an irregular, jagged pattern. The cabin was the usual two-room affair but with a hall through the center and a lean-to in the back. The walls were papered with newspapers and, although there was a motley collection of objects and furniture, everything was scrupulously clean.

Ryna * was blind from cataracts and had not been feeling very well; so she had just got up from bed. Although her body was bent and very feeble, her mind was still clear.

"Ise bout eighty-five yeahs ole, but I caahn tell zackly. I belong tuh duh Coupers wen I wuk on duh plantation. It bin sech a long time I mos stop studyin bout dem days. But I membuh we use tuh hab good times."

In answer to our inquiry regarding any Africans whom she had known during plantation days, Ryna told us, "Alexanduh, Jummy, an William, dey is all African. I membuh ole William well an he tell me lots bout times in Africa. Dey

* *Ryna Johnson, Harrington, St. Simons Island.*

ain weah no cloze, he say, but a leedle clawt string roun em.

"William say dat dey ain hab much trouble gittin tings tuh eat in Africa cuz so much grow free. Dey cut duh tree an let duh suhrup drain out. Duh women tie duh leedle chillun an duh babies on tuh deah back tuh carry em roun.

"He say wen dey come in duh boats tuh ketch em, dey trail a red flag an dey ain use tuh see red an das duh way dey git duh load. William he talk funny talk. He hab funny wud fuh tings. I use tuh know some ub em, cuz he teach em tuh me but it so long, missus, Ise fuhgit. But I membuh he say pot call 'sojo' an watuh 'deloe' an he call fyuh 'diffy.' He sho did dat, but das all I kin membuh. Ef uh study bout em, maybe I kin membuh some mo."

We wanted a description of William, the African.

"William a good size man, heaby set. He hab two leedle line mahk on he right cheek." [14]

Ryna mused: "Tings is sho change. Wen we is young, we use tuh hab big frolic an dance in a ring an shout tuh drum. Sometime we hab rattle made out uh dry goad an we rattle em an make good music." [23, 25]

We wondered if she, too, remembered the Buzzard Lope and she assured us, "Yes'm, sho I knows it. Ebrybody knows it." [17]

Shortly afterward the conversation turned to conjure and the old woman told us, "I sho heah plenty bout da ting. Way back we hab plenty discussion bout root makuhs.[22, 48] I membuh my huzbun Hillard Johnson speak bout a root makuh in Darien wut make duh pot bile widout fyuh. My huzbun he frum Sapelo. He could tell yuh bout sech tings ef he wuz libin."

A short distance away lived Charles Hunter,* whose small board house was set well back from the road. The front yard enclosed by a wire fence was planted with a profusion of brightly colored flowers along the sandy walk leading to

---

* *Charles Hunter, Harrington, St. Simons Island.*

the house. Across the road to the left was a field which had been planted in corn.

Charles, a medium-sized, intelligent man, very black of skin and rather small-featured, talked to us about his people.

"Dey is long libin people," he began. "Muh fathuh lib until he a hundud an muh mothuh wuz ninety wen she die. Muh gran, she name Louise an come frum Bahama Ilun.* She lib tuh hundud an fifteen. Das duh way dey do an I guess I'll do duh same."

Did the people around Harrington believe in the old customs the way his mother and grandmother had believed in them?

"Yes'm, dey sticks tuh em but duh times is changin an yuh hab tuh change wid em. Duh unduhtakuh come now an mone lakly he bring yuh back tuh duh chuch an dey ain no watch an singin."

In the course of our talk he told us that the river baptisms were held by members of the local churches. "Yes'm, we still baptize in duh ribbuh," Charles said. "We hab one not long ago. We hab tuh wait till a Sunday wen a ebb tide come at a good time, cuz it duh ebb tide wut carry yuh sin away." [63]

Charles confirmed what the other residents had told us regarding conjure.

"Well, dey's some belieb in cunjuh an some wut dohn. Dey's lots wut say sickness ain natchul an somebody put sumpm down fuh yuh.[15] I ain belieb in it much muhsef but dey's curious tings happen. Now, wen I wuz a boy deah's a root makuh wut lib yuh name Alexanduh. He wuz African an he say he kin do any kine uh cunjuh wut kin be done an he kin cuo any kine uh disease.[48] He wuz a small man, slim an bery black. Alexanduh say he could fly.[68b, 69c] He

* A number of slaves accompanied their masters from the West Indies to this country. It was also the custom for slave ships to stop at the Bahamas en route to America with a cargo.

say all his fambly in Africa could fly. I ain seen em fly muhsef but he say he could do it all right. We's sked ub im wen
we's boys an use tuh run wen we see im come."

During the interview Emma, Charles' wife, hovered nearby,
seemingly very much interested in the proceedings. Finally
we asked her to come and talk to us. Although she said that
she was too young to remember much of the old times, she
gave us some recollections regarding superstitions and African customs.

"Now muh gran Betty she wuz African an she plant benne
seed. Once yuh staht plantin benne, yuh got tuh plant em
ebry yeah aw yuh die. I tell yuh who kin tell yuh sumpm
bout ole times an das Chahls Murray. He ain tell me how
ole he is but I ketch he age jis duh same. Yuh go down tuh
duh main road a lill way an duh road spring off tuh Chahls
Murray house."

Emma also told us how to reach Ben Sullivan, one of the
oldest men living on the island.

From Hunter's we turned left on a lane flanked by a
thicket of low trees and bushes. After about two or three
miles we came to a clearing where there was a scattering of
houses and sheds.

A tall, spare man was plowing in a field to the left of the
road. We hailed him and asked him if he could help us find
Ben Sullivan. He left his mule and plow and came over to
the car. He was tall, as straight as a soldier, with a lean
agility that bespoke youthfulness. Over his long jaws and
rather straight features his copper skin was smooth.

"Ise Ben Sullivan," * he said, and we were puzzled.

"But," we said, "the Ben Sullivan we are looking for is an
old man."

"Ise duh only Ben Sullivan," he answered. "Ise eighty-
eight."

It seemed incredible that this active, intensely alive man

* Ben Sullivan, St. Simons Island.

could really be so old. We asked him who his people were and what he remembered about the old times.

"We belong tuh duh Coupers. Ise son tuh Belali. He wuz butluh tuh James Couper at Altama. I membuh we hab lots uh time tuh play wen we's chilluns." He smiled pleasantly at the memory.

This man, too, remembered native Africans he had known, for he told us, "I membuh lots uh Africans, but all ub em ain tame. But I knowd some ub em wut is tame an I knowd one tame Indian."

We asked again about old Alexander, the African root maker.

"Yes'm, I membuh him. He wuz a lill black man an he belong tuh duh Butlers but I ain know him well cuz we's diffunt people. Now ole man Okra an ole man Gibson an ole Israel, dey's African an dey belong tuh James Couper an das how I knows em. Dey tell us how dey lib in Africa. Dey laks tuh talk. It funny talk an it ain so easy tuh unnuhstan but yuh gits use tuh it. Dey say dey buil deah own camp deah an lib in it.

"Ole man Okra he say he wahn a place lak he hab in Africa so he buil im a hut. I membuh it well. It wuz bout twelve by foeteen feet an it hab dut flo an he buil duh side lak basket weave wid clay plastuh on it. It hab a flat roof wut he make frum bush an palmettuh an it hab one doe an no winduhs. But Massuh make im pull it down. He say he ain wahn no African hut on he place.

"Ole Israel he pray a lot wid a book he hab wut he hide, an he take a lill mat an he say he prayuhs on it. He pray wen duh sun go up an wen duh sun go down. Dey ain none but ole Israel wut pray on a mat. He hab he own mat. Now ole man Israel he hab shahp feechuh an a long pointed beahd, an he wuz bery tall. He alluz tie he head up in a wite clawt an seem he keep a lot uh clawt on han, fuh I membuh, yuh could see em hangin roun duh stable dryin."

179

Asked if he remembered any other Africans who tied their heads up, the old man told us, "I membuh a ole uhmun name Daphne. He didn tie he head up lak ole man Israel. He weah loose wite veil on he head. He wuz shahp-feechuh too an light uh complexion. He weah one ring in he eah fuh he eyes.[27] I hab refrence to it bein some kine uh pruhtection tuh he eyes. Wen he pray, he bow two aw tree times in duh middle uh duh prayuh."

We asked about the music they used to have and what they used for dancing in the old days.

"We ain dance den duh way dey dances now. We dance roun in a succle an den we dances fuh prayin.[19a] I membuhs we use tuh hab drums fuh music an we beat duh drum fuh dances.[23]

"Now, ole man Dembo he use tuh beat duh drum tuh duh fewnul,[24] but Mr. Couper he stop dat. He say he dohn wahn drums beatin roun duh dead. But I watch em hab a fewnul. I gits behine duh bush an hide an watch an see wut dey does. Dey go in a long pruhcession tuh duh buryin groun an dey beat duh drums long duh way an dey submit duh body tuh duh groun. Den dey dance roun in a ring an dey motion wid duh hans.[18] Dey sing duh body tuh duh grabe an den dey let it down an den dey succle roun in duh dance.

"Dey ain hab no chuch in doze days an wen dey wannuh pray, dey git behine duh house aw hide someweah an make a great prayuh. Dey ain suppose tuh call on duh Lawd; dey hadduh call on duh massuh an ef dey ain do dat, dey git nine an tutty.

"Dey ain marry den duh way dey do now. Attuh slabery dey hadduh remarry. Dey hab big baptizin in duh ribbuh lak dey do tuhday an dey dip em on duh ebb tuh wash duh sins away an duh preachuh he make a great prayuh tuh duh ribbuh.[63]

"Ole man Okra he a great un fuh buil drum.[25] He take a calf skin an tan it an make duh side uh maple. Ise pretty

180

sho it wuz maple. He stretch em obuh it good. It wuz bout eighteen inches wide an fifteen inches deep wen he finish it. He beat it wid a stick. Ole man Okra he sho kin chase a drum. Ole man Jesse he frum Africa, too, an he make he own drum."

When we asked Ben if he remembered any African words, he replied, "I know dat deah wuz a ole man, it bin so long I caahn relate his name, at duh plantation wut wehn roun wid ole man Okra an I membuh well he call all duh fish an ting uh duh ribbuh by duh name uh 'nyana' an den I heah pancake call 'flim.' Muh granmothuh Hettie, duh mothuh uh muh mothuh Bella, he come from Africa too an he huzbun come frum Africa. He name wuz Alex Boyd. Alex wuz bery small felluh but heaby an he hab dahk skin an shahp-feechuch. Yes, ma'am, he talk African but he stuttuh so he dohn talk much roun us chillun, cuz we make fun at im, an as I say befo, I wuz small lad den. Alex wuz knock-kneed an he tie he head up in a clawt."

Had his grandmother, Hettie, ever talked to him about Africa, we wanted to know.

Ben told us, "Many time. He tell some tings I membuh. He say he mus be bout tutteen aw foeteen wen dey bring im frum Africa. He say deah wuz great talk bout comin tuh dis country an some men tell em it would take only two aw tree days tuh git deah. Dey wuz all happy tuh come. Him an lot uh friens come tuhgedduh.

"Wen Hettie fus come, he say he feel worried cuz he couldn unnuhstan duh talk yuh an many udduh tings bein so diffunt frum he own country. He hab two sistuhs an tree brothuhs but dey couldn git a chance tuh come. He hab mo refrence tuh he mothuh dan tuh he fathuh. An he say dat in Africa he lib in a 'groun house.' It wuz a squeah house, an he say dat he didn lib close tuh a salt ribbuh but weah deah wuz a lot uh wile swamp. Wen he fus come tuh dis country, he didn unnuhstan bout fish. But he tell a lot bout monkey an parakeet. An, too, he say nuttn ebuh die way. Duh crops jis come back ebry yeah widout habin tuh be planted.

"Das all I membuh Hettie tellin bout Africa. Muh fathuh's fathuh come frum Africa too but wen muh fathuh Belali wuz a small young lad, muh granfathuh wehn tuh Dungeness on Cumberland Ilun tuh trade in slabes an nebuh wuz seen agen. It wuz muh fathuh Belali dat made rice cakes."

When asked about his father's mother, Ben continued, "Muh fathuh's mothuh lib at Altama. Huh name wuz Luna, but muh fathuh's fathuh wuz a unmarried man. Deah's many tings I do not membuh, it wuz sech a long time ago. I know dat wen deah wuz tuh be a buryin, dey alluz bury duh dead at night at duh plantation. Dey alluz come in frum duh tas befo dahk.

"In doze days deah wuz no way tuh git tuh Savannah cep by boat an wen Mr. Couper wannuh go, he use a boat bout fifty foot long an bout six foot wide. He take six strong oahsmen an dey would make it in ten aw twelve hours. I heahd tell ub a house buil by a man frum Africa, wid cawn stalks an mud an wid a straw filluh."

The flying story about old Alexander, the root maker, had interested us and we asked if Ben Sullivan had heard of it.

"I ain heahd specially bout him but Ise heahd plenty Africans talk bout flyin. Deah's plenty ub em wut could fly.[68c, 69b] I sho heahd em talk bout great doins an Ise heahd ole Israel say duh hoe could wuk by itsef ef yuh know wut tuh say tuh it.[39] It bin a long time sence Ise tought bout tings lak dat, but ef uh studies bout em, dey comes back tuh me."

On the way back from Harrington to St. Simons village we stopped at Nora Peterson's * small cabin to talk with her. Nora, the daughter of Tom Floyd, an African who came to

* *Nora Peterson, St. Simons Island.*

this country on the *Wanderer* in 1858, is a nice looking, middle-aged woman, pleasant and up to date. She told us about her father.

"I wuz bery lill wen he died—not mone bout fo yeah ole, uh spec. I do know he come frum Africa. I membuhs dat an uh membuh muh Uncle Slaughtuh wuz his brothuh an he come frum Africa, too. I nebuh heahd him talk much bout it but maybe uh wuz too lill tuh membuh."

Although she had been so young at the time of her father's death, the woman still retained a vivid picture of him and she gave us the following description:

"He wuz shawt an dahk, an heaby buil. Yuh see, he wuzn but bout sixty yeah ole wen he died. Muh mothuh wuz Charity Lewis an uh got one brothuh, Caesar Prince, but he's younguh dan me an dohn membuh nothin."

From Nora's we went to the old tabby slave house of Floyd White * who was related to her. Floyd was of middle height, black, and of a powerful build. When we were uncertain and groping as to the right questions to ask, Floyd was clear and helpful.

"Ise nephew tuh Charity Lewis, so Nora is muh cousin, but Ise olduhn Nora an I membuh ole Tom Floyd well. I bout fifteen wen he die. He wuz shawt an tick set. I tinks he wuz Ibo. He used tuh whoop an holluh. He say dey do da way in Africa. He wuz doctuh too an he could cut yuh wid a knife an cop yuh. I wish he wuz yuh right now tuh cop me. I sho needs it an it make yuh feel lots bettuh.[48] I heah him talk plenty bout Africa but I caahn membuh so much ub it cuz uh wuz young boy den. He say he lib in a hut on a ribbuh an dey eat coconut an bread wut grow on a tree. Dey plant yam ebry seben yeah an dey dohn hadduh wuk it. Dey hab peanut an banana. He call it by anudduh name but I caahn membuh it. I seen plenty ub African peo-

* *Floyd White, St. Simons Island.*

183

ple an dey all say dey plant duh crop an dey dohn hadduh wuk it. I heah lot ub em tell how dey git obuh yuh. Dey trap em on a boat wid a red flag."

Old Tom Floyd was not the only root doctor Floyd could remember. There were many others, he said, some still living and plying their trade.[48]

"I knows a root makuh now," he told us. "Uncle Quawt, he root makuh. Does yuh know him?"

We replied that we had known Quarterman for some time but that he had never told us he could work roots.

"Maybe he ain tell yuh but he kin wuk em all right.[48] He kin put a cunjuh on wid a goofa bag as good as anybody. Now, I tell yuh bout im. Deah's two felluhs in Brunswick wut does a lill killin an wen duh case is call, two buzzud light on duh cote house an wen duh men come up befo duh jedge, he let um go free. Now, Uncle Quawt, he had sumpm tuh do wid dat. Dey ain so many root makuhs lef."

Floyd, too, had heard of Alexander, the old African root maker.

"Yes'm, Ise heahd much bout im. He wuz still libin wen I wuz a boy. Ise heahd em tell plenty uh tales bout im. Dey say duh boat leab fuh Savannah an Alexanduh he yuh. He say good-bye frum yuh an tell em tuh go on widout im but he say he see em deah an wen duh boat git tuh Savannah, Alexanduh he in Savannah on duh dock tuh ketch duh line."

Pleasant memories associated with the social activities of the past caused Floyd to ponder abstractedly for a time. Finally he roused himself and told us, "We use tuh dance roun tuh a drum an a rattle goad. Dey could make good drum frum hawg an bass drum frum cow.[25] Doze days dey ain only beat duh drum fuh dancin; dey beat it on duh way tuh duh grabe yahd.[24] Dat wuz fuh duh det mahch wen dey use tuh carry duh body in a wagon. Dey hab lot uh singin den too an dey hab singin at duh baptizin. Den dey baptize em in duh ribbuh jis lak dey does now. Dey sing wid all duh

184

candidates walkin in wite robes tuh duh ribbuh an duh preachuh he dip em on duh ebb tide an he pray duh ribbuh tuh take duh sin away.[63] Dey ain mine gittin wet in duh ribbuh.

"Heahd bout duh Ibo's Landing? Das duh place weah dey bring duh Ibos obuh in a slabe ship an wen dey git yuh, dey ain lak it an so dey all staht singin an dey mahch right down in duh ribbuh tuh mahch back tuh Africa, but dey ain able tuh git deah. Dey gits drown."

St. Marys

THE NEGROES OF ST. MARYS LIVE SCATTERED ABOUT the town and its outskirts. In the past few years many of the very old people have died and there remain only a few who are past eighty years old. We went to see Hettie Campbell,* who was only seventy-two. Her mother had belonged to Dr. Wright of St. Marys and all her ante-bellum knowledge had been imparted to her by her mother and her stepfather, Andrew King. When we drove up she was sitting on the porch of her small house. The front garden was a packed dirt yard with formal plantings of flowers and shrubbery. During most of our talk Hettie's son, Horace,** stood in the doorway, half interested in and half amused by the conversation.

We asked Hettie to tell us about the old times.

"I remembuh Uncle Patty an Ahnt Rachel. They wuz frum Africa. Aftuh the waw wen they move from the plantation, they lived in a house on the watuhfront an they use tuh talk funny tuh each othuh so none of us chilluns couldn unduhstan em. I dohn remembuh so much bout em cuz uh wuz mighty lill then, but Henry Williams he remembuhs all right. Henry's eighty-seven yeahs ole.

"I do remembuh the big times we use tuh have wen I wuz young. We does plenty uh dances in those days. Dance roun in a ring. We has a big time long bout wen crops come in an evrybody bring sumpm tuh eat wut they makes an we

* Hettie Campbell, St. Marys. Deceased autumn, 1939.
** Horace Campbell, St. Marys.

186

all gives praise fuh the good crop an then we shouts an sings all night.[38] An wen the sun rise, we stahts tuh dance. It ain so long since they stop that back in the woods but these young people they does new kines uh dances."

Horace interjected here, "I seen em do those dances back in the woods but not yuh."

We asked what sort of music they had for the dances.

"They mosly have guitah now," said Hettie, "an we use tuh use guitah too, but we makes em frum goad an we beats drums too. We makes em frum coon hide stretched ovuh hoops.[25] Muh step-fathuh, Andrew King, who lived down the Satilla Rivuh, use tuh tell me how it wuz in the ole days. He tell me they bring a boatload of them Africans ovuh frum a ilun tuh theah plantation. That wuz jis befo the waw an they wuz runnin frum the Yankees."

We asked if she had known any families who refused to eat certain kinds of food.

"Thas a hahd un, ma'am. Mos people eat wut they kin git but I knowd Chahlotte Froman who wouldn tech chicken. They all say that chicken wuz a duhty animal an they ain gonuh eat em.[65] They keeps chicken cuz frizzle chicken is a wise chicken. It sho kin fine wut you caahn fine."[13a]

We asked about conjure.

Horace laughed and said, "I tell yuh, ma'am, they's mo doin of cunjuh up roun Savannah than theah is in these pahts. I jis bin up theah an I ain nevuh heahd so much talk of it in muh life. Theah's a lot of ole customs still roun an we've all heahd bout em an knows bout em but theah ain nobody much wut's ole nuff tuh pay much tention tuh em." Horace smiled with the superiority of the younger generation.

Later we visited Henry Williams,* (Plate XIX), whose little house (Plate XX) sat back in a clump of tall, overgrown brush that grew close to the dilapidated paling fence.

* Henry Williams, St. Marys.

187

Henry, who sat on his sunny porch, was strong and healthy looking for his eighty-seven years. The shabbiness of his clothes contrasted with the splendor of the naval cap on his head. Two little neighbors, Enoch and Artie Jones, were playing in the yard, (Plate XXI).

When we told Henry that we wanted to know about old times, he launched into eager conversation.

"I belong tuh William Cole wut live at Oakland Plantation but it wunt long befo the waw an then I wuz free an come tuh town. Wen I wuz bout twelve, I hep Daddy Patty in his tannin yahd ovuh theah on the watuh by the cimiterry. Patty wuz a shoemakuh too an use tuh make all kines uh things out uh hides an skins."

We asked him to tell us all he could remember about Uncle Patty and his wife.

"Well, they's both frum Africa an as I remumbuh they's Ibos. They wuz bout middle height an heavy buil. I ain suttn bout Ahnt Rachel but Daddy Patty belong tuh ole man Arnow an I think he bought im at a sale an bring im down yuh. They use tuh talk tuh each othuh in a language wut we couldn unduhstan an Patty use tuh alluz be singin a song, 'a-shou-tu-goula.'

"Daddy Patty, he use tuh talk tuh the mens in the tannin yahd bout weah he come frum. He ain talk tuh me but I heah im. He say they ain hadduh plant but once a yeah cuz evrything grows wile. They buns gumbo fuh wood. He say they live in 'boo-boo-no' made out uh sticks an straw thas plastuhed with mud. Fus they digs a big flat celluh bout a foot deep an packs the earth down smooth an tight. Thas the flo. Then they leans the sticks tuh the centuh an they puts the straw an the mud on em an it come out lak a beehive an thas weah they lib.

"They buil a big 'boo-boo-no' fuh the chief. Patty he wuz the chief son an he have three straight mahks slantin down on he right cheek an that wuz a bran tuh show who he wuz.[14]

He wuz the waw chief son and doze mahks tell whut tribe he belong tuh. Wen I knowd im, he stay down in a lill house on the alley neah the ribbuh. I sho heahd im talk a lot. Ise hole duh hide fuh im wen he scrapes em with a scrapuh. Patty say all the people suppote the king by plantin cassaba an givin the king some uh the cassaba."

We asked Uncle Henry about the dances and the customs of long ago.

"I sho see dances wut give thanks fuh the crop [38] an we prays in the night an dance wen the sun rise. I know the Buzzud Lope too.[17] I seen em do that an they use tuh have big Satdy night doins. Roun Christmas we git three days' holiday an theah's plenty uh dances an shoutin then. We goes tuh the ownuh an gits a ticket an we all gathuhs at the same place an we shouts an kick up with each othuh, but wen yuh ticket out, ef yuh dohn come back, the patrol will git yuh an then yuh gits whipped."

We asked him about witch doctors and taboos.

"I tell yuh, missus, they ain many wut knows bout roots yuh tuhday. Some does come tuh sell hans an chahms [8] an they's a heap uh signs fuh the bad an good luck ef I have time tuh study bout em. Now the Jordan family, ole man Jordan, he dohn let none uh his family eat rabbit. Theah's the ole man an Ahnt Tillah an theah chillun, Sally an Austin. He use tuh tell the boy, 'Dohn yuh go shoot no rabbits roun yuh; we dohn none of us eats rabbit. Thas bad luck fuh us.' He sho wuz strick bout it." [65]

We questioned the old man further about his recollections of the beliefs and practices of his ancestors. It appeared, however, that for the present, his discourse had come to a close.

After a moment's hesitation he answered us with, "I ain think bout doze ole days so much lately, miss, but wen uh gits tuh studyin bout em, lots uh things comes back tuh me."

We went by to talk with Charity Lucas, a fine looking up-standing, middle-aged Negro woman. She told us she did not know much about her father's people,—they had come from around Carolina,—but her mother and her mother's people had come from around Waycross and she herself had been born in Waycross. She said that the coast Negroes were very different from the interior people. She had heard talk of conjure and spirits around St. Marys but she didn't believe much in it herself; she had not been brought up that way.

Her son Robert (Plate XXII), a tall, lithe, powerful young Negro of about twenty-five, was rather taciturn. He had heard of these things but didn't care to speak of them and didn't believe in them much anyway.

Charity advised us to go to see old Jim Myers. "Now theah's one that's ole an'll be able tuh tell yuh plenty. He's neahly ninety and sho likes tuh talk."

We asked if his memory were good. "Yes'm, it's as good as mine. I guess it's bettuh."

We asked for directions and she told us how to go, ten miles deep into the woods off from the St. Marys-Kingsland highway.

Our road and what later turned out to be a pine needle wagon track carried us through Marianna, John Houstoun McIntosh's plantation, through Sweetwater Hammock and on through other settlements to Mush Bluff Island where old Jim Myers lived. The last mile we had to walk, owing to some swampy patches in the wagon track. A Negro boy of about eleven sauntered around a bush, and his eyes popped open in frightened surprise at strangers appearing so suddenly in the woods.

"Does Jim Myers live near here?" we asked.

"Right theah roun the cawnuh of the path," he said, and we came suddenly upon the house, a three room unpainted, board cabin sitting about two feet off the ground on large, sturdy oak stumps. The front steps were three oak logs of increasing diameter that made a massive if difficult tread to the door. The house was in a large grove of oak trees and the usual plows, iron pots, and implements were scattered about the hard packed, sand yard. Jim Myers owned a good deal of land and there was a well-to-do feeling about the whole place, though it was old-fashioned and isolated in the extreme.

Uncle Jim * (Plate **XXIII, XXIV**) came down the log steps to greet us. His bare feet manipulated the round treads easily. He was a big man, slightly bent from rheumatism, very black with a white fringe of a beard. His eyes were rheumy with age. Around his ankles were two brass wires, which helped to take the pain out of his legs.[12b]

"Uncle Jim," we said, "tell us about the times when you were a boy."

Uncle Jim laughed in condescending good humor. "Lawd, missus, thas so long ago I ain thought bout them days in a long time and theah ain much tuh tell. Ise bawn jis twenny mile from yuh on Mr. John Tompkins' plantation and I lived roun yuh all muh life. I bin heah on Mush Bluff Ilun a long time."

We asked him if he had known any Africans when he was a young man.

"Yes'm, I sho knowd plenty of em. Theah wuz a lawg house that belonged to Mr. Hallowes wich use tuh set right ovuh theah in them woods until about ten yeahs ago. That was the house that they kep the wile Africans in. It had big ion rings in the flo. They chained them wile Africans theah till they wuz tame. They'd take em out one by one and they'd give em a stick an put em in the fiel with people wut knowd how tuh wuk and that way they lun how too. They sked to give em a hoe. It's shahp and they might frail roun with it."

* Jim Myers, Mush Bluff Island.

We asked Uncle Jim if he could see spirits. "No'm, I ain nevuh seen em. I wuzn bawn with a caul [4] an I caahn see em. Now, muh brothuh he kin see em cuz he wuz bawn with a caul. He see em all the time. Spirits is alluz roun in time of fewnuls an wen a pusson die, we have a settin-up and then we leave sumpm wut we got tuh eat in a dish by him to eat [54] —that is, we use tuh do that—an we put salt on em in the ole days an we go up to em an we put our hands on theah chest to bid em feahwell." [31]

We asked Uncle Jim if they used to have night funerals in the old days. "No'm, we alluz have our fewnuls in the day time but my great granmothuh, now, she say in Africa they have night fewnuls."

We asked him to tell us more of his African great grand-mother.

"Muh great gran, huh name wuz Bina; thas all we know uh by. She brought up muh mothuh cuz muh gran got bun up in uh house wen muh mothuh wuz two days ole."

We asked him if he remembered her well. "Yes'm, I wuz a big boy about fifteen wen she die an they all say she wuz a hundud an thutty yeahs ole at that time. She sho ole, I know dat, but she remembuh plenty. She tell us chillun so much I caahn remembuh all them things."

We asked again about night funerals. "She jis say they have em at night but she didn say wy. She did say they alluz kill a wite chicken at the time they go to bury em an they take the blood an feathuhs an they do sumpm special with em but I ain unduhstood how it is.[35a, b] I tell you wut she tell me, how she get heah on a big boat an she lan down theah on Cumberland Ilun on a big dock in the time of Mr. Nightingale an she say they put em in a lill pick house to keep em safe an the chimbly of that same lill house is standin about two hundud yahds out in the rivuh off Cumberland tuhday."

We asked if she had told him how they lived in Africa

and what kind of house they lived in. "She ain speak of
wut kine uh house but she do speak of monkeys. They have
monkeys all roun em and they dohn have tuh do no plantin
cuz evrything is wile and they pick it off the trees."

We asked him if he could remember any African words
he had heard his grandmother use. "They wuz funny wuds,"
he laughed, "I ought tuh be able to remembuh em but I
caahn. She use tuh sing songs with African wuds. Ef I
could study about em, I might remembuh some but now you
ask me I jis caahn git em tuh mine. She did sing a chuch
song wut have wuds we could unduhstand, an then in the
middle of it she say 'yeribum, yeribum, yeribum, by,' and
looked like wen she come to the en of each stanza, she sing
'yeribum, yeribum, yeribum, by.' It sho is a long time ago,
them days."

Later we followed a deeply rutted sand road which led
westward in the direction of Folkston. Few cars traveled
this way and once during our trip we encountered an old
fashioned two-wheeled ox cart whose driver guided his oxen
deftly to one side in order to let us pass.

About three or four miles out on the road we turned in a
gate and drove to the side of Shadwick Rudolph's * house.
The old man greeted us smilingly. At first glance he did
not appear to be the eighty-six years he claimed, but on
closer observation we noticed that his eyes were dimmed from
age. He talked with us for some time, telling us among
other things, "I belong tuh Mr. Dave Bailey. He own
Woodbine Plantation. Muh granfathuh, his name wuz Jim.
He come ovuh tuh this country frum Africa. He tell me
that ovuh theah they have houses made of palmettuh.

"Then, ole Nanny Mammy, she live at the plantation too,
and she come frum Africa. She alluz set down tuh wuk;
no mattuh wut kine uh wuk, she set down tuh do it. Nanny
Mammy use tuh set down in the middle of the flo of uh house

* *Shadwick Rudolph, Folkston Road, near Woodbine.*

193

wen she go tuh eat an she alluz eat out of a wooden bowl. Sometimes she use a spoon, but mos of the time she jis eat with uh finguhs. Muh granfathuh use tuh set with uh an talk. They talk a lot an speak the African wuds an souns. I ain know wut they talk bout, mosly bout the times in Africa I think. One soun aw wud I membuh they say wuz 'cupla' but wut it mean I sho dohn know.

"Fuh the longes time I have a wooden bowl [70] bout lak the one Nanny Mammy have. It wuz holluhed out jis as smooth, an it wuz made of some kine uh dahk wood. Not long ago muh wife say she ain see da bowl in monuh yeah. She think mebbe one uh the chillun, muh grans I mean, mustuh misplace it someway.

"Theah's a lot uh things I membuh at the plantation. Muh grandmothuh, Sally, she make the bes rice cakes. She make em with brown shuguh. She ain mix em up with honey. I seed em make home-made drums theah too. They stretch a sheep-hide ovuh a roun bucket.[25] Then they beats the drum in the fewnul cession wen they mahches tuh the buryin groun.[24] Long then wen a pusson die they have a settin-up [37a] an have a suppuh too.[37b, c] Theah wuz an still is pussons wut put a dish uh food out on the poach fuh the spirit, but some of em take cooked food tuh the grave an leave it theah fuh the spirit.[58] They say, too, that a frizzle chicken kin dig up any kine uh cunjuh.[13] Theah's a lot uh talk bout cunjuh these days mung the young folks, even mo than in the ole days." [15]

A short while later, our interview concluded, we thanked the old man for the information and took our leave. Looking back we saw him sitting on the steps of his house, his gray head bent, to all appearances lost in a reverie of the past.

Appendix

◇◇◇◇◇◇◇◇◇◇◇◇◇

1. *Burial at home*

a *Basden says of the Ibo:* "The desire of every Ibo man and woman is to die in their own town or, at least, to be buried within its precincts. For a long period it was very difficult to persuade a man to travel any distance from his native place, and if he were in need of medical assistance an Ibo would seldom agree to go from home in spite of assurances that he would be able to have better treatment elsewhere. In case of death occurring at a distance, if it can be done at all, the brethren will bring the body home for burial. It may be that this cannot be done for several days, according to distance and other circumstances."
Among the Ibos of Nigeria, pp. 115–16.

b *Bosman says of the Coast of Guinea:* "The Negroes are strangely fond of being buried in their own Country; so that if any Person dies out of it, they frequently bring his Corpse home to be buried, unless it be too far distant."
Description of the Coast of Guinea, p. 232.

c *Meek says of Nigeria:* "When a man dies at a distance from his home his body is always taken back, when possible, to his home, wrapped up in mats covered by a cloth and placed on a bier or cradle, which is carried on the shoulders of his relatives. The reason assigned for this is that the dead must not be severed from the company of other ancestors—they should be buried close to their living descendants on whom they are dependent for nourishment. Moreover, it is important that the ritual traditional to the

kindred should be carried out accurately. This cannot be done by strangers."
Law and Authority in a Nigerian Tribe, p. 309.

d *Nassau says of the Bihe country:* "It is considered essential that a man should die in his own country, if not in his own town. On the way to Bailundu, shortly after leaving Bihe territory, I met some men running at great speed, carrying a sick man tied to a pole, in order that he might die in his own country."
Fetichism in West Africa, p. 228.

2. *Burial of sections of body*

a *Burton says of Gelele:* "Amongst the Egbas and various tribes of the Congo family . . . , various small parts of the body are brought home to be reinterred."
A Mission to Gelele, King of Dahome, II, 165.

b *Ellis says of the Gold Coast:* "*Toh-fo*, 'one lost' is a ceremony held when a person has met with death, and the body has either been destroyed or cannot be found; for instance, when a man has been burned to death and the body reduced to ashes, or when one has been drowned and the body cannot be recovered. . . . In the case of a man destroyed by fire, some of the ashes of the burned body, or of the house in which it was consumed, are placed in the coffin with similar ceremonies.

"In this ceremony a fragment of the corpse is always interred if possible; and, if no portion of it can be found, some earth, water, or other substance from the locality in which the death occurred."
The Tshi-Speaking Peoples of the Gold Coast of West Africa, p. 223.

3. *Burial of relatives and strangers*

a *Pearce says of West Africa:* "There is a strong feeling of kinship in Africa and only relatives may be buried in the same piece of ground together." (Interview with John Pearce of Hinesville, Ga., an ex-missionary in West Africa.)

4. *Caul*

a *Beckwith says of Jamaica:* "A baby born with a caul has
the power to see duppies without the duppies' harming him.
Parkes was born with a caul and attributed his frequent
visions of ghosts to this circumstance."
Black Roadways, p. 57.

b *Herskovits says:* "Born with a caul is significant in
Dahomey, West Africa, Dutch Guiana, Jamaica, and proba-
bly everywhere among the New World Negroes."
From correspondence dated October 10, 1938.

c *Peterkin says:* "Animals have 'second sight' and can see
spirits, but only people born with cauls over their faces have
this keen vision."
Roll, Jordan, Roll, p. 206.

d *Beckwith says:* "The caul is also connected with sym-
pathetic magic of a healing, rather than an injurious kind.
It should be removed and carefully parched over a hot brick
and a bit put into the baby's tea to prevent convulsions due
to the irritation of a ghost."
Black Roadways, p. 57.

e *Herskovits says of Haiti:* "A child born with a caul is believed to be strong in combating all evil spirits. The caul
is dried and reduced to powder, and the infant is given some
of the powder in water two or three days after birth."
Life in a Haitian Valley, p. 95.

f *Herskovits says of Dahomey:* "A child born with a caul—
'with a veil over its face'—who follows the first child after
twins, is called, if a boy Wusŭ, if a girl Wúmé. The child
born after such a one is called Wŭsâ or Wuhwê, according
to sex. If the child with the caul does not follow the first
child born after twins, then the names given are Kesŭ or
Kesî; the child who follows one of these is called Kesâ, if a
boy. No special name is given a girl born immediately after
a child with a caul."
Dahomey, I, 264.

5. *Charms, made of animals, insects*

a *Herskovits says of Dahomey:* "Thus from the earth, from trees and shrubs, from rocks, and from the bodies of animals and humans the Dahomean obtains materials for his *gbŏ*, while from the *Azizǎ* and other spirits of the forest, from Lεgbá, the Fá Group, Dạ, and the Great Gods, he obtained knowledge of how to endow them with effective power."
Dahomey, II, *287.*

b *Leonard says of West Africa:* "These are procured from or made with the spines of certain animals, porcupines more especially, compounded with potash, iron filings, and other inorganic matters, which are reduced to a powder. In this form they are supposed to be communicated invisibly with such celerity and exactness against a person, that blood poisoning supervenes."
The Lower Niger and Its Tribes, p. 500.

c *Melville and Frances Herskovits say of the Paramaribo Negro:* Fiofio, as envisaged in this belief, is the name of an insect and also of a spirit which, taking the shape of this insect, enters human bodies, causing illness and sometimes death. It comes as a result of family quarrelling which does not end in reconciliation. Strictly speaking, it is the extending of gestures of friendship or intimacy at a later date, when the bitterness of the quarrel has either passed or is masked, which brings on the illness. Such gestures of intimacy or friendship include accepting food that is offered, or a caress, or borrowing some kind of wearing apparel, or asking and receiving any other favor, and the resulting illness comes to either one or both of the persons who had participated in the quarrel."
Suriname Folk-Lore, p. 53.

6. *Charms, counter*

a *Farrow says of the Yoruba:* "The power of 'medicine' (*ogun*) exercised through a certain channel may be neutralised or overcome by a superior power of *ogun* through another channel. Van Gennep tells us that in Madagascar

fady (the local name for 'taboo') may be broken by one who has a higher power known as *hasina*. So in Yoruba, a stronger 'medicine' is employed to overcome, or counteract, an evil one, or a curse incurred through a broken *ewo* ('taboo'). This is the explanation of the use of 'charms,' whether material (as amulets), vocal, or actionary. It is the invocation of a higher power, or a fuller measure of the same power."
Faith, Fancies and Fetich, p. 121.

b *Herskovits says of Dahomey:* "Súkpíkpâ, *brings danger to another.* a. This *gbŏ* is essentially a 'counter' against sorcery. Actually, it demonstrates the principle which will be developed at greater length in the succeeding pages, that the line between good magic and bad magic is difficult to determine, since evil can be done by a charm otherwise good, if it is directed toward an evil end, and good by an evil charm, if properly handled. This *gbŏ* is called *agbą́ngba* 'outside'—and consists of a piece of wood first split in two, and then, after the ingredients are placed between the pieces, tied together with cord and fastened by passing the end through, and tying but not knotting it. One end is colored green. If a man who is strong in magic power is angry with the owner, and it is deemed likely that an attempt may be made to kill him with magic, the owner takes this charm, inserts it in the ground near his house, puts a stone on top of it and the evil magic is thereby not only prevented from becoming effective, but any evil attempted will rebound on him who has sent it."
Dahomey, ii, 269.

c *Melville and Frances Herskovits say of Dahomey:* "No matter how strong the magic, somewhere there is stronger magic which not only can overcome it, but may, in certain cases, turn back its effect on the person who invoked the original magic. This is true not only of evil charms, but of protective ones as well. Thus, we have in lengthy detail, information concerning a charm which a man buries in his field to protect it. Against this there is an evil 'counter'

which will not only allow its user to steal from the field, but brings evil on the rightful owner. Against this bad magic there is, in turn, an elaborate 'counter-counter,' which brings the thief to book."
An Outline of Dahomean Religious Belief, p. 65.

7. *Charms, foot-track*

a *Puckett says of the Gold Coast:* "On the Gold Coast it is believed that a man may be harmed by a 'medicine' made from the dust picked up from his foot-tracks. . . ."
Folk Beliefs of the Southern Negro, p. 220.

8. *Charms, general*

a *Brown says of the Bantu tribes:* "As the Bechuana believe that no misfortune befalls one naturally, but is always the effect of malevolence on the part of the living or the dead, so they also strongly believe that good fortune can only be maintained by means of charms."
Among the Bantu Nomads, p. 137.

b *Ellis says of the Ewe of West Africa:* "Magic powders are very numerous. One kind, when blown against a door or window, causes it to fly open, no matter how securely it may be fastened; another, when thrown upon the footprints of an enemy, makes him mad; a third, used in the same way, neutralizes the evil effects of the second; and a fourth destroys the sight of all who look upon it.

"Magic unguents (iro) are not uncommon. They and the powders are obtained from the priests, and must be rubbed on the body of the person who is to be influenced by them. Some are believed to compel a man to lend money, but their more common property is to constrain the unwilling fair to listen favourably to the amorous proposal."
The Ewe-Speaking Peoples of the Slave Coast of West Africa, p. 94.

c *Herskovits says:* "In Dahomey magic charms are sold by professional workers of magic."
Life in a Haitian Valley, p. 31.

d *Herskovits says of Dahomey:* "Magic charms form another type of personal property. As has been noted, these charms, which include herbs and other medicines, are held by tradition to have been revealed chiefly to hunters in the bush. When a hunter had learned how to make a given charm, or had been taught how to use a certain leaf to cure some disease, this knowledge was then his property and had salable value. When he was sought out for a charm to achieve a specific purpose—to protect a man on a journey, or to make of him a successful trader, or to insure the death of an enemy—if the hunter detailed the contents of the charm, how to put the ingredients together, the situation in which it would become effective and any formulae necessary to set it in operation, this knowledge then became the property of the purchaser as well as the vender. . . . To the professional dealers in charms, then, these comprise a stock in trade that is their property and potential wealth; for others, while the charms they own are property, they do not represent a source of income."
Dahomey, i, *81–82.*

e *Kingsley says of West Africa:* "Charms are made for every occupation and desire in life—loving, hating, buying, selling, fishing, planting, travelling, hunting, etc."
Travels in West Africa, p. 448.

f *Melville and Frances Herskovits say of the Suriname Negro:* "That is, people are spoken of as 'buying luck' or 'wearing luck,' and comments are heard about the importance of carrying one's 'luck' when walking alone at night, when going on a journey, when wooing a woman, or seeking work, or combating the effect of black magic."
Suriname Folk-Lore, p. 99.

g *Nassau says of the Gabun territory:* "For every human passion or desire of every part of our nature, for our thousand necessities or wishes, a fetich can be made, its operations being directed to the attainment of one specified wish, and limited in power only by the possible existence of some more powerful antagonizing spirits."
Fetichism in West Africa, p. 85.

201

h *Talbot says of the Ibibio tribes:* "Ibokk are, for the most part, made for defensive purposes, for protection against ill-wishers or evil messengers, but are sometimes procured from 'doctors' to harm an enemy."
Life in Southern Nigeria, p. 21.

i "There is what may be termed a 'white art' as well as a 'black art,' and the great majority of fetiches and charms are intended to *protect* from evil, and not to *attack* innocent folk."
The Geographical Journal, xxxi, *607.*

9. *Charms, graveyard dirt*

a *Pearce says of West Africa:* "Juju bags containing graveyard dirt and other material which had had a spell put upon it by juju are effective for either good or evil purposes. A bag of this sort worn around the neck, as a Catholic wears a scapula, serves as a protection from the spells of enemies. However, if a man wishes to work evil on his enemy, he may purchase a juju bag containing evil powder, and through it cast a spell on his enemy."
(Interview)

10. *Charms, hair and nails*

a *Ellis says of the Ewe:* "Hence it is usual for pieces of hair and nails to be carefully buried or burned, in order that they may not fall into the hands of sorcerers; and whenever a king or chief expectorates, the saliva is carefully gathered up and hidden or buried."
The Ewe-Speaking Peoples of the Slave Coast of West Africa, p. 99.

b *Meek says of the Jukun:* "Sorcerers also capture and injure or kill souls in a variety of ways, notably by acting on the hair, nail-parings or excreta of a person, the soul substance being regarded as immanent in these. If a person wishes to injure another he has merely to obtain a piece of his enemy's nails and hand them to a sorcerer, who, if he knows his work, will speedily cause the death of the former owner of the nail-parings. For this reason a Jukun always

hides or buries his hair and nail cuttings. Some Jukun burn these, but others would refrain from doing this on the ground that the burning would cause a scorching of his soul."
A Sudanese Kingdom, p. 298.

c *Milligan says of the Mpongwe:* "The parings of finger-nails, the hair of the victim and such things are powerful ingredients in these 'medicines.' An Mpongwe, after having his hair cut, gathers up every hair most carefully and burns it lest an enemy should secure it and use it to his injury. When sickness continues for a length of time they usually conclude that some offended relation has caused an evil spirit to abide in the town."
The Fetish Folk of West Africa, p. 39.

d *Nassau says of the Bantu:* "So fearful are natives of power being thus obtained over them, that they have their hair cut only by a friend; and even then they carefully burn it or cast it into a river."
Fetichism in West Africa, p. 83.

e *Nassau says of the Benga, the Mpongwe, and the Fang:* "If it be desired to obtain power over some one else, the oganga must be given by the applicant, to be mixed in the sacred compound, either crumbs from the food, or clippings of finger nails or hair, or (most powerful!) even a drop of blood of the person over whom influence is sought. These represent the life or body of that person."
Fetichism in West Africa, p. 83.

f *Nassau says of the Banita region:* "Sitting one day by a village boat-landing in the Banita region, about 1866, while my crew prepared for our journey, I was idly plucking at my beard, and carelessly flung away a few hairs. Presently I observed that some children gathered them up. Asking my Christian assistant what that meant, he told me: 'They will have a fetich made with those hairs; when next you visit this village, they will ask you for some favor, and you will grant it, by the power they will thus have over you."
Fetichism in West Africa, p. 83.

g *Nassau says of the West Coast natives:* "Lately a fellow missionary told me that in a conversation with certain natives, professed Christians, they admitted their fear lest their nail-clippings should be used against them by an enemy, and candidly acknowledged that when they pared their nails they threw the pieces on the thatch of the low roof of their house."
Fetichism in West Africa, p. 104.

h *Talbot says of the Ibibio tribes:* ". . . witches and wizards try to obtain hair, nail-clippings, or a piece of cloth long worn by the person whom they desire to injure."
Life in Southern Nigeria, p. 65.

i *"Ekanem, witness for prosecutor, stated on oath:* 'I remember Ofuo Afaha Eke telling me that Tomkpata had come to his mother in a dream and cut off some of her hair. So next day she went to him and said that he must restore her soul.' Ofuo Afaha Eke, sworn, stated: 'Tomkpata is my elder brother, I complained to him that my mother had dreamed a dream in which she saw him cut off her hair with scissors. From this we knew that he was trying to snare her soul.' "
Life in Southern Nigeria, p. 122.

11. *Charms and bad luck signs, house and property*

a *Burton says of Dahome:* "Every house has its 'fetish' hanging up, and every man has a 'fetish' charm about his person. There is a devil fetish for driving away evil spirits, and another for bringing good luck."
A Mission to Gelele, King of Dahome, ii, 361.

b *Ellis says of the Yoruba:* "An *onde* for the protection of the person is worn on the body, being tied round the wrist, neck, or ankle, or placed in the hair. Others, for the protection of property, are fastened to houses, or tied to sticks and stumps of trees in cultivated plots of ground. In consequence of their being tied on to the person or object they protect, the word *edi*, which really means the act of tying or binding, has now the meaning of amulet or charm, just as

in Ewe the word *vŏ-sesa* (amulet) is derived from *vŏ* and *sa*, to tie or bind."
The Yoruba-Speaking Peoples of the Slave Coast of West Africa, p. 118.

c *Farrow says of the Yoruba:* "Charms and amulets of various kinds are greatly used by the Yorubas. The Bale, or head-chief, of Ogbomosho, being of a particularly nervous and superstitious nature, had not only a number of tutelary gods guarding the threshold of his dwelling, but had laid in the ground, from one side of his compound to the other, chains and other charms to render each person who approached him powerless to do any evil. Charms for the protection of property are fastened to the houses, etc. They may consist of sticks, stumps of trees, etc."
Faith, Fancies and Fetich, p. 123.

d *Beckwith says:* "Other acts are to be avoided lest they pay the penalty of death to the immediate family. Never add to a house or cut down an old tree."
Black Roadways, p. 87.

12. *Charms, medicinal*

a *Delafosse says of the African in general:* "Belief . . . in the power of amulets and talismans is legendary among the Negroes. There is not one of them, whatever his religion, who does not wear on his body several 'gris-gris,' of which one is to preserve him from such and such a malady, a second from the evil eye."
Negroes of Africa, pp. 236–37.

b *Ellis says of the Yoruba:* "Another word sometimes used to express amulet is *ogun*, which, however, more properly means medicinal preparation, poison, or magical drug."
The Yoruba-Speaking Peoples of the Slave Coast of West Africa, p. 118.

c *Melville and Frances Herskovits say of the Bush Negro of Dutch Guiana:* "We had not been long in her hut before we noticed the iron arm-band she wore. It was, we knew, a '*tapu*'—a magical preventive which, in this instance,

warned its wearer of danger, and kept her from harm in a combat."
Rebel Destiny, p. 288.

d "Obia, then, is the spirit; obia is the preventive and curing agent; obias are the charms that are worn by people to help them."
Rebel Destiny, p. 321.

13. *Chicken and cock superstitions*

a *Herskovits says:* "Frizzled chickens are prized both in Africa and in the New World for their ability to find and scratch up evil magic buried against the owner."
From correspondence dated October 10, 1938.

b *Rattray says of Ashanti:* "A cock crowing at midnight or long before dawn is immediately killed, as it is considered unlucky."
Ashanti Proverbs, p. 80.

14. *Cicatrization*

a *Herskovits says of Dahomey:* "Another form which these positive injunctions take has to do with facial cuts, which vary from sib to sib. Thus the Adjalénû make no cuts at all. The Hwedánu who live in Whydah, make two cuts on each cheek. The Agblomenu, who are considered a group of autochthonous inhabitants of the plateau of Abomey, make three cuts on each side of the face, one on the temple called *àdjàkàsí* (tail of a rat), and two on the cheek, both in front of the ear. The Gedevĭ, another aboriginal group near Abomey, distinguish themselves by means of three cuts on each temple. At the present time all Dahomeans are supposed to have three cuts on the temple, though the Agblomenu have suppressed the two of these three and only cut the 'rat's tail.' "
Dahomey, I, 162.

b "Twelve sets of cuts constitute a complete cicatrization."
Dahomey, I, 292.

c "The last design is placed between the breasts, and often takes the form of a series of links or of straight lines radiating from a central point."
Dahomey, i, 295.

d *Livingstone says of South Africa:* "They mark themselves by a line of little raised cicatrices, each of which is a quarter of an inch long; they extend from the tip of the nose to the root of the hair on the forehead."
Missionary Travels and Researches in South Africa, p. 576.

15. *Conjure, illness and death*

a *Ellis says of the Yoruba:* "They consequently attribute sickness and death, other than death resulting from injury or violence, to persons who have for bad purposes enlisted the services of evil spirits, that is to say, to wizards and witches."
The Yoruba-Speaking Peoples of the Slave Coast of West Africa, p. 117.

b *Meek says of the Jukun:* "Sudden deaths, especially of young people, are usually regarded as the work of sorcerers (*ba-shiko* or *ba-shibu*). If the deceased had been noted for his disrespect to his seniors his death would be ascribed to offended ancestors, and he would go to his grave with 'bloodshot eyes'; but otherwise it is thought that one who had died suddenly had met his death by the foul means of witchcraft and would take vengeance in his own time."
A Sudanese Kingdom, pp. 223–24.

c *Milligan says of a Mpongwe tribe:* "Sickness and death, they believe, may be caused by fetish medicine, which need not be administered to the victim, but is usually laid beside the path where he is about to pass."
The Fetish Folk of West Africa, p. 39.

d *Nassau says of West Africa:* " 'According to native ideas, all over Africa, such a thing as death from natural causes does not exist. Whatever ill befalls a man or a family, it is always the result of witchcraft, and in every

case the witch-doctors are consulted to find out who has been guilty of it.' "
Fetichism in West Africa, p. 117.

e *Talbot says of the Ibibio tribes:* "When a man falls sick because his soul has gone forth and is being detained by an enemy, or when he believes that such an one is trying to entice it from out his body, he, in turn, goes to a Juju man known to have the power of seeing clearly."
Life in Southern Nigeria, p. 121.

f *Talbot says of the Yoruba:* "The Yoruba, like all other tribes here, considered that a large number of deaths was due to witchcraft or ill-will on the part of some enemy, and when many people died of famine or sickness, a general meeting was held and resort had to divination to find out the guilty persons, who were at once killed or offered in sacrifice to one of the Orisha."
The Peoples of Southern Nigeria, III, 474–75.

16. *"Daddy"*

a *Hutchinson says of the Ethiopian:* "The appellative 'Daddy' is used by the Africans as expressive of their respect as well as confidence."
Ten Years' Wanderings among the Ethiopians, p. 22.

17. *Dances, buzzard lope, etc.*

a *Cuney-Hare says of the Bushman:* "They possess a variety of dances pertaining to social customs, each of which has its appropriate chant. One dance imitates the actions of different animals."
Negro Musicians and Their Music, pp. 10–12.

b *Melville and Frances Herskovits say of the Bush Negro of Dutch Guiana:* "Those who danced for the buzzard had no machetes, but went about in a circle, moving with bodies bent forward from their waists and with arms thrown back in imitation of the bird from which their spirit took its name."
Rebel Destiny, p. 330.

c "Bush and town invoke the buzzard, *Opete,* so named in Ashanti, and sacred everywhere in West Africa. . . ."
Rebel Destiny, Preface, X.

d "The men were dancing to the great Kromanti spirits; the tiger-jaguar—and the buzzard, two of the three forms which the dreaded Kromanti *obia* can take. 'Obia! Huh! Huh!' one ejaculated, imitating the tiger, as his dancing became wilder and wilder."
Rebel Destiny, p. 17.

18. *Dances, funerals*

a *Moore says of a Mandingo funeral:* "They begin with Crying, and at Night they go to Singing and Dancing, and continue so doing till the Time they break up and depart."
Travels Into the Inland Parts of Africa, p. 130.

b *Rattray says of Ashanti:* "People from a far place who were related to the deceased and people from towns near by, also form their own companies. They dance the war-dances in the morning, and at 'the mouth' of evening, when the sun is slanting, they circle the grave. It is now that the corpse is taken to the grave."
The Tribes of the Ashanti Hinterland, p. 194.

19. *Dances, religious significance*

a *Rattray says of Ashanti:* "Dancing in Africa invariably has a religious significance."
Religion and Art in Ashanti, p. 184.

b *Talbot says of the Sudanese tribes:* "Among Nigerians, however, it would appear that the god was not evolved out of the dance, but was there first and the dance was developed as a method of worship, of attaining union with him, and of exerting an influence with *his help* on the fertility of men and of crops."
The Peoples of Southern Nigeria, III, 803.

20. *Day names*

a *Beckwith says of Jamaica:* "According to an old custom recorded from the African Gold Coast, every child receives at birth a name depending on the day of the week on which it is born.

> *Friday*   Cuffee   (Coo-fee)"

Black Roadways, p. 59.

b *Ellis says of the Tshi-Speaking native:* "Every child, from the moment of birth, is given a name which is derived from the day of the week on which it is born."
The Tshi-Speaking Peoples of West Africa, p. 219.

c *Rattray says of Ashanti:* "As soon as it is born, all the old women shout, 'Hail so-and-so,' at once naming the infant after that particular day of the week upon which it is born. This name, which is sometimes called 'God's name,' will ever after be the child's natal day name. To this, as will be noted presently, will later be added a patronymic, and possibly later on in life one or more 'strong names' (*mmerane*)."
Religion and Art in Ashanti, pp. 56–57.

21. *Days, lucky and unlucky*

a *Ellis says of the Tshi-Speaking native:* "There are national and tribal lucky and unlucky days, and individuals also have days which they consider lucky and unlucky for themselves. Kwoffi Karikari considered Thursday an unlucky day, and would never commence any undertaking on a Thursday. Kidjo Monday, which falls early in February, is considered by the Ashantis the luckiest day of the year. Their most unlucky day is the anniversary of the Saturday on which Osai Tutu was slain in an ambush near Acromanti in 1731."
The Tshi-Speaking Peoples of the Gold Coast of West Africa, p. 220.

22. *Diviners, Divining, Seed Casting, Etc.*

a *Delafosse says:* "Numerous fortune-tellers predict the future and reveal hidden things, by means of processes,

many of which strangely resemble those which our own clairvoyants employ."
Negroes of Africa, p. 237.

b *Herskovits says of Dahomey:* "A third type, called *agɔ̃kwíka*, employed two magically treated *agô* seeds tied to the ends of a cord long enough to go about the neck of the accused, and the seeds were buried lightly in the ground. Such was the spiritual power in these seeds, that if the accused was guilty of the crime, he could not remove them from the ground; if he succeeded in rising, he was declared innocent."
Dahomey, ii, 18.

c "In this myth, not only is the explanation found of how the prevalent system of divination came to man, but the principal outlines of the practices which characterize the Fá cult are to be discerned—that is, the sixteen palm-kernels employed in throwing the lots, the sixteen combinations in which they may fall, and which foretell the future. . . ."
Dahomey, ii, 206.

d "The details of this system by means of which the future is foretold may now be considered. In essence, Fá is based on the interpretation, by reference to appropriate myths, of the permutations and combinations obtained by the diviner when he manipulates the sixteen palm-kernels he employs for this purpose. Before him as he works lies a rectangular wooden tray, on which powdered white clay or meal has been sprinkled. In one hand he holds his sixteen palm-kernels, and with great rapidity brings the hand which holds them into the palm of the other one, leaving either one or two seeds for an instant before they are once more picked up and the process is repeated. As soon as he has glimpsed the one or two kernels in his left hand, the right, with the palm-kernels, closes down upon it and the two clasp the seeds. The index and second fingers of the right hand are, however, left free and with these he describes

211

marks in the white powder on the board in front of him. Moving his fingers away from him, he makes a double line for each single kernel, a single line if two seeds are left. The process is repeated eight times for a complete reading." *Dahomey,* II, *209–10.*

e *Rattray says of the Ashanti:* "The soothsayer, oracle man, or diviner, as will be seen presently, takes a leading part in the everyday life of these people. He is consulted on almost every conceivable occasion. Hardly anything can be done until he has been asked. He is really a *medium,* a 'go-between' in the land of the living and the world of spirit ancestors. The root of the word used to describe this person is generally the same as that found in the word for shrine. The people consult him at some shrine, the spirit in which guides him and directs his answers."
The Tribes of the Ashanti Hinterland, I, *44.*

23. *Drums*

a *Melville and Frances Herskovits say of the Paramaribo Negro:*

"Drums are the most important instruments in both Town and Bush, and the drummers, in these as in all Negro cultures, achieve a virtuosity of performance and an intricacy of rhythm that come of long practice. It was impossible to obtain satisfactory recordings of drumming which would reveal the complexity of these rhythm-patterns, chiefly because, lacking electrical recording apparatus, the inner rhythms which in combination give a steady beat are lost, and only the points where the notes of the several instruments coincide can be discerned.

"The drums have more than a musical significance in this culture. Tradition assigns to them the threefold power of summoning the gods and the spirits of the ancestors to appear, of articulating the messages of these supernatural beings when they arrive, and of sending them back to their habitats at the end of each ceremony. Both in Town and in

the Bush, the dancers who are the worshippers,—one of the most important expressions of worship is dancing—face the drums and dance toward them, in recognition of the voice of the god within the instruments."
Suriname Folk-Lore, pp. 520–21.

b *Milligan says of the West African:* "The fact is, however, that the only one of his musical instruments which the African regards with profound respect is his dearly beloved *tom-tom*—the drum to which he dances."
The Fetish Folk of West Africa, p. 77.

24. *Drums, funeral*

a *Herskovits says of Dahomey:* "Outside the house the funerary zɛ̀li, a pottery drum, is played day and night. The drummers are the members of the *dókpwê* of the quarter where the dead man lived, or if he was a villager, of his village, and it is the head of this *dókpwê* who is the commanding *dókpwégâ* at the funeral."
Dahomey, I, 355.

b *Melville and Frances Herskovits say of the Bush Negro of Dutch Guiana:* "That night whenever we stirred in our sleep we strained for the sound of the drums, but the wind blew from the east, and though Gankwe, where the dead man lay in state, was but a ten-minute run down the rapids, we could hear nothing. In the morning, however, we heard them plainly, heard the invocations drummed by the grave diggers on their way to the burial ground deep in the bush on the opposite bank."
Rebel Destiny, p. 3.

c *Livingstone says of South Africa:* "Drums were beating over the body of a man who had died the preceding day, and some women were making a clamorous wail at the door of his hut, and addressing the deceased as if alive. The drums continued beating the whole night, with as much regularity as a steam-engine thumps, on board ship."
Missionary Travels and Researches in South Africa, p. 467.

25. *Drums, manufacture of*

a *DuPuis says of Ansah:* "The large drums were carried on the heads of men, and beaten in that posture; but the small ones were slung as kettle drums. These added to calabashes and gourds filled with shot or small stones, concave bits of iron, and striking sticks, will give an idea of the national taste in harmonic matters."
Journal of a Residence in Ashantee, p. 43.

b *Ellis says of the Gold Coast:* "Drums are made of the hollowed sections of trunks of trees, with a goat's or sheep's skin stretched over one end. They are from one foot to four feet high, and vary in diameter from about six to fourteen inches. Two or three drums are usually used together, each drum producing a different note, and they are played either with the fingers or with two sticks. The lookers-on generally beat time by clapping the hands."
The Tshi-Speaking Peoples of the Gold Coast of West Africa, p. 326.

c *Herskovits says of Haiti:* "Drums, iron, and rattles are indispensable for a *vodun* dance. The drums, of the characteristic hollow-log African type, tuned with pegs inserted in the sides and reinforced with twine wound about the stretched heads of cow-hide or goat-skin, are played in batteries of three, the largest being called *manman*, the middle the *seconde*, and the smallest the *bula*."
Life in a Haitian Valley, pp. 181–82.

d *Herskovits says of Dahomey:* "Generally the drums are of the usual African type, made of a hollowed-out log with a more or less crudely carved foot, its head of animal skin being attached to pegs inserted into the body of the drum, just below its upper end. The drum-head is tightened by driving these pegs into the drum until the required note is sounded, since by this method the skin is stretched to produce the desired tone. Ordinarily the attachment of the head to the pegs is by means of strips of the skin itself; in some forms, however, a cord attachment is used. A small barrel drum, the only one of its kind observed, about eight-

een inches high and twelve inches in diameter, and which does not have a foot, is used in the Sagbatá rites. The other more conventional drums range from two feet in size to a length of five feet and more."
Dahomey, II, *318.*

e *Moore says of the Mandingo:* ". . . with him came two or three Women, and the same Number of Mundingo Drums, which are about a Yard long, and a Foot, or twenty Inches diameter at the Top, but less at the Bottom, made out of a solid Piece of Wood, and covered, only at the widest End, with the Skin of a Kid. They beat upon them with only one Stick, and their left Hand, to which the Women will dance very briskly."
Travels Into the Inland Parts of Africa, p. 64.

f *Ward says of the Bakongo country:* "The natives were drumming on a goat-skin stretched tightly across the mouth of a hollowed-out log, and dancing round a fire lighted in their midst, one man singing a refrain, while others took up the chorus ; and the mingled sound of the voices and the distant beating of other drums in neighboring villages helped to keep me awake."
Five Years with the Congo Cannibals, p. 68.

g *Beckwith says:* "The beating of the gombay drum is a familiar accompaniment of death."
Black Roadways, p. 83.

26. *Drum Messages*

a *Rattray says of Ashanti:* "A great deal is heard in Africa about the wonderful way in which news can be passed on over great distances in an incredibly short space of time. It has been reported that the news of the fall of Khartum was known among the natives of Sierra Leone the same day, and other equally wonderful instances are quoted to show that the native has some extraordinary rapid means of communicating important events. It must, however, be remembered that most of the instances that one hears quoted are incapable of verification, and would, moreover, probably be found to have been much exaggerated. Having said this much, however, it must be admitted that these natives have a means of intercommunication which often inspires wonder and curiosity on the part of Europeans. One of such means of communication is by drumming.

"This idea the European will readily grasp, and being familiar with various means of *signalling*, will suppose that some such a method might be adapted to drums; but among the Ashantis the drum is not used as a means of *signalling* in the sense that we would infer, that is by rapping out words by means of a prearranged code, but (to the native mind) is used to sound or speak the actual words."
Ashanti Proverbs, pp. 133–34.

b "I first became interested in this difficult subject many years ago. At that time it was generally known that the Ashanti, in common with certain other West Coast peoples, were able to convey messages over great distances and in an incredibly short space of time by means of drums, and it was thought that their system was based upon some such method as that with which Europeans are familiar in the Morse code."
Ashanti, p. 242.

27. *Earrings*

a *Beckwith says of the Jamaica Negro:* "Parkes says that men who 'deal in spirits' wear a red flannel shirt, or a crosspiece of red under their ordinary clothes, and generally gold earrings. Not all men who wear earrings are Obeah Men; fishermen, for example, generally wear one earring. The gold is said to 'brighten their eyes to see ghosts,' but also a gold earring is put on to improve the natural sight."
Black Roadways, p. 108.

28. *Earth thrown in grave*

a *Brown says of the Bantu Nomad, (the Bechuana):* "A pit is dug and into it the body is lowered in the sitting position. The grave is then filled in, each person present slowly

pouring earth onto the body and around it with their hands until the grave is full."
Among the Bantu Nomads, p. 67.

b *Meek says of Nigeria:* "Loose earth is then thrown in on the body, together with the mat and cloth. Even very young sons must throw in a little earth, as evidence that they had taken a share in their father's burial rites. The last handfuls are thrown in with the back turned to the grave, as a sign that they had finished with the dead man."
Law and Authority in a Nigerian Tribe, pp. 307–08.

29. *Echo of speech*

a *Herskovits says of Haiti:* "With the benediction, the *action de grâce* came to an end, and the solemn, tired voice of the *prêt savanne* was heard intoning a hymn, which, in the usual fashion, was repeated by the assembled group until, without interlude, without even a pause, the interpolations of the chorus gradually changed, so that the rhythm became African, and, with the transition, the *vodun* priest took over the leadership. The *hungan* began by repeating several times the phrase which throughout the entire ceremony was to punctuate all its climaxes, '*Grâce* [et] mise'corde,' and the family murmured it in response."
Life in a Haitian Valley, p. 161.

30. *Farewell to corpse (spoken to)*

a *Melville and Frances Herskovits say of the Bush Negro of Dutch Guiana:* "Now the ceremony was drawing to a close, and the leave takings were to be said. . . . Distinctly the low voice of Sedefo came to us as he addressed the corpse:

> '*The hour has come when we must part from you. What the Earth has decreed we cannot help. We have done for you what we could. We have given you a funeral worthy of you. You must care for us, and you must deliver us from all evil that may come upon us.*'"
Rebel Destiny, p. 18.

31. *Farewell to corpse (touched)*

a *Pearce says of the Gold Coast of West Africa:* "The mourners sit around the body with their hands upon it, and chant a farewell dirge."

32. *Fig, sacred*

a *Rattray says of Ashanti:* "The chief here—in answer to my question—said that the fig tree was a famous sanctuary, and that any one sentenced to death who escaped there would be safe."
Ashanti, pp. 128–29.

33. *Folk Tales*

a *Rattray says of Hausa folk tales:* "Stories and traditions collected through the medium of an interpreter are amusing, and might prove of interest in the nursery, though much would have to be omitted or toned down, as savage folk-lore is often coarse and vulgar according to our notions."
Hausa Folk-Lore Customs, Proverbs, Etc., i, *Author's Note,* xi.

34. *Forest-dwelling forces*

a *Farrow says of the Yoruba:* "Certain trees are particularly sacred. The silk-cotton tree (Yoruba *peregun*) is highly venerated throughout West Africa 'from the Senegal to the Niger,' probably because of its majestic appearance, for it is of little utility, the timber being soft, and its cotton possessing neither strength nor durability. This tree often grows to a stupendous height, approximating 300 feet, far out-topping all other trees of the forest."
Faith, Fancies and Fetich, p. 16.

b *Herskovits says of Dahomey:* "The psychological liaison between the gods and magic, however, is revealed in the character of the semi-divine spirits who are believed to people the forest—Mínonâ, Hoho, the *abikŭ* and the *azizą*."
Dahomey, ii, *260.*

c *Kingsley says of the Bantu tribes:* "In some part of the long single street of most villages there is built a low hut in which charms are hung, and by which grows a consecrated plant, a lily, a euphorbia, or a fig."
Travels in West Africa, p. 452.

d *Leonard says of Southern Nigeria:* "Groves and woods, and those portions of the bush close to every town which are reserved as burial-grounds, are considered sacred and worship is paid to either the spirits or the deities who inhabit or preside over them."
The Lower Niger and Its Tribes, p. 298.

35. *Fowl, sacrifice of*

a *Ellis says of the Yoruba:* "After this invitation to be gone, the fowl, called *adire-iranna*, is sacrificed, which, besides securing a right-of-way for the soul, is supposed also to guide it. The feathers of the fowl are scattered around the house, and the bird itself carried out to a bush-road, where it is cooked and eaten."
The Yoruba-Speaking Peoples of the Slave Coast of West Africa, p. 160.

b *Leyden says of the Mandingo territory:* "The journey was marked by nothing remarkable, except the sacrifice of a white chicken, which was offered by Johnson, the interpreter, to the spirits of the woods, described as a powerful race of white beings, with long flowing hair."
Historical Account of Discoveries and Travels in Africa, I, 339.

c *Meek says of Nigeria:* "The next rite is known as Eku-ibu-ocha, a phrase which seems to mean 'Making the face (of the dead man) white (*i.e.* radiant).' Women of the deceased's family bring a cock fastened to a string of cowries and one of the women who is considered especially lucky (*e.g.* whose children are all alive), or some person previously indicated by the deceased, holds or hangs the cock over the dead man's head. When the cock shakes its wings (a sign of acceptance by the deceased), it is taken out and hung at

the door of the hut or on a branch of an *oterre* tree in the compound. After a while it is taken down and its neck is drawn, the blood being allowed to drip on to the ground at the threshold. The fowl is then cooked and eaten by the female relatives. The intention in leaving the fowl hung up is, apparently, to give the deceased time to see and receive the offering."
Law and Authority in a Nigerian Tribe, pp. 303–04.

d *Rattray says of Ashanti:* "The eldest son supplies a sheep and a fowl which are killed in the yard of the compound (*dundon*) and grain-food is prepared which is called *sanfana* (in Dagomba, *sore segam*, literally 'food for the road'). The sextons and others attending the funeral partake of this food, and a portion of the grain-food and a leg of the fowl are also placed in a calabash which is set down in the room where the corpse had been laid prior to interment."
The Tribes of the Ashanti Hinterland, II, 460–61.

36. *Funeral, proper observance*

a *Ellis says of the Yoruba:* "It is considered the greatest disgrace to a family not to be able to hold the proper ceremonies at the death of one of their number, a notion which is comprehensible when we remember how much the welfare of the soul of the deceased is supposed to depend upon their performance. Hence families not unfrequently reduce themselves almost to beggary in order to carry them out, or pawn or sell their children to raise the money necessary."
The Yoruba-Speaking Peoples of the Slave Coast of West Africa, p. 161.

b *Leonard says of the Ibo:* "All Ibo place great faith in the due and proper observance of the funeral ceremony, for they are of the opinion that it enables the soul to go to God and to find its final destination, and that without this sacred rite the soul is prevented by the other spirits from eating, or in any way associating with them, and in this manner, from entering into the Creator's presence. So in this way it becomes an outcast and a wanderer on the face of the earth,

haunting houses and frequently burial grounds, or is forced perhaps to return to this world in the form or body of some animal."
The Lower Niger and Its Tribes, p. 142.

c *Meek says of Nigeria:* "The spirit of a dead Ibo is considered to hover round his home, or wander aimlessly in the underworld, until the final funeral rites have been performed."
Law and Authority in a Nigerian Tribe, p. 314.

d *Milligan says of the Mpongwe of Gaboon:* "The spirit of the deceased knows all that is going on and is supposed to be very sensitive in regard to the amount of mourning and the details of the funeral."
The Fetish Folk of West Africa, p. 148.

37. *Funerals, wakes—importance, social activity*

a *Herskovits says of Dahomey:* "A death-watch is now provided to see to it that the body is not left unattended. This watch is kept with rigid care, especially when the body is in the hands of the members of the *dókpwê* who actually carry out the ritual of the funeral. This is because of the opportunity a corpse affords anyone who is desirous of obtaining the means for working magic by capturing the soul of the deceased, since a bit of the dead man's cloth, or, better still, some of his hair or nail-parings might easily be taken and used to this end. Furthermore, with such material, or with a cloth placed inside the mouth of the corpse to absorb some of the moisture remaining there, charms of great power and therefore great value could be made."
Dahomey, I, 353.

b *Leonard says of the Ibo and other tribes:* "Although the death of a man is in reality a great loss to his household or even to the community, the occasion of his obsequies is regarded as an event of great entertainment to the community at large. It is looked upon as a circumstance in which the family honour is concerned in a distinctly two fold sense, affecting its reputation in this world as well as in the next.

For the reception of the soul of the deceased in spiritland and his final prestige are altogether dependent on the grandeur and liberality of the human entertainment."
The Lower Niger and Its Tribes, pp. 157–58.

c *Talbot says of the Sudanese tribes:* "A wake invariably takes place, the duration and grandeur of which depend upon the wealth of the family. Animals—including cows if these can be afforded—are slain in profusion, while palm wine and gin are provided in plenty, and in old days, rum. Cannons and guns are fired off to give notice to the ghosts that a 'big man' is coming, and plays are performed by the clubs and societies of which the deceased was a member. In fact, funerals provide the best opportunity for festivals, 'plays,' dances and performances in general."
The Peoples of Southern Nigeria, III, 473.

38. *Harvest festivals*

a *Ellis says of the Tshi-Speaking native:* "Yam, or Harvest Festivals.—These appear to be festivals held for the purpose of returning thanks to the gods for having protected the crop. There are apparently two; one held in September, when the yam crop is ripe, and another, called *Ojirrah*, in December, when it is planted. A minor festival, called *Affi-neh-dzea-fi*, which is held in April, appears, however, to be of the same nature. The September festival lasts a fortnight, and is commenced by a loud beating of drums. It is called by the Ashantis *Appatram*, and no new yam may be eaten by the people till the close of the festival."
The Tshi-Speaking Peoples of the Gold Coast of West Africa, p. 229.

b *Meek says of Nigeria:* "Public sacrifice to Ala may be offered periodically at the beginning of the agricultural season, before clearing new land, or after clearing old, before planting yams, or at the end of the yam harvest.
Law and Authority in a Nigerian Tribe, p. 26.

c *Rattray says of Ashanti:* "There appear to be at least three great festivals which are held by the Talense in connexion with the crops and harvest."
The Tribes of the Ashanti Hinterland, ii, *358–59.*

d *Talbot says of the Ibibio tribes:* "At the time of new yam planting, people came from far and near to beg protection and increase for their crops and herds. On such occasions the brow of the chief priest is bound with a fillet of white cloth, which may not be taken off till the time of sacrifice comes round again. He marks all the people with white chalk, as a sign that they have attended the festival and asked the blessing of the genius of the pool."
Life in Southern Nigeria, p. 38.

39. *Hoe, magic*

a *Rattray repeats a Hausa folk tale:* "When he struck one blow on the ground with the hoe, then he climbed on the hoe and sat down, and the hoe started to hoe, and fairly flew until it had done as much as the hoers. It passed them, and reached the boundary of the furrow."
Hausa Folk-Lore Customs, Proverbs, Etc., i, *74–76.*

b *Rattray tells an Ashanti folk tale:* "The Hoe turned over a huge tract (of land). Then they stopped work and went off, and the Porcupine took the hoe and hid it. And Kwaku, the Spider, saw (where he put it). He said, 'This hoe that I have seen, to-morrow very, very early I shall come and take it to do my work.' Truly, very, very, very early, the Spider went and got it; he took to his farm. Now, the Spider did not know how to make it stop, and he raised his song:

'Gyensaworowa, Kotoko, saworowa.
Gyensaworowa, Kotoko, saworowa,
Gyensaworowa.'

And the Hoe, when it commenced hoeing, continued hoeing. And it hoed until it came too far away. Now it reached the Sea-god's water. Thence it came to the Land of White-men-far, and the White men took it, and looked at it, and made

others (like it). That is how many (European) hoes came among the Ashanti. Formerly it was only Kotoko, the Porcupine, who had one."
Akan-Ashanti Folk-Tales, p. 43.

40. *Hog, sacrifice of*

a *Beckwith says of Jamaica:* "When they come to the Grave, which is generally made in some Savannah or Plain, they lay down the Coffin, or whatever the Body happens to be wrapt up in; and if he be one whose Circumstances could allow it (or if he be generally liked, the Negroes contribute among themselves) they sacrifice a Hog."
Dark Roadways, p. 79.

41. *Images*

a *Cruickshank says of the Gold Coast of Africa:* "They also mould images from clay, and bake them. We have seen curious groups of these in some parts of the country. Upon the death of a great man, they make representations of him, sitting in state, with his wives and attendants seated around him."
Eighteen Years on the Gold Coast of Africa, p. 270.

b *Ellis says of the Ewe:* "The head is sometimes of wood, rising like a cone; the mouth extends from ear to ear, and is garnished with the teeth of dogs, or with cowries to represent teeth; the eyes are also represented by cowries. The arms of the figure are invariably immensely long, while the legs are short and the feet large."
The Ewe-Speaking Peoples of the Slave Coast of West Africa, p. 42.

c *Guillaume and Munro say:* "He is especially fond of giving a flashing regard to the eyes by inserting beads, shells, stones or bits of metal."
Primitive Negro Sculpture, p. 29.

d "Constructed like a building of solid blocks, a typical negro statue is itself a solid, a full, substantial block, set with convincing, massive reality in its own space. Its effect

does not depend, as that of much other sculpture does, on elaborate superficial decoration scratched upon a weak and vaguely realized mass. There is rarely a sense of overdecoration or pretense, a feeling of inner rottenness, as though, one could squash the whole fabric between the hands, or scrape off its ornaments at a stroke. Surface decorations there may be in profusion, but they are based upon a firm foundation and integrated with it, to form an unyielding and immovable structure."
Primitive Negro Sculpture, p. 37.

e *Kingsley says of the West African:* "He cuts from a tree a moderately thick branch which he carves into a rude resemblance of the human figure; usually these figures are simply cylindrical pieces of wood, from ten to fourteen inches in length and from three to four in diameter. Two or three inches from one end, which may be called the top, the stick is notched so as to roughly resemble a neck, and the top is then rounded to bear some rough distant resemblance to a head."
Travels in West Africa, p. 510.

f *Leonard says of the Ibo and other tribes:* "It is quite impossible to understand the spiritual conception and the god-idea of these natives unless we possess a knowledge of that peculiarly personal system of society out of which it has evolved and developed; and we recognise that the gods are but the shadows or spirits, so called, of mortals. They are rude but perfect pictures of the very worshippers in whose own human image they have been either kneaded out of clay or carved out of wood."
The Lower Niger and Its Tribes, p. 433.

g "Not so the barbarian, however. With him the Ju-Ju or emblem is no child's play, no mere outlet for a state of activity which he is not particularly desirous of, not even a safety-valve by which the accumulated steam of his pent-up emotions might escape, but a matter of life and death, connecting, as it does, one to the other, *i.e.* himself and household to the household in the spirit. To natural man this grotesque image of clay or wood is no mere toy, no senseless figure, that he moulds or carves for amusement during his hours of leisure, simply to kill time with.

"So this bundle of repressed but irrespressible emotions appeals to his household doll, as to an association—not in a merely abstract but in a personal sense, as a lifelong association, to which, connected and related as he is, from a twofold aspect, he is doubly bound. He appeals to it, as to a familiar object, embodying, as it does, his familiar and guardian spirit, not because he merely thinks or hopes this to be so, but because in all sincerity he feels and believes it to be the case. More than this, because he believes it to be the spirit of his father or grandfather, who, in accordance with the divine instructions, occupies the position of communicator and mediator between the human and spiritual households."
The Lower Niger and Its Tribes, p. 384–85.

h "Small figures and images, such as are mentioned above, purporting and believed by the natives to contain the spirits of the defunct, and occupying exactly the same status as the Aryan 'Pitris' or 'Fathers' and the Roman Lares and Penates, are also made and venerated by all the Delta tribes. Food and liquid offerings are regularly placed on graves or at the monuments erected, or the symbols that have just been referred to, for the use of the departed spirits."
The Lower Niger and Its Tribes, p. 183.

i *Rattray says of Ashanti:* "The priestly class and the *sumankwafo*, the doctors in *suman*, demanded for their professional purposes figures in human or animal forms; this resulted in the carving of *Sasabonsam, mmoatia* and, finally, human figures; in all of these the genius of the people found an outlet for latent artistic talent."
Religion and Art in Ashanti, p. 269.

42. *Memorial (second funeral)*

a *Farrow says of the Yoruba:* "In June of each year the Annual Egun festival is held, for seven days. It is the Yo-

ruba 'All Souls' festival, when mourning is repeated for all those who have died during the last few years. Egungun is specially powerful in Ibadan, even as Oro is in Abeokuta."
Faith, Fancies and Fetich, pp. 79–80.

b *Leonard says of the Ibo and other tribes:* "The Lamentation or Second Burial.—This is conducted on much the same lines as the first, except that a greater entertainment is provided and the expenses incurred are heavier.

"In a spiritual sense, however, the rite is one of infinitely greater importance, because it is a special memorial service held over the deceased in order to release him from the thraldom of the region of the dead in which all souls are confined, where they exist on leaves or grass just like the brute beasts, and to usher him triumphantly, as befits his birth, into the abode of his fathers in the world of spirits.
"For the universal belief on this point is that no human soul can attain to the peaceful ancestral habitations without this rite of second burial. Hence the great aversion shown by a community towards those who fail to observe this holy sacrament."
The Lower Niger and Its Tribes, pp. 159–60.

c *Meek says of Nigeria:* "The Ekwa-Ozu rites are commonly referred to in English as 'The Second Burial,' though there is no apparent reason for the use of this expression.
"The responsibility for performing the rites falls mainly on the principal heir, who should endeavour to carry them out within a year of the dead man's death. But the period may be extended, if the deceased's family has been unable to find the necessary means, and cases have occurred of the final funeral rites being postponed for as much as ten or twenty years."
Law and Authority in a Nigerian Tribe, p. 314.

d *Talbot says of the Ibibio tribes:* "This first burial, generally called Mkpa Owo, is followed, from six months to two years later, by the Ewonga or Usiak Ekkpo, the second burial, with which the obsequies are completed and without

which the deceased is thought to be unable to take his proper position in the realm of the dead."
Life in Southern Nigeria, p. 142.

43. *Mortars*

a *Monteiro says of Angola:* "These mortars are made of soft wood, mostly of the cotton wood tree, which is easily cut with a knife; for scooping out the interior of the mortars the natives use a tool made by bending round about an inch of the point of an ordinary knife, which they call a "locombo."
Angola and the River Congo, p. 167.

44. *Owl, hooting of*

a *Ellis says of the Vais:* "The Vais consider the owl the king of all witches. They believe that some old king transformed himself into the owl and became the king of witchcraft. The owl is called húhu. Whenever the cry of this bird is heard they tremble with fear. It is said when an owl sits upon a home at least one of its inmates is sure to die."
Negro Culture in West Africa, p. 66.

b *Nassau says of West Africa:* "Then, concerning owls; see that your camp at night is not disturbed by the cry of the Kulu (spirit of the departed), that warns you that one of you is going to die."
Fetichism in West Africa, pp. 195–96.

45. *Palm cabbage, palm wine*

a *Bridge says of the West Coast of Africa:* "Palm wine is the sap of the tree; and its top furnishes a most delicious dish, called palm-cabbage. The trunk supplies fire-wood and timber for building fences. From the fibres of the wood is manufactured a strong cordage, and a kind of native cloth; and the leaves, besides being used for thatching houses, are converted into hats. If nature had given the inhabitants of Africa nothing else, this one gift of the palm-tree would have included food, drink, clothing, and habitation,

and the gratuitous boon of beauty, into the bargain."
Journal of an African Cruiser, p. 106.

b *Burton says of Gelele:* "The palm, after being felled, is
allowed to lie for a couple of days, the cabbage is removed
for food, and in its place a pipe, generally a bit of papaw-
stalk, conducts the sap into the calabash below. At times,
to make the juice flow more freely, a lighted stick is thrust
into the hole, which is afterwards scraped clear of charred
wood. This "toddy" is the drink of the maritime regions,
where it is most impudently watered, and we shall not taste
it beyond the Agrime swamp."
A Mission to Gelele, King of Dahome, i, pp. 128–29.

46. *Possession*

a *Basden says of the Ibo:* "The more one listens to native
music, the more one is conscious of its vital power. It
touches the chords of man's inmost being, and stirs his
primal instincts. It demands the performer's whole attention and so sways the individual as almost to divide asunder,
for the time being, mind and body. . . . Under its influence,
and that of the accompanying dance, one has seen men and
women pass into a completely dazed condition, oblivious and
apparently unconscious of the world around them."
Among the Ibos of Nigeria, p. 192.

b *Ellis says of the Gold Coast:* "The drums strike up, and
the priest commences his dance, leaping, bounding, and turning and twisting round and round, until he works himself into
a real or simulated condition of frenzy, with foam dropping
from the mouth, and eyes wildly rolling."
*The Tshi-Speaking Peoples of the Gold Coast of West
Africa, p. 125.*

c *Ellis says of the town of Forhudzi:* "A god was beginning
to take possession of him. . . . In the meantime the trem-
bling increased, and soon the priest was shuddering as if in
an ague fit. Every portion of his body seemed to shake; the
head, arms, legs, abdomen, and pectoral muscles, all quiver-

ing violently. He leaned forward and appeared to be endeavoring to vomit, doubtless to give the idea that his body was struggling to expel the god which was now supposed to possess him. A little foam appeared on his lips, and from time to time saliva fell on the ground. Next, with open mouth and protruding tongue, and with eyes wildly rolling, he worked himself, still seated and quivering violently, into the middle of the arena."
The Tshi-Speaking Peoples of the Gold Coast of West Africa, p. 132.

d *Herskovits says of Haiti:* "Fundamentally, to be possessed by a *loa* means that an individual's spirit is literally dispossessed by that of the god. Personalities undergo radical change in accordance with the nature of the deity, while even the sex of the one possessed is disregarded if it differs from that of the god, so that, for example, a woman 'mounted' by Ogun is always addressed as Papa Ogun. One wears the colors of the god and the ornaments he likes, eating and drinking those things he prefers, and otherwise manifesting his peculiar characteristics—rolling on the earth, if possessed by Damballa or chattering incessantly if by Gede."
Life in a Haitian Valley, p. 146.

e *Leonard says of the Ibo and other tribes:* "This possession by spirits, although not confined to any particular tribe or tribes in the Delta, is said to be much more common among the Ijo and Brassmen, and women are afflicted in a considerably greater proportion than men. These possessions— which are invariably made by the Owu or water spirit—may occur at any time, or in any place, and as soon as a woman jumps up and begins to talk a strange language—usually either Okrika or Kila—it is the first as it is a sure indication that she has become possessed. The fact that in many instances the obsessed person in her normal state is unable to speak the tongue which, when possessed, she speaks quite fluently, is naturally looked upon as direct evidence that it is the investing spirit who speaks and not the woman herself. So, too, a girl or woman who through excessive shyness is

230

too coy to dance in public, develops, when under the influence of the Owu, an excess of boldness, which enables her to do things that under ordinary conditions she would not dream of doing. This boldness is to these natives merely the confirmation of a pre-existing conviction that it is not the person that is doing these things but the spirit who has invaded and obsessed her.

"It is further believed that persons so afflicted are possessed of physical strength which is altogether superhuman, so that when they become violent and uncontrollable they are scarcely to be overcome by half a dozen or more able-bodied men."
The Lower Niger and Its Tribes, pp. 227–28.

f *Meek says of the Yaku:* "As the dance proceeds they are one by one assailed with convulsive shiverings, wave their arms, strike themselves and throw themselves on the ground like demented persons."
A Sudanese Kingdom, p. 278.

47. *Possessions on grave*

a *Burton says of Dahome:* "At the end of the funeral customs, especially in the Old Calabar River, a small house is built upon the beach, and in it are placed the valuables possessed by the departed—some whole, and others broken,—statues, clocks, vases, porcelains, and so forth."
A Mission to Gelele, King of Dahome, ii, p. 262.

b *Nassau says of the Benga, the Mpongwe and the Fang:* "Formerly also slaves carried boxes of the dead man's goods, cloth, hardware, crockery, and so forth, to be laid by the body, which in those days was not interred, but was left on the top of the ground covered with branches and leaves."
Fetichism in West Africa, p. 218.

c *Talbot says of the Ibibio:* "Next a table and some of the finest pieces of household furniture, together with jars, dishes, and bowls of old china, were carried thither and set in order. When all had been arranged, the coffin was carefully

lowered down the shaft, borne through the passage and laid upon the resting-place so reverently prepared."
Life in Southern Nigeria, p. 154.

48. *Root doctors*

a *Cardinall says of the Gold Coast:* "With the belief that spiritual agents are the cause of misfortune and sickness, it follows that medical treatment consists generally in charms. There are certain men considered most proficient in the curative art. These are the *liri-tina* (Kassena), *tiindana* (Nankanni), *tinyam* (Builsa), (owner of medicine). Their medicines are drawn from the bush, and are usually bitter-tasting grasses, herbs, and barks. For poultices the same herbs are used mixed with shea-butter and charcoal and ashes. Usually they are covered with cow-dung. It is said that the stronger the smell the more easily will the evil spirit causing the sickness be driven away."
The Natives of the Northern Territories of the Gold Coast, p. 46.

b *Cruickshank says of the Gold Coast native:* "The natives of the Gold Coast have no despicable knowledge of the qualities of herbs. A collection of these was, at one time, sent home for analysis; and it was found generally that they possessed some qualities calculated to be of use in alleviating the diseases for which the natives applied them."
Eighteen Years on the Gold Coast, II, 147.

c *Leyden says of the interior sections of West Africa, such as the Congo, the banks of the Senegal and the Gambia, etc.:* "The magicians appear to have been resorted to universally in cases of malady, which proved a hard trial on the faith even of the steadiest converts. When their children or near relations were seized with illness, they immediately began to cast a longing eye towards their old method of cure; and if they had not recourse to it, they even incurred reproach among their neighbors, as suffering their relation to die, rather than incur the expence of a magician."

Historical Account of Discoveries and Travels in Africa,
I, *120.*

d *Meek says of Nigeria:* "The believer in witchcraft feels
he has a right to protect himself by every means in his
power, and chief among these is the employment of a witch-
doctor . . . [who] is therefore considered just as essential
in most negro communities as a medical practitioner is
amongst ourselves, and, though some witch-doctors may
abuse their powers for selfish ends, as a class they are regarded as champions of morality."
Law and Authority in a Nigerian Tribe, p. 345.

e *Nassau, quoting Menzies' History of Religion, p. 73, says
of the Benja, the Mpongwe, the Fang, and other West African tribes:* " 'There is generally a special person in a tribe
who knows these things, and is able to work them. He has
more power over spirits than other men have, and is able to
make them do what he likes. He can heal sickness, he can
foretell the future, he can change a thing into something
else, or a man into a lower animal, or a tree, or anything; he
can also assume such transformations himself at will. He
uses means to bring about such results; he knows about
herbs, he has also recourse to rubbing, to making images of
affected parts in the body, and to various other arts. . . .
It is the spirit dwelling in him which brings about the wonderful results; without the spirit he could not do anything.' "
Fetichism in West Africa, pp. 86–87.

f *Ward says of the Bakongo tribes:* "It is a general belief
with the Bakongo that all sickness is the result of witchcraft
exercised by some member of the community, and the services of the charm-doctor are employed to discover the individual who is *ndoki, i.e.,* bedeviled, and guilty of devouring
the spirit of the unfortunate invalid; and in the event of the
sick person dying, the medicine-man is deputed by the relatives of the deceased to find out the witch who has 'eaten the
heart.' "
Five Years with the Congo Cannibals, p. 39.

49. *Sewing on clothes*

a *Puckett says of West Africa:* "In West Africa one dare
not sew his cloth while it is on his body lest his relative die."
Folk Beliefs of the Southern Negro, p. 405.

50. *Serpents*

a *Beckwith says of Jamaica:* "The snake is the 'baddest of
all,' anyone will affirm, but as there are seldom to be found
snakes in Jamaica today this takes one back in the history
of obeah to the days of *ob*, to the voodoo, and the Obeah
Man of the past who carried 'A staff carved with snakes or
with a human head on the handle, a cabalistic book and a
stuffed snake.' "
Black Roadways, p. 122.

b *Leonard says of Southern Nigeria:* "Reptiles, snakes, and
crocodiles particularly are much more utilised as emblems,
simply, it is to be presumed, because they are more in evidence in the forests and rivers of the Delta than any other
species of animals, consequently must have appealed to the
natives as the most convenient and suitable repositories for
the ancestral manes."
The Lower Niger and Its Tribes, p. 317.

c *Melville and Frances Herskovits say of Dahomey:* "The
next personal spirit or force we are to describe is one less
esteemed than feared. It is called Dą, which signifies 'serpent.' What is the power of Dą? All serpents are Dą but
not all serpents are worshipped. Quintessentially, Dą represents the principle of mobility, of sinuosity. 'All things
which curve, and move, but have no feet, are Dą.' "
An Outline of Dahomean Religious Beliefs, p. 56.

d *Melville and Frances Herskovits say of the Paramaribo
Negro:* "The most prevalent types of *winti* among women
in particular are those associated with the snake, and since
these enter into all the categories of *winti*, we list them after
the gods of the Sky and Earth. Of these we have *Dagowe,
Papa, Vɔdų, Hɛi-grɔ, Aboma, Aninine, Alado, Sinero, Koro-
wena, Kwɛnda, Tobochina,* and *Cheno.* The term *Dagowe*

often serves, in the town, as a generic term for all the snake spirits, though the *Dagowe*, snake, properly speaking, is one of the constrictor group found in the colony, and is believed by the natives to inhabit both land and water. This is, of course, good observation on their part, for this characteristic of all snakes of the boa type is well-known. Not all snakes are sacred, yet no one will kill a snake."
Suriname Folk-Lore, pp. 63–64.

e *Talbot says of the Ibibio tribes:* "Each great Ibibio Juju man is supposed to keep one such serpent familiar in his house, in the 'bush' where secret rites are celebrated, or in some place by the waterside. It is called Kukubarakpa, and, by virtue of this agent, much of the magician's power is said to come to him. The possession of a snake is also supposed to bring riches, though its magic is thought to be of no avail during the season of storms."
Life in Southern Nigeria, p. 17.

51. *Serpents, dream of*

a *Leonard says of Southern Nigeria:* "A snake seen in a dream implies a host of enemies seeking to destroy the dreamer's life. Nightmare is caused by the visitation of an evil or it may be antipathetic spirit."
The Lower Niger and Its Tribes, p. 147.

52. *Sneezing*

a *Puckett says of the Ewe:* "Sneezing is regarded as a bad omen by the Ewe tribes of Africa because it indicates that the indwelling spirit is about to quit the body, affording an opportunity for a homeless spirit to enter in and cause illness. A similar belief leads the Calabar natives to exclaim, 'Far from you!' when a person sneezes, with an appropriate gesture as if throwing off some evil."
Folk Beliefs of the Southern Negro, p. 453.

53. *Spider stories*

Melville and Frances Herskovits say of the Suriname Negro: "Though few tales have been recorded, these play an impor-

tant role in the life of the Suriname Negroes. They are, whatever their nature, called *Anqnsi-tɔri*, the stories of Anansi, the Twi trickster-hero, who, like in Curaçao and Jamaica, has survived his migration to the western hemisphere to be here, as on the Gold Coast, the most important single character in the folk-tales of the Negroes of these regions."
Suriname Folk-Lore, p. 138.

54. *Spirits, animals*

a *Ellis says of the Yoruba:* "The souls of the dead are sometimes reborn in animals, and occasionally, though but rarely, in plants."
The Yoruba-Speaking Peoples of the Slave Coast of West Africa, p. 133.

b *Herskovits says of Haiti:* "*Baka* appear as small bearded human-like figures with flaming eyes, or as cattle, horses, asses, goats, bears (?) and dogs."
Life in a Haitian Valley, p. 241.

55. *Spirits, dwarfs*

a *Cardinall says of the Gold Coast:* "They are *kyikyiri* (Kassena), *kukru* (Builsa), and *chichirigu* (Nankanni). Sometimes they are visible to men, and in appearance resemble the *mmotia* of the Ashanti, ill-shapen dwarfs . . . they annoy travellers by night by 'throwing stones at them.'"
The Natives of the Northern Territories of the Gold Coast, pp. 27-28.

56. *Spirits, existence after death*

a *Campbell says of the Aku, Yoruba tribes:* "They believe in the spirit after death, and in its power of being present among the living for good or evil purposes."
A Pilgrimage to My Motherland, p. 75.

b *Cruickshank says of the Gold Coast native:* "They are unanimous in thinking that there is in man a spirit which survives the body. This spirit is supposed to remain near

the spot, where the body has been buried. They believe it to have a consciousness of what is going on upon earth, and to have the power of exercising some influence over their destiny."
Eighteen Years on the Gold Coast of Africa, II, 135.

c *Melville and Frances Herskovits say of the Bush Negro of Dutch Guiana:* "As in Africa, the spirit of the dead is powerful for good or evil, and the rites of death must be carried out as tradition demands, so that the dead man may feel he has received honor among the living and proper introduction to the world of the dead."
Rebel Destiny, p. 4.

57. *Spirits, faces turned backward*

a *Cardinall says of the Gold Coast:* ". . . the spirits turned their faces to the back of the head."
The Natives of the Northern Territories of the Gold Coast, p. 34.

58. *Spirit, food for*

a *Cole says of West Africa:* "The spirits of the dead, as well as genii, are also honored and adored. Food, tobacco, and rum are placed on the graves for the departed, and their aid is requested at the taking of a journey, or in times of need."
A Revelation of the Secret Orders of Western Africa, p. 39.

b *Herskovits says of Dahomey:* "Food is brought in the dishes from which the dead ate when alive, and each meal is given to the *akɔvi* on guard, who takes three morsels and puts them down one after the other near the corpse. She also allows water to drop three times nearby, and then tells the wife of the deceased to gather up and remove everything that has been put down. The dead man's pipe must now be placed next to him; tobacco is put into it, and it is smoked for the enjoyment of the dead man by the *akɔvi* and the wife who watch the body."
Dahomey, I, 356.

c *Hutchinson says of the Efik:* "Amongst the Efik tribe, who are the residents here, there exists a practice of cooking food and leaving it on the table of a fabric called the 'devil house,' which is erected near the grave of a man or woman. The food is placed there in calabashes, and it is believed that the spirit of the deceased, with those of the butchered serfs who are her or his fellow-travelers, frequently came to partake of it in their journey to the world of spirits, whither they are supposed to be travelling."
Ten Years' Wanderings Among the Ethiopians, pp. 206–07.

d *Nassau says of West Africa:* "When affairs are going wrong in the villages, and the people do not know the cause, offerings of food and drink are taken to the grave to cause the spirit to cease disturbing them, and prayers are made to it that it may the rather bless them."
Fetichism in West Africa, p. 220.

e *Rattray says of Ashanti:* "An Ashanti never drinks without pouring a few drops of the wine on the ground for the denizens of the spirit world who may happen to be about (also some for 'fetishes'). Food is constantly placed aside for them."
Ashanti Proverbs, p. 37.

f "If you see your ancestor in a dream lying dead, as he did on the day of his death, then you know that there is going to be another death in your clan; otherwise, to be visited by an ancestor only means that he is hungry and you place food upon his stool."
Religion and Art in Ashanti, pp. 193–94.

59. *Spirits and ghosts, general*

a *Kingsley says of the West Coast of Africa:* "Accounts of apparitions abound in all the West Coast districts, and although the African holds them all in high horror and terror, he does not see anything supernatural in his 'Duppy.' It is a horrid thing to happen on, but there is nothing strange about it, and he is ten thousand times more frightened than puzzled over the affair. He does not want to 'investigate' to see whether there is anything in it. He wants to get clear away, and make ju-ju against it, 'one time.'

"These apparitions have a great variety of form, for, firstly, there are all the true spirits, nature spirits; secondly, the spirits of human beings—these human spirits are held to exist before as well as during and after bodily life; thirdly, the spirits of things."
Travels in West Africa, p. 509.

b *Melville and Frances Herskovits say of the Suriname Negro:* "When going home late from *winti*-dances, we were led away from certain thoroughfares, and went a roundabout way to avoid a corner, or a tree, or a house, because these were known to be 'bad' places,—that is to say, they were haunted. At least two persons accompanied us home, so that, in returning to their own homes, they would not have to walk the streets alone. The hours that are dangerous are mid-day, from 5:30 to 6:30 in the evening, and from 12:30 to 1:30 at night."
Suriname Folk-Lore, p. 111.

c *Rattray says of Ashanti:* "Sasabonsám. Deriv. *bonsam*, a devil, or evil spirit (*not* the disembodied soul of any particular person, just as the fetish is not a human spirit).
Its power is purely for evil and witchcraft. The *obayifo* is perhaps its servant, as the terms are sometimes synonymous."
Ashanti Proverbs, p. 47.

60. *Spirit, guardian of entrance (Legba)*

a *Herskovits says of Haiti:* ". . . they proceeded slowly to the gateway, where a ceremony was held for Legba, the guardian of entrances, that he might permit the other *loa* to pass."
Life in a Haitian Valley, pp. 172–73.

b "Even at the church, however, where all go to offer the prayers that are the central observances of the fête, the many candles placed on the rocks at the entrances are usu-

ally for St. Anthony; that same St. Anthony who, it will be recalled, is the *loa* named Legba, the guardian of all entrances."
Life in a Haitian Valley, p. 286.

61. *Spirit, guardian of buried treasure*

a *Herskovits says of Haiti:* "*Baka* are often employed to guard buried money. 'In this country, when you find money buried in jars, it is an affair of *baka*. There is never one jar, but always two or three, and you must call a *hungan* to find out which one you may take and which you must not touch. Generally the finder is allowed to take half of the treasure, for if he took all he would be tormented by the *baka* who had been left as guardian. Such jars, it is said, are usually found with human bones beside them or under them, and tradition has it that the slave-owners who are believed to have been strong in magic customarily killed the most evil slave on a plantation that his spirit might keep watch over the jars. If the owner never returned, the spirit of the slave, as a 'sold *baka*,' remained to wreak vengeance upon anyone who dared disturb his charge."
Life in a Haitian Valley, pp. 242-43.

62. *Spirits, plat-eye*

a *Johnson says of St. Helena:* "In the Georgetown section plat-eye is used to signify a ghost or spook. Its etymology is uncertain, and it may be an instance of an Africanism surviving in a restricted area."
Folk Culture on St. Helena Island, South Carolina, p. 58.

b *Nassau says of West Africa:* "Another manifestation is that of the uvengwa. . . . It is the self-resurrected spirit and body of a dead human being. It is an object of dread, and is never worshipped in any manner whatever. Why it appears is not known. Perhaps it shows itself only in a restless, unquiet, or dissatisfied feeling. It is white in color, but the body is variously changed from the likeness of the original human body. Some say that it has only one eye, placed

in the centre of the forehead. Some say that its feet are webbed like an aquatic bird. It does not speak; it only wanders, looking as if with curiosity."
Fetichism in West Africa, p. 71.

63. *Spirits, river*

a *Cardinall says of the Gold Coast:* "Spirits of rivers and water-holes are greatly respected. They are most powerful spirits, too. They can slay men and they can bring much good fortune. To them are brought many sacrifices of fowls and goats, etc. It is said that these spirits live below the river-bed."
The Natives of the Northern Territories of the Gold Coast, p. 34.

b *Melville and Frances Herskovits say of the Paramaribo Negro:* "A fourth group of *winti* are those which are associated with the river. This group, as all others, overlap the Snake gods, since the constrictor lives in the water as well as on land. However, there are other gods, among them the *kaimą*, which are peculiar to the rivers alone. The river-gods are headed by the *Liba-Mama*, or *Watra-Mama*, respectively Mother of the River, or Mother of the Water, who, again, is not referred to by name. Among the Saramacca tribe of Bush-Negroes, the river-gods go under the generic name of Tonε, and this name, like the name from the interior for the gods in general, is also sometimes employed in Paramaribo."
Suriname Folk-Lore, pp. 64–65.

c *Meek says of Nigeria:* "At Eha-Amufu (Nsukka Division) there is a river-cult, the priest of which is known as the Atama Ebe. Ebe is the spirit of the river and controls the fish, who are regarded as the spiritual counterparts of the inhabitants of Eha-Amufu. The big fish are the counterparts of the principal men of the village group, while the fry are the counterparts of persons of no consequence. When a villager dies a fish dies, and when a fish dies a villager dies. It is taboo, therefore, to catch fish in the river, and

much annoyance has been caused by visits of foreign fishermen who disregard the local scruples. Ebe, the spirit of the river, being the guardian of the fish, which are his children and messengers, is regarded as the giver of children to men, and is thus the object of public and private worship."
Law and Authority in a Nigerian Tribe, p. 38.

64. *Stealing from grave*

a *Nassau says of the interior tribes of the West Coast:* "A noticeable fact about these gifts to the spirits is that, however great a thief a man may be, he will not steal from a grave. The coveted mirror will lie there and waste in the rain, and the valuable garment will flap itself to rags in the wind, but human hands will not touch them. Sometimes the temptation to steal is removed, by the donor fracturing the article before it is laid on the grave."
Fetichism in West Africa, p. 232.

65. *Taboos*

a *Bosman says of Guinea:* "Each Person here is forbidden the eating of one sort of Flesh or other; one eats no Mutton, another no Goats-Flesh, Beef, Swines-Flesh, Wild-Fowl, Cocks with white feathers, &c. This Restraint is not laid upon them for a limited time, but for their whole Lives: And if the Romanists brag of the Antiquities of their Ecclesiastical Commands; so if you ask the Negroes why they do this, they will readily tell you, because their Ancestors did so from the beginning of the World and it hath been handed down from one Age to another by Tradition. The Son never eats what the Father is restrained from, as the Daughter herein follows the Mother's Example; and this Rule is as strictly observed amongst them, that 'tis impossible to persuade them to the contrary."
Description of the Coast of Guinea, pp. 154–55.

b *Burton says of the Dahomean:* "Some are allowed to eat beef, others only mutton; many are prohibited to touch the flesh of goats. Poultry is permitted to some, eggs to others."
A Mission to Gelele, King of Dahome, ii, 361–62.

c *Ellis says of the Ewe:* "The usual reverence is paid by the members of a clan to the animal or plant from which the clan takes its name. It may not be used as food, or molested in any way; but must always be treated with veneration and respect. The general notion is that the members of the clan are directly descended from the animal, or plant, eponymous."
The Ewe-Speaking Peoples of the Slave Coast of West Africa, p. 100.

d *Ellis says of the Tshi:* "With some races the reverence originally felt for the deceased ancestor, and in later times transferred to the animal for which he was named, culminates in the animal being regarded as a tutelary deity, and consequently a being to be worshipped and propitiated by sacrifice; but in other cases—and this is almost always the case with the family divisions of the natives of the Gold Coast—an abstention from the use of the flesh of the animal whose name the family bears, is sometimes the only remaining sign of any feeling of reverence or respect."
The Tshi-Speaking Peoples of the Gold Coast of West Africa, p. 206.

e *Melville and Frances Herskovits say of the Suriname Negro:* "An illness may be caused by . . . an unconscious violation, arising out of the fact that a man's mother had never told him the name of his true father, and consequently he had been observing food taboos which were not his own and had been neglecting to observe those which were his, since, as we have seen, these personal food taboos are inherited from the father."
Suriname Folk-Lore, pp. 59–60.

66. *Teeth, children born with*

a *Meek says of Nigeria:* "Children born feet first or with teeth or any deformity were also destroyed, on the ground that they were incarnations of evil spirits."
Law and Authority in a Nigerian Tribe, pp. 290–91.

b *Thomas says of the Ibo of Nigeria:* "Not only twins, but many other children are, or were, exposed because of some circumstance connected with their birth or development. For example, a child born with teeth is regarded as a monster who will bring misfortune on its father—perhaps the belief may be that it will devour him. . . ."
Anthropological Report on the Ibo-Speaking Peoples of Nigeria, I, pp. 10–11.

67. *Twins*

a *Melville and Frances Herskovits say of the Suriname Negro:* "Twins, and the child born after twins, who is called *Dosu,* and children born feet foremost, are in a category by themselves, and they are often spoken of as *ogri,* . . . bad."
Suriname Folk-Lore, p. 42.

b *Meek says of Nigeria:* "And twins were allowed to die or were deliberately killed by being enclosed in a pot or ant-hill. For the Ibo hold the common belief that the birth of twins is an indication of the disfavour of the spirits, and a punishment, possibly of adultery. Twin-births are regarded as non-human, and it is a common belief that the *chi* or accompanying soul of a twin is the *chi* of an animal. After the birth of twins a diviner is consulted to ascertain which spirit or ancestor had been offended, and sacrifice is offered to appease his wrath."
Law and Authority in a Nigerian Tribe, p. 291.

c *Nassau says of Africa:* "All over Africa the birth of twins is a notable event, but noted for very different reasons in different parts of the country. In Calabar they are dreaded as an evil omen, and until recently were immediately put to death, and the mother driven from the village to live alone in the forest as a punishment for having brought this evil on her people.

"In other parts, as in the Gabun country, where they are welcomed, it is nevertheless considered necessary to have special ceremonies performed for the safety of their lives, or, if they die, to prevent further evil."
Fetichism in West Africa, p. 206.

68. *Witches, animal form*

a *Herskovits says of Dahomey:* "The *azɔndato*, as such practitioners are called, are spoken of in whispers, and are said to be organized into a close guild. They exercise power over the souls of those who have not had proper burial and therefore wander about the earth discontented, and over these souls procured by 'killing' their owners in the manner described above. These *azɔndato* are to be recognized by their blood-shot eyes, and Dahomeans stealthily point out two or three such persons in the market-place who usually may be remarked to be doing somewhat better business than those who sit near them. These dangerous individuals change into bats at night, or assume other animal forms and go forth to hold council together or to perform their dark deeds."
Dahomey, ii, *287*.

b *Meek says of Nigeria:* "Witches (*amozu*) and wizards (*ogboma*) have also animal counterparts, and so assume the forms of owls, lizards, vultures, and numerous species of night-birds. Consequently, if a night-bird comes and rests on a house, the owner loses no time in trying to drive it away or shoot it; and if he fails he will seize his *ofo* and call on his ancestors or any local deity to rid him of his enemy. A witch always assails at night. By magic means she attacks the throat, so that the victim is paralysed and cannot move or speak, and in the morning may be found lying senseless and naked outside his hut. . . . Witches can penetrate into a house through the smallest cracks in the wall, and can assume the form of the smallest insect. Flies and other creatures which bite are witches or the agents of witches, and if a person is severely bitten he may consult a diviner, who will order the patient to offer sacrifice to propitate some witch, and induce the witch to remove the spell by transferring it to some one else. Witches can poison food or infect it with sorcery, and if any one eats a meal cooked by a witch he will become seriously ill or die. Moth-

ers, therefore, advise their children to avoid eating food outside their own homes."
Law and Authority in a Nigerian Tribe, pp. 79–80.

c *Talbot says of Southern Nigeria:* "Witches often change into leopards and other animals."
The Peoples of Southern Nigeria, ii, 219.

d "Witchcraft seems to have been more dreaded in the Oru clan than among any other Ibo. . . . They can change into crocodiles, fish, leopards, bush-cows, snakes and goats."
The Peoples of Southern Nigeria, ii, 213.

e *Farrow says:* "The witch-doctor is, of course, a privileged person. He is called in to trace the source of disease and death, for these are generally attributed to witchcraft, unless they are evidently caused by the vengeance of Shopono (smallpox), Shango, or some similar deity. Various forms of disease are described as 'snakes inside' (*ejo-inu*), 'an insect' (*kokoro*), etc., and it is supposed that these have been introduced by a foe through the agency of witchcraft."
Faith, Fancies and Fetish, p. 125.

69. *Witches, riding victims*

a *Ellis says of the Vais:* "There is a belief, as I have stated, among the Vais that witches come to your house and ride you at night,—that when the witch comes in the door he takes off his skin and lays it aside in the house. It is believed that he returns you to the bed where he found you, and that the witch may be killed by sprinkling salt and pepper in certain portions of the room, which will prevent the witch from putting on his skin. Just before they go to bed it is a common thing to see Vais people sprinkling salt and pepper about the room."
Negro Culture in West Africa, p. 63.

b *Leonard says:* "In Brass the natives firmly believe that witches exist, and that certain persons by natural operations—or rather by co-operation with natural forces—possess the power of inflicting disease, injury, or death upon their neighbours. These individuals are divided into two classes—the harmful and the harmless.

"The former are said to go out of their houses at night, and to hold meetings with demons and their colleagues, to determine whose life is next to be destroyed. This is done by gradually sucking the blood of the victim through some supernatural and invisible means the effect of which on the victim is imperceptible to others."
The Lower Niger and Its Tribes, p. 486.

c *Rattray says of Ashanti:* "Men and women possessed of this black magic are credited with volitant powers, being able to quit their bodies and travel great distances in the night. Besides sucking the blood of victims, they are supposed to be able to extract the sap and juices of crops."
Ashanti Proverbs, p. 48.

70. *Woodcarving and weaving*

a *Herskovits says:* "In West Africa, the development of techniques of all kinds is the greatest on the continent. The Benin bronzes, the brass-work of Dahomey, the weaving of the Ashanti, or the wood carving of the Ivory Coast, Dahomey, and Nigeria are famous, while pottery of a high grade, basketry, and iron work are found everywhere."
Social History of the Negro, p. 221.

b *Herskovits says of the Bush Negro:* "In the villages of the Bush Negroes the artist holds an enviable position, and the good carver is sought after in marriage and often wins the most desirable young woman for his wife. This is because Suriname woodcarving is a part of all phases of life."
Social History of the Negro, p. 247.

c *Herskovits says of Dahomey:* "But, as stated, the greatest proportion of objects are intended for some specific end. The spotted hyena, for example, formed a handle for the staff of a chief. The two wands with human figures on them are employed in the Fá cult. The three figures in the background of the same plate, representing a woman, an animal,

and a bird respectively, support cups which hold the seeds employed in the Fate cult. . . ."
Dahomey, ii, *370.*

d "Wood-carving is the most democratic, and the most widely practiced, of all the arts. It constitutes the one mode of artistic expression open to all men in Dahomey, for, as in many cultures, wood-carving is not a technique permitted to women. In addition, however, to the democratic nature of the art it pervades the daily life of the people to a greater degree than any other art-form, and a catalogue of the uses to which the objects carved in wood are put by the Dahomeans would touch upon all elements of Dahomean culture. Carvings thus catalogued would range from the artistic statuettes found in the shrines of the gods and the smaller human figures used as *gbŏ*, the beautifully carved cups which hold the palm-kernels employed in the Fá cult, and the carefully worked handles of the Xɛvioso axes, all of which indicate the association of wood-carving with religion, to the mortars, stools, and other decorated objects used in the everyday round of life."
Dahomey, ii, *363.*

e "Among these forms are plastic and graphic arts, music, dancing and a wide range of oral literature. In the former group wood-carving is the most widespread and the most commonly practised. As will be indicated in detail below, carvings in wood enter many phases of life. Statues of the gods, human forms which, as *gbŏ*, protect the owner and his household, and the implements of the Fate cult, are all a part of the religious life. The sceptres of King and chiefs, and the elaborately carved stools on which they sat were indispensable symbols of rank and succession. The wands of office and stools of sib-chiefs associate this art with social organisation, especially where the totem animal is figured, while even the *adji* game-boards of the Dahomeans are embellished by the carvings of the artist."
Dahomey, ii, *311.*

f *Melville and Frances Herskovits say of the Bush Negro of Dutch Guiana:* "There were other carvings which we bought —a large rice-carrying tray, and some food stirrers, one of which was especially fine, made as it was of two small paddles with miniature blades, the handles joined by a wooden ring-chain, and all of this carved out of one piece of wood."
Rebel Destiny, p. 277.

g "Few things on the river seemed to the outsiders more characteristic of the life of the Saramacca people than these carvings which were met with everywhere, however small the village, however poor the home. When the seasonal rains came, men incised their desires on wood, which later told the legend of procreation, or safety on the river, or a curse invoked against a woman if she proved unfaithful; or something of humor, such as a man bidding for a girl's favor, and she refusing him, while up above intertwined were a man and woman, symbolizing the ultimate consummation with the proper suitor."
Rebel Destiny, pp. 277–78.

h *Talbot says of the Sudanese tribes:* "Carving in wood is common among all tribes, but is for the most part rather crude. In all cases articles were as far as possible made from the solid block; never nailed or glued together."
The Peoples of Southern Nigeria, III, 928.

i "The varieties of woven work include checker, twilled and wicker; others are plaited, and there are several sorts of coiled basketry. The oblong market baskets used by the women, particularly among the Ibo and many of the Semi-Bantu tribes, closely resemble those of the Ancient Egyptians."
The Peoples of Southern Nigeria, III, 938.

Glossary

◇◇◇◇◇◇◇◇◇◇◇◇

ahmeen—spoken in a prayer
ameela—spoken in a prayer
anansi, An Nancy—spider
balonga—watermelon
belambi, hakabara, mahamadu—spoken in a prayer
boo-boo-no—circular African house of sticks and straw, plas-
  tered with mud
cop—to cut, to bleed
cunjuh—magical practices, the casting of spells
de big raid—War Between the States
deloe—water
diffy—fire
dose—conjure mixture
figlin water—wine
flim—pancake
gran—grandfather, grandmother
ground house—African dwelling
gumbo—okra
hakabara—spoken in a prayer
han—a magic charm carried to insure good luck
heaby root—a powerful spell
hoodoo—magical practices, the casting of spells
juba haltuh—water bucket
line scahs—tribal marks
maduba—mistress
ma-foo-bey—ejaculation of surprise
mahaba—master
maulin a bumba—thunder
mojo—charm

mosojo—sojo—pot
nayam—to eat
nyana—seafood
planted—place an evil charm
plat-eye—especially dreaded ghost
put down—place an evil charm
rootin—casting an evil charm
saraka—flat rice cakes
settin-ups—wakes
shadduh—ghost
shoutin—rhythmic beating of hands and feet
skinskon—expression of anger
strikin roun—working conjure
tabby—a mixture of lime and oyster shell, used for building
   material
totem, taboo—forbidden article of food
tuh fix—cast a spell
voodoo—magical practices, the casting of spells
wukin roots—curing by magic

Informants

◇◇◇◇◇◇◇◇◇◇◇◇◇

Anderson, Alec, *Possum Point*, Sterling.

Anderson, Rachel, *Possum Point*, Sterling.

Baker, Lawrence, *Darien*, Darien.

Baker, Ophelia, *Sandfly*, R. F. D., Savannah.

Basden, Isaac, *Harris Neck*, Harris Neck.

Basden, Liza, *Harris Neck*, Harris Neck.

Bates, Henry, *Frogtown and Currytown*, 1118 Waldburg Street, Savannah.

Baynes, Lee, *Sandfly*, R. F. D., Savannah.

Bivens, John, *Sandfly*, R. F. D., Savannah.

Blackshear, John, *Brownville*, 625 Grapevine Avenue, Savannah.

Boddison, George, *Tin City*, Savannah.

Branch, Susie, *White Bluff*, R. F. D., Savannah.

Brown, Evans, *Yamacraw*, West Broad Street School, Savannah.

Brown, Katie, *Sapelo Island*, Sapelo.

Brown, William, *Brownville*, Florence Street, Savannah.

Butler, Bruurs, *Grimball's Point*, Grimball's Point.

Bryant, Ryna, *Springfield*, R. F. D., Savannah.

Bryant, Stephen, *Springfield*, R. F. D., Savannah.

Campbell, Horace, *St. Marys*, St. Marys.

Campbell, Hettie, *St. Marys*, St. Marys. (deceased)

Carter, Jerome, *Frogtown and Currytown*, 443 Jefferson Street, Savannah.

Cohen, Ozie, *Tin City*, Savannah.

Coleman, Preston, *Frogtown and Currytown*, 532 Charles Street, Savannah.

Collier, James, *Brownville*, 806 W. 39th Street, Savannah.

Cook, Tressie, *Brownville*, 911 W. 38th Street, Savannah.

Cooper, James, *Yamacraw*, Port Wentworth.

Davis, Ellie, *Sandfly*, R. F. D., Savannah.

Davis, Sophie, *White Bluff*, R. F. D., Savannah.

Dawson, Minnie, *Pin Point*, R. F. D., Savannah.

Delegal, Tony, *Brownville*, R. F. D., Savannah.

Dorsay, Ellen, *Yamacraw*, 515 W. Congress Street, Savannah.

Edwards, William, *Brownville*, West Broad and 32nd Streets, Savannah.

English, Emma, *Brownville*, 628 W. 36th Street, Savannah.

Gamble, Henry, *Frogtown and Currytown*, 519 West Broad Street, Savannah.

Gilbert, Phoebe, *Sapelo Island*, Sapelo.

Gibson, Mary Liza, *Grimball's Point*, Grimball's Point.

Grace, Bishop, *Brownville, House of Prayer*, 643 Bismark Street, Savannah.

Grant, Rosa, *Possum Point*, Sterling.

Grovernor, Julia, *Sapelo Island*, Sapelo. (deceased)

Grovernor, Katie, *Sapelo Island*, Sapelo.

Grayson, London, *White Bluff*, R. F. D., Savannah. (deceased)

Hall, Serina, *White Bluff*, R. F. D., Savannah.

Hall, Shad, *Sapelo Island*, Sapelo.

Hamilton, Carrie, *Yamacraw*, 530 West President Street, Savannah.

Haynes, Henry, *Brownville*, 41st and Harden Streets, Savannah.

Haynes, John, *Old Fort*, 933 Wheaton Street, Savannah.

Higgins, Harry, *Brownville*, 1810 West Broad Street, Savannah.

Holmes, S. B., *Old Fort*, 716 E. Perry Street, Savannah.

Houston, Tonie, *Tatemville*, R. F. D., Savannah.

Hunter, Mary, *Old Fort*, 548 E. St. Julian Street, Savannah.

Hunter, Charles, *St. Simons Island*, St. Simons.

Hunter, Emma, *St. Simons Island*, St. Simons.

Jackson, F. J., *Grimball's Point*, Grimball's Point. (deceased)

Jackson, Della, *Grimball's Point*, Grimball's Point.

Jenkins, Albert, *Brownville*, 627 W. 36th Street, Savannah.

Jenkins, Lizzie, *Sandfly*, R. F. D., Savannah.

Johnson, Anna, *Harris Neck*, Harris Neck.

Johnson, Dorothy, *Springfield*, 1201 Murphy Avenue, Savannah.

Johnson, Ryna, *St. Simons Island*, St. Simons.

Jonah, Uncle, *Sunbury*, Sunbury.

Jones, Ellen, *Springfield*, near 1304 Stiles Avenue, Savannah.

Jones, Esther, *Tatemville*, 308 W. 46th Street, Savannah.

Jones, Fred, *Yamacraw*, 607 W. Congress Street, Savannah.

Jones, Nero, *Sapelo Island*, Sapelo.

Jones, Thursday, *Brownville*, 39th Street near Florence Street, Savannah.

Kelsey, D. C., *Frogtown and Currytown*, 521 West Gaston Street, Savannah.

Lewis, Nathaniel John, *Tin City*, Savannah.

Lewis, Jane, *Darien*, Darien.

Linder, Julian, *Brownville*, 612 W. 36th Street, Savannah.

Little, George W., *Brownville*, 737 W. 34th Street, Savannah.

Little, Preacher, *Sapelo Island*, Sapelo.

Major, Martha, *Yamacraw*, 542 W. York Street, Savannah.

Maxwell, Susan, *Possum Point*, Sterling.

McCarts, Katie, *Old Fort*, 744 Hull Street, Savannah.

McCullough, Priscilla, *Darien*, Darien.

McKen, Millie, *Frogtown and Currytown*, 409 W. Duffy Street, Savannah.

McNichols, Robert, *Brownville*, E. 39th Street, Savannah.

McQueen, Peter, *Wilmington Island*, R. F. D., Savannah.

Mikell, William, *Brownville*, 616 W. 32nd Street, Savannah.

Miller, Anna, *Frogtown and Currytown*, 1018 Cuyler Street, Savannah.

Miller, H. H., *Tatemville*, 46th and Pearl Streets, Savannah.

Moore, James, *Tin City*, Savannah.

Munroe, Emma, *Tin City*, Savannah.

Myers, Jim, *St. Marys*, Mush Bluff Island, R. F. D., St. Marys.

Nelson, Christine, *Tin City*, Savannah.

Newkirk, William, *Tatemville*, R. F. D., Savannah.

Noah's Ark, *Old Fort*, Peace Mission, Joe and Harmon Streets, Savannah.

Page, Martha, *Yamacraw*, 606 Zubly Street, Savannah.

Parker, Allen, *Tatemville*, R. F. D., Savannah.
Peace, Sister Patience, *Old Fort*, Peace Mission, Joe and Harmon Streets, Savannah.
Peterson, Nora, *St. Simons Island*, St. Simons.
Pinckney, Robert, *Wilmington Island*, R. F. D., Savannah.
Postell, Florence, *Brownville*, 928 W. 51st Street, Savannah.
Quarterman, Wallace, *Darien*, Darien. (deceased)
Ralph, Marion, *Brownville*, 2411 Harden Street, Savannah.
Redmond, Professor, *Frogtown and Currytown*, West Broad Street, Savannah.
Reese, Bessie, *Brownville*, 2408 Harden Street, Savannah.
Roberts, Elizabeth, *Sunbury*, Sunbury.
Rogers, William, *Darien*, Darien.
Ross, Lee, *Brownville*, R. F. D., Savannah.
Royal, Bessie, *White Bluff*, R. F. D., Savannah.
Rudolph, Shadwick, *St. Marys*, R. F. D., Woodbine. (Folkston Road)
Sallins, Rosa, *Harris Neck*, Harris Neck.
Sampson, Mattie W., *Brownville*, W. 32nd Street, Savannah.
Singleton, Charles, *Springfield*, R. F. D., Savannah.
Singleton, Justine, *Tatemville*, R. F. D., Savannah.
Singleton, Paul, *Tin City*, Savannah.
Small, Celia, *Wilmington Island*, R. F. D., Savannah.
Smith, Clara, *Springfield*, 1139 W. Duffy Street, Savannah.
Smith, Crawford, *Brownville*, 1704 Ogeechee Avenue, Savannah.
Smith, George, *Sapelo Island*, Sapelo.
Smith, Thomas, *Yamacraw*, 37 Ann Street, Savannah.
Snead, Margaret, *Pin Point*, R. F. D., Savannah.
Sneed, Prince, *White Bluff*, R. F. D., Savannah.
Stephens, Josephine, *Harris Neck*, Harris Neck.
Stevens, Emma, *Sunbury*, Sunbury.
Stevens, Mary, *Sunbury*, Sunbury.
Sullivan, Ben, *St. Simons Island*, St. Simons.
Tattnall, Gene, *Wilmington Island*, R. F. D., Savannah.
Tattnall, Jack, *Wilmington Island*, R. F. D., Savannah.
Taylor, Reuben, *Eulonia*, Eulonia.
Thorpe, Ed, *Harris Neck*, Harris Neck.

Triumphant Virgin, *Old Fort*, Peace Mission, Joe and Harmon Streets, Savannah.

Waldburg, Dick, *Tatemville*, R. F. D., Savannah.

Ward, Beatrice, *Brownville*, 832 W. 35th Street, Savannah.

Washington, James, *Springfield*, R. F. D., Savannah.

Washington, Ben, *Eulonia*, Eulonia.

Washington, Sara, *Eulonia*, Eulonia.

West, Chloe, *Frogtown and Currytown*, 623 W. Waldburg Lane, Savannah.

White, Floyd, *St. Simons Island*, St. Simons.

Wilcher, Alfred, *Brownville*, 610 W. 31st Street, Savannah.

Williams, Dye, *Old Fort*, Peace Mission, Joe and Harmon Streets, Savannah.

Williams, Henry, *St. Marys*, St. Marys.

Williams, Rosanna, *Tatemville*, R. F. D., Savannah.

Wilson, Cuffy, *Sapelo Island*, Sapelo.

Wilson, Jack, *Old Fort*, 272 McAlister Street, Savannah.

Wing, Catherine, *St. Simons Island*, St. Simons.

Wright, Richard, *Tatemville*, R. F. D., Savannah.

Bibliography

Bancroft, Frederic. *Slave Trading in the Old South.* Baltimore: J. J. Furst Co., 1931.

Basden, George Thomas. *Among the Ibos of Nigeria.* Philadelphia: J. B. Lippincott Co.; London: Seeley, Service & Co., Ltd., 1931.

Beckwith, Martha Warren. *Black Roadways.* Chapel Hill: The University of North Carolina Press, 1929.

Bennett, John. "Gullah: A Negro Patois," *South Atlantic Quarterly.* Part I, October, 1908; Part II, January, 1909.

Bosman, William. *Description of the Coast of Guinea. Divided into the Gold, the Slave and the Ivory Coasts.* London: Printed for F. Knapton, A. Bell, R. Smith, D. Midwinter, W. Haws, W. Davis, C. Strahan, B. Lintott, T. Round, and F. Wale, 1705.

Bridge, Horatio. *Journal of an African Cruiser.* New York: George P. Putnam & Co., 1853.

Brown, J. T. *Among the Bantu Nomads.* London: Seeley, Service & Co., Ltd., 1926.

Burton, Richard Francis. *A Mission to Gelele, King of Dahome.* London: Tinsley Brothers, 1864. I, II.

Campbell, Dugald. *In the Heart of Bantuland.* Philadelphia: J. B. Lippincott Co.; London: Seeley, Service & Co., Ltd., 1932.

Campbell, Robert. *A Pilgrimage to My Motherland.* New York: Thomas Hamilton; Philadelphia: the Author, 1861.

Cardinall, Allan Wolsey. *The Natives of the Northern Territories of the Gold Coast, Their Customs, Religion and Folklore.* London: George Routledge & Sons, Ltd.; New York: E. P. Dutton & Co., 1920.

Cole, J. Augustus. *A Revelation of the Secret Orders of Western Africa.* Dayton: United Brethren Publishing House, 1886.

Cruickshank, Brodie. *Eighteen Years on the Gold Coast of Africa.* London: Hurst & Blackett, 1853. II.

Cuney-Hare, Maud. *Negro Musicians and Their Music.* Washington: The Associated Publishers, Inc., 1936.

Danquah, Joseph Boakye. *Gold Coast: Akan Laws and Customs and the Akin Abuakwa Constitution.* London: George Routledge & Sons, Ltd., 1928.

Delafosse, Maurice. *Negroes of Africa.* Washington: The Associated Publishers, Inc., 1931.

Du Chaillu, Paul B. *Explorations and Adventures in Equatorial Africa.* New York: Harper & Bros., 1871.

DuPuis, Joseph. *Journal of a Residence in Ashantee.* London: Printed for Henry Colburn, 1824.

Ellis, A. B. *The Tshi-Speaking Peoples of the Gold Coast of West Africa.* London: Chapman & Hall, Ltd., 1887.

——. *The Ewe-Speaking Peoples of the Slave Coast of West Africa.* London: Chapman & Hall, Ltd., 1890.

——. *The Yoruba-Speaking Peoples of the Slave Coast of West Africa.* London: Chapman & Hall, Ltd., 1894.

Ellis, George W. *Negro Culture in West Africa.* New York: The Neale Publishing Co., 1914.

Farrow, Stephen S. *Faith, Fancies and Fetich.* New York and Toronto: The Macmillan Co., 1926.

Geographical Society, The Royal. *The Geographical Journal,* XXXI (1908). London: Edward Stenford.

Gonzales, Ambrose E. *The Black Border.* Columbia: The State Co., 1922.

Guillaume, Paul and Munroe, Thomas. *Primitive Negro Sculpture.* New York: Harcourt, Brace & Co., 1926.

Harvard African Expedition. *The African Republic of Liberia and the Belgian Congo.* Edited by Richard P. Strong. Cambridge: Harvard University Press, 1930.

Herskovits, Melville J. "Social History of the Negro," *Handbook of Social Psychology.* Edited by Carl Murchison. Worcester: Clark University Press, 1935.

——. *Life in a Haitian Valley.* New York and London: Alfred A. Knopf, 1937.

——. *Dahomey.* New York: J. J. Augustin, 1938. I, II.

——, and Herskovits, Frances S. *An Outline of Dahomean Religious Belief.* New York: American Anthropological Assn., 1933.

——, and Herskovits, Frances S. *Rebel Destiny.* New York and London: Whittlesey House, 1934.

——, and Herskovits, Frances S. *Suriname Folk-Lore.* New York: Columbia University Contribution to Anthropology, XXVIII, 1936.

Hutchinson, Thomas J. *Ten Years Wanderings Among the Ethiopians.* London: Hurst & Blackett, 1861.

Johnson, Guy B. *Folk Culture on St. Helena Island, South Carolina.* Chapel Hill: The University of North Carolina Press, 1930.

Kingsley, Mary H. *Travels in West Africa.* New York: The Macmillan Co., 1897.

Leonard, Major Arthur Glyn. *The Lower Niger and Its Tribes.* New York: The Macmillan Co., 1906.

Leyden, John. *Historical Account of Discoveries and Travels in Africa.* Edinburgh: Printed by George Ramsey & Co., for Archibald Constable & Co.; London: Longman, Hurst, Rees, Orme & Brown, 1817. I, II.

Livingstone, David. *Missionary Travels and Researches in South Africa.* New York: Harper & Bros., 1858.

Mayer, Brantz. *Captain Canot: or Twenty Years of an African Slaver.* New York: D. Appleton & Co., 1854.

Meek, C. K. *A Sudanese Kingdom and Ethnographical Study of the Jukun-Speaking Peoples of Nigeria.* London: Kegan Paul, Trench, Trubner & Co., Ltd., 1931.

——. *Law and Authority in a Nigerian Tribe.* London, New York, Toronto: Oxford University Press, 1937.

Miller, Janet. *Jungles Preferred.* Boston, New York: Houghton, Mifflin Co., 1931.

Milligan, Robert H. *The Fetish Folk of West Africa.* New York: Fleming H. Revell Co., 1912.

Monteiro, Joachim John. *Angola and the River Congo.* New York: Macmillan & Co., 1876.

Moore, Francis. *Travels Into the Inland Parts of Africa.* London: Edward Cave, St. John's Gate, 1738.

Nassau, Rev. Robert Hamill. *Fetichism in West Africa.* New York: Charles Scribner's Sons, 1904.

Newspapers:
Columbia Museum and Savannah Advertiser.
Georgia Gazette (Savannah).
Savannah Evening Press.
Savannah Morning News.

Park, Mungo. *Travels in the Interior of Africa.* New York: J. Tiebout, 1800.

Peterkin, Julia. *Roll Jordon Roll.* New York: Robert O. Ballou, 1933.

Puckett, Newbell Niles. *Folk Beliefs of the Southern Negro.* Chapel Hill: The University of North Carolina Press, 1926.

Rattray, Capt. Robert Sutherland. *Ashanti.* Oxford: The Clarendon Press, 1930.

——. *Akan-Ashanti Folk-Tales.* Oxford: The Clarendon Press, 1930.

——. *Ashanti Proverbs.* Oxford: The Clarendon Press, 1916.

——. *Religion and Art in Ashanti.* Oxford: The Clarendon Press, 1927.

——. *The Tribes of the Ashanti Hinterland.* Oxford: The Clarendon Press, 1932. I.

——. *Hausa Folk-Lore Customs, Proverbs, etc.* Oxford: The Clarendon Press, 1913. I.

Records in United States Post Office, Federal District Court, Savannah, Georgia:

May 8, 1815, United States vs. Schooner Hal.

January, 1818, Extract: Appraisement of Negroes in the Schooner *Syrena.*

July 18, 1818, U. S. District Court at Savannah, Huquiel De Casto vs. Ninety-five African Slaves in the Brig. *Jusee Nazarene.*

1819, The United States vs. *Isabella*—Libel.

June 3, 1819, Brutus Privateer vs. *The Tentatirra* and slaves.

February 8, 1820, John H. Henly, Esq. vs. The Schooner *Syrena*.

April 27, 1820, Charles Mulvey vs. The Slaves of the *Politina*.

May 30, 1820, The U. S. vs. *The Nuestra Siegnora de Belin*.

July, 1820, Case of the *Antelope* Otherwise the *Gen. Remirez* and Cargo.

August 22, 1821, United States vs. Robert Hoy, John Low and Robert Forsyth.

December 23, 1822, In Admiralty, Libel Decree; Juan Madrazo vs. The Cargo of the *Isabolits*.

December 24, 1823, Libel for Restitution Juan Madrazo vs. African Proceedings.

The Wanderer Trial: U. S. (1859).

Singer, Caroline and Eldridge, and LeRoy, Cyrus. *White Africans and Black*. New York: W. W. Norton & Co., Inc., 1929.

Talbot, Percy Amaury. *Life in Southern Nigeria*. London: Macmillan & Co., Ltd., 1923.

——. *The Peoples of Southern Nigeria*. London: Oxford University Press, 1926. I, III, IV.

Thomas, Northcote Whitredge. *Anthropological Report on the Ibo-Speaking Peoples of Nigeria*. London: Harrison and Sons, 1913.

Ward, Herbert. *Five Years With the Congo Cannibals*. London: Chatto & Windus, Picadilly, 1891.

Weeks, John H. *Among the Primitive Bakongo*. London: Seeley, Service & Co., Ltd., 1914.

Williams, Rev. John G. *De Ole Plantations*. Allendale, S. C., 1896.

Index

Africans (*continued*)
Natives (*continued*)
William, 175.
Yaruba, 161, 166.
African prayer rituals, 121, 141, 144, 145, 156, 161, 165, 168, 171, 172, 179, 180, 187.
African slave trade, 17, 74, 105, 116, 187, 192.
Altama Plantation, 179, 182.
Anderson, Alec, 138–42.
Anderson, Rachel, 139–42.
Animals
Alligator, 70, 129, 152.
Ant, 27.
Bear, 167.
Bird, 75, 117, 157.
Bug, 30, 36, 96.
Bull, 124.
Buzzard, 28, 109, 110, 157, 184.
Cat, 6, 80, 96, 167.
Chicken, 18, 101, 136, 145, 147, 167, 171, 192.
Cow, 124, 184.
Cricket, 41.
Crocodile, 26.
Crow, 28, 101.
Deer, 124.
Dog, 18, 21, 34, 37, 69, 70, 80, 96, 99, 168.
Frog, 41, 58, 70, 136, 152.
Hog, 101, 124, 160, 184.
Insect, 80.
Lion, 167.
Lizard, 21, 41, 53, 58, 70, 160, 161.
Mole, 129.
Monkey, 181, 193.
Owl, 4, 18, 68, 75, 99, 101, 171.
Ox, 160.
Parakeet, 182.
Rabbit, 160, 161, 189.
Rat, 4.
Sheep, 96.
Snake, 14, 26, 29, 41, 43, 53, 70, 77, 83, 90, 117, 136, 148, 167.
Spider, 56, 57, 107, 108, 156, 157, 169.
Turtle, 26.
Worm, 25, 101.
Animal stories, 79, 110, 111, 160, 161, 171.

Apparitions
Dwarfs, 15, 40, 63, 64, 96, 97, 157.
Ghosts, 2, 5, 7, 15, 17, 18, 19, 23, 24, 29, 30, 33, 34, 35, 44, 57, 60, 63, 123, 124, 128, 129.
Head turned backwards, 69.
Headless spirits, 40, 44, 79, 114, 123.
Plat-eye, 136.
Shadows, 34, 36, 44, 160, 168.
Spirits, 5, 6, 7, 15, 16, 19, 29, 30, 35, 36, 40, 41, 59, 62, 66, 68, 69, 70, 76, 77, 79, 80, 91, 95, 96, 97, 109, 114, 121, 124, 127, 128, 135, 136, 140, 157, 165, 171, 192.
Witches, 4, 6, 7, 16, 17, 18, 19, 20, 24, 25, 34, 35, 44, 45, 57, 58, 59, 60, 80, 95, 96, 108, 119, 121, 140, 157.
Arnow, 188.
Ashcake, 69.
Atwood, 174.
Austin (Jordan), 189.

B

Bahamas, The, 162.
Bailey, Mr. Dave, 193.
Baker, Lawrence, 154–57.
Baker, Ophelia, 90–91.
Baptism, river, 92, 112, 113, 122, 125, 131, 141, 143, 144, 156, 177, 180, 184, 185.
Barnard, Mr., 105.
Barrett, Huger, 147.
Basden, Catherine, 131.
Basden, Isaac, 121.
Basden, Liza, 123–28.
Baskets, 8, 26, 52, 121.
Bates, Henry, 34.
Baynes, Lee, 92, 94, 95, 96, 97.
Belali (*see* Belali Sullivan)
Bella, 181.
Birth customs, 125, 126, 128.
Bivens, John, 92.
Black cat bone, 58, 102.
Blackbeard Island, 76, 79.
Blackshear, John, 51.
Blood, 84.
Blue, Mr., 150.
Bo-Cat, 84, 87.
Boddison, George, 20.

Whiskey, 14, 41.
White, Floyd, 183.
Wilcher, Alfred, 53.
Wiley, Capt., 99.
Wiley, George, 99, 100.
William, Catfish Tom, 98.
Williams, Dye, 3.
Williams, Henry, 186, 187, 188, 189.
Williams, Rosanna, 70–2.
Wilson, Cuffy, 164, 168.
Wilson, Jack, 6.
Wilton Bluff Plantation, 18.
Wine, palmetto, 52, 110.
Wing, Catherine, 173–74.
Wings for sale, 42.

Witches, 4, 6, 7, 16, 17, 18, 19, 20, 24,
25, 34, 35, 44, 45, 57, 58, 59, 60,
80, 95, 96, 108, 119, 121, 140, 157.
Woodbine Plantation, 193.
Woodcarving, 26, 33, 52, 53, 67, 70,
162, 194.
Wright, Dr., 186.
Wright, Richard, 67.
Words, African, 24, 32, 66, 76, 79,
106, 116, 121, 131, 144, 161, 162,
165, 168, 176, 181, 188, 193, 194.
Worms, 25, 101.

Z

Zapala (Sapelo), 158.